# The author

Ann Hoffmann has spent the greater part of her professional life working with or for writers. After a first job in publishing, she travelled widely in Europe and, on returning to England, spent four years as secretary/researcher to the well-known writer, the late Robert Henriques. In 1966 she established a research service for authors, which she ran until 1987. She now devotes the bulk of her time to researching and writing her own books; these include *The Dutch: How They Live and Work*, *Bocking Deanery*, *Lives of the Tudor Age* and *Majorca*.

In this expanded and revised edition of *Research for Writers*, Miss Hoffmann writes knowledgeably from personal experience on a variety of sources of information, on research methods, on some of the pitfalls to be avoided by the 'novice' researcher, on the particular problems facing writers of fiction and non-fiction and on the impact of the new technology on research.

# Research for
# Writers

### Books in the 'Writing Handbooks' series

Freelance Writing for Newspapers • Jill Dick

The Writer's Rights • Michael Legat

Writing for Children • Margaret Clark

Writing Comedy • John Byrne

Writing Crime Fiction • H.R.F. Keating

Writing Dialogue for Scripts • Rib Davis

Writing Erotic Fiction • Derek Parker

Writing Fantasy Fiction • Sarah LeFanu

Writing about Food • Jenny Linford

Writing Historical Fiction • Rhona Martin

Writing Horror Fiction • Guy N. Smith

Writing for Magazines • Jill Dick

Writing a Play • Steve Gooch

Writing Popular Fiction • Rona Randall

Writing for Radio • Rosemary Horstmann

Writing Romantic Fiction • Daphne Clair
and Robyn Donald

Writing for the Teenage Market • Ann de Gale

Writing for Television • Gerald Kelsey

Writing a Thriller • André Jute

Writing about Travel • Morag Campbell

### Other books for writers

Writers' & Artists' Yearbook

Word Power: a guide to creative writing • Julian Birkett

Interviewing Techniques for Writers and
Researchers • Susan Dunne

Rewriting: a creative approach to
writing fiction • David Michael Kaplan

SIXTH EDITION

# Research for

# Writers

## Ann Hoffmann

A & C Black • London

Sixth edition 1999

Under the title *Research for Writers* the third, fourth and fifth editions were published in 1986, 1992 and 1996 by A & C Black (Publishers) Limited, 35 Bedford Row, London WClR 4JH

ISBN 0–7136–4156–8

Previously published under the title *Research: a handbook for writers and journalists*
First edition 1975 Midas Books
Second edition 1979 A & C Black (Publishers) Limited

© 1999, 1975, 1979, 1986, 1992, 1996 Ann Hoffmann

The photograph on the front cover is reproduced with permission by Tony Stone Images.

Printed in Great Britain by Creative Print Design (Wales), Ebbw Vale

# Contents

Principal Abbreviations used in this Book    xi

**Author's Note**    xiv

1    **The Writer as Researcher**    1–8

2    **Organisation and Method**    9–41
Costs of Research    9
Equipment    12
   Computers    14
   Photocopiers    17
Organisation of Material    18
   Electronic storage    18
   Card indexes    19
   Loose sheets and notebooks    19
   Working chronologies    20
   Filing    21
Research Methods    23
   Using the Internet and email    23
   Using libraries    28
   Note-taking    31
   Photocopying    32
   Copyright    33
   Use of portable equipment in libraries    36
   Interviewing    37

3    **Basic Sources of Information and their Location**    42–78
Printed Sources    42
   Books    42
   Copyright and reference libraries    44
   Special libraries    47
   Catalogues and guides    48
   Bibliographies    49
   Electronic and other book information services    49
   Tracing books    51
   Obtaining out-of-print books    51

Newspapers and Periodicals   53
  Tracing newspapers and periodicals   54
  Indexes to newspapers   56
  Indexes to periodicals   57
  Press cuttings   58
Official Publications   58
Miscellaneous   59
  Translations   60
  Street and telephone directories   60
  Maps   61
Unpublished Sources   61
  Manuscripts and private papers   61
  Public records   63
  Theses   64
  Broadcast and televised material   65
  Filmed and recorded material   66
  Oral history collections   67

4   **Factual and Historical Research**   79–91
Factual Research   79
  Sources of factual information   80
  Getting hold of experts   83
Historical Research   84
  Conflicting authorities   86
  Dates   86
  The use of periodicals in historical research   87

5   **Research for Fiction Writers and Dramatists**   92–115
The Modern Novel   92
  Background   92
  People   93
  Language   95
The Historical Novel   96
  Places   99
  Dates   99
  Weather   100
  Language   101
  Cost of living, currencies and wages   101
  Fashion, etiquette and food   102
  Transport and travel   103
Children's Fiction   104
Crime Fiction   105
Science Fiction   105
Finding out about Published Fiction   105

6   **Biography and Autobiography**   116–36
    Private Papers   118
    Printed and Other Sources   120
        Biographical dictionaries   120
        Bibliographies   122
        Obituaries   123
        Diaries, letters and memoirs   123
        School and university records   124
        Service records   124
        Business records   125
        Members of Parliament and government officials   126
        Public speeches and broadcasts   126
        Travel   127
    Further Research   127
    Special Problems   129
        Names   129
        Dating letters   129
        Verbal information   131

7   **Family and Local History**   137–56
    Using County Record Offices, Archaeological Societies
        and Other Collections   139
    Family History   140
        Verifying births, marriages and deaths   141
        Parish registers   144
        Marriage indexes   145
        Divorce records   146
        Wills and administrations   146
        Census returns   147
        Other records   148
    Local History   150
    Depositing Papers   152

8   **Specialist Research**   157–61
    Genealogy   158
    Picture Research   159
    Translation   160
    Research Fees   161

9   **Information from and about Foreign Countries**   162–79
    Short List of Foreign Source-material   166

10  **Preparation for the Press**   180–90
    Prelims   181
    Notes and References   182
    Bibliography   182

Preparation of the Typescript    182
The Copy-Editing Process    184
Proof-correction    185
The Index    185
A Last Word of Advice    188

**Appendix I: Selective List of Major Sources in the
    United Kingdom    191–221**
The Copyright Libraries    191
Public Record Offices    192
General Register Offices    193
Manuscript Collections/Registers of Archives    193
County Record Offices/Regional Archives Centres    194
University Libraries with Important Manuscript
    Collections    202
Cathedral Archives and Libraries    204
Other Major Reference Libraries    204
Private Subscription Libraries    205
Short List of Subjects and Sources    205

**Appendix II: Reference Books for the Writer    222–9**
Suggested Basic Reference Library for the Writer    223

**Index    230**

**Personal Notes    242**

# Principal Abbreviations used in this Book

| | |
|---|---|
| AGRA | Association of Genealogists and Record Agents |
| APGI | Association of Professional Genealogists in Ireland |
| ASGRA | Association of Scottish Genealogists and Record Agents |
| Aslib | Association for Information Management (formerly called the Association of Special Libraries and Information Bureaux) |
| BAC | Business Archives Council |
| BALH | British Association for Local History |
| *BBA* | *British Biographical Archive* |
| BBC | British Broadcasting Corporation |
| BFI | British Film Institute |
| BHI | British Humanities Index |
| BL | British Library |
| BLAISE | British Library Automated Information Service |
| BNF | Bibliothèque Nationale de France |
| *BNB* | *British National Bibliography* |
| *BNI* | *British Newspaper Index* |
| BT | British Telecom |
| CD-ROM | Compact Disk-Read Only Memory |
| *DNB* | *Dictionary of National Biography* |
| DSC | British Library Document Supply Centre |
| FAQ | Frequently Asked Questions |
| FFHS | Federation of Family History Societies |
| FRC | Family Records Centre |
| GRO | General Register Office |
| HMSO* | Her Majesty's Stationery Office |
| ICA | International Council on Archives |
| IGI | International Genealogical Index |
| IHR | Institute of Historical Research |
| ISP | Internet service provider |
| IT | Information technology |
| ITC | Independent Television Commission |
| ITI | Institute of Translation and Interpreting |

| | |
|---|---|
| *KIST* | *Keyword Index to Serial Titles* |
| LA | Library Association |
| n.d. | no date |
| N.S. | New Style (dates) |
| NSA | National Sound Archive |
| *OED* | *Oxford English Dictionary* |
| ONS | Office for National Statistics |
| OPAC | Online Public Access Catalogue |
| O.S. | Old Style (dates) |
| PCC | Prerogative Court of Canterbury (wills) |
| PCY | Prerogative Court of York (wills) |
| PRA | Picture Research Association (formerly SPREd) |
| PRO | Public Record Office |
| SFEP | Society of Freelance Editors and Proofreaders |
| STB | British Library Science, Technology and Business Service |
| TSO* | The Stationery Office Ltd |
| URL | Uniform Resource Locator |
| WWW | World Wide Web |

*Prior to 1 October 1996 the acronym HMSO was used for the government executive agency which undertook various trading activities, including publishing. Since that date HMSO has been used for Her Majesty's Stationery Office, an administrative unit within the Cabinet Office. The Stationery Office Ltd (TSO) is a private sector publishing company which on 1 October 1966 acquired the publishing operation of the government agency HMSO.

Note: For the sake of brevity and to avoid the clumsy repetition of 'he' and 'she' throughout the book, writers/researchers are referred to by the one pronoun, 'he'. No offence is intended to the female person.

# Important Note re changes to telephone codes

From 22 April 2000 new area codes and prefixes will apply in London, some provincial cities and Northern Ireland. Until that date either the former or the new numbers may be dialled. The telephone numbers stated in this edition are those which apply from 22 April 2000.

For London, the area code is now 020; the prefix for former 0171 numbers is 7, and for former 0181 numbers it is 8. After 22 April 2000 it will not be necessary to include the area code 020 if you are dialling locally.

The other changes, bringing the numbers up to eight digits, are: Cardiff: area code 029, all numbers prefixed by 20; Coventry: area code 024, all numbers prefixed by 76; Portsmouth: area code 023, all numbers prefixed by 92; Southampton: area code also 023, all numbers prefixed by 80. The code throughout Northern Ireland will be 028, with various prefixes to the number (i.e. for Belfast 028 plus prefix 90).

# Author's Note

When I embarked on this project in 1975 it was with the idea of setting down, for freelance writers faced with the daunting task of researching for publication for the first time, some practical notes on methods and sources that would start them off along the right lines and at the same time help them to avoid some of the pitfalls. Although the book has grown in the process, and this sixth edition enables me to revise the text once again, it was never intended to be – nor, considering the vast sources available to the modern writer, can it ever be – more than a guide. No one researcher can do more than scratch the surface, let alone compile a comprehensive research manual. Even had I now a team to assist me and the space of a CD-ROM to fill it would be a thankless task, given the need to keep it up to date with the thousands of new reference works, in electronic and microform as well as in print, that are published each year. Not only would such a manual have to be priced beyond the means of the very people my little book is intended to reach, it would defeat my prime purpose, which has always been to point the way and to encourage the researcher to *research*. The danger of making too much information available too easily and too speedily is that the recipient may be tempted to sit back, accept what is offered as gospel and not bother to delve further.

Researching, like writing, is an individual, creative and selective process. It cannot be 'taught'. In his quest for original material – and who does not dream of stumbling upon a cache of hitherto unknown, unpublished papers or the answer to a problem that has baffled scholars for several generations? – the writer never ceases to learn. All the time he is probing, absorbing, adding to his store of knowledge of sources of information largely by trial and error. Either he has a 'nose' for it or he has not. If not, unless he has time on his hands, he would be well advised to use the services of a professional. An elementary grasp of sources can of course be gleaned from a textbook and a few days' intensive study in a good reference library; this has immense value as a springboard. After that he is on his own. Invariably he will find himself, at different stages of his research, thrust into the unaccustomed roles of student, librarian, interviewer, detective and private investigator, and much else besides.

Throughout the compilation of this and previous editions, therefore, I have kept in mind the many time-consuming problems likely to be encountered by a novice writer/researcher, whether he is concerned with fiction or non-fiction. I have dared to suggest, from my own experience, ways in which these problems may be tackled. Like all craftsmen, I have my favourite tools – principally those tried and trusted reference works that served me well during my years as a professional researcher. Over the last decade I have taken on board many of the newer, electronic aids. Laying these out alongside one another on the work bench, as it were, for fellow craftsmen to pick up, handle and use as they see fit, has been a joy and a challenge. They may not constitute the particular assortment that a colleague would select – indeed, they are a somewhat mixed bag, being drawn in the main from my own research activities and thus inclined more to the factual, historical and biographical than to the scientific or technical. But I can vouch for them absolutely as loyal and steadfast helpmates, and I am confident that they will go on for some time yet to help others to solve some of those alarming and often seemingly insoluble conundrums that have the nasty habit of cropping up at the worst possible moment in a writer's working day. If, in the long term, there may result books and features and theses that are not only better researched, but researched with less strain and less burning of the midnight oil on the part of their authors than was once the norm, then the putting together of this book, the sixth time round, will have achieved its purpose.

Most professional writers and journalists now make full use of the new information technology (IT). Terms such as 'database', 'online', 'CD-ROM', 'World Wide Web' and 'email' no longer need explanation. Many of those 'technophobics' who not so long ago were still maintaining a stubbornly 'anti-computer' stance have since succumbed, have successfully mastered the new skills and now navigate, 'surf' or 'trawl' the Internet regularly along with the rest. The younger generation of writer-researcher, computer-literate almost from the cradle, takes for granted speedy access to information and the facility, when armed with little more than a mouse and a modem, to communicate and exchange ideas internationally at relatively low cost. Never before has so much source material been so instantly (and relatively inexpensively) accessible. The problem today is not the quantity of information available at the press of a key, but the *quality* of that information – or, to phrase it differently, the *quantity of misinformation* lying in wait for the unwary.

Increasingly 'the Net' encroaches on our professional and domestic lives, so that we are getting to the point where there will soon be very little that can be accomplished without it. Nevertheless, as individual writers and researchers, I feel very strongly that we should treat the Internet with caution. More importantly, I believe that as individuals we must remain free to make use only of those elements of IT that work for us personally. No more. We should never feel we *have* to 'go online' simply to 'keep up' with friends and colleagues, or because the media tells us how wonderful it is. And *never* if we become so worried about the skills involved that the problems of which key to press, and in what sequence, start to interfere with the creative process.

Already the Internet impinges on pretty well every aspect of our daily routine, be it in banking, shopping, travelling, writing, or any other activity, and regardless of whether or not we ourselves are 'online'. As book buyers or researchers every time we enter a bookshop or library we have the benefit of a computerised catalogue. Even if we are not yet ourselves online there are opportunities to take advantage of library computer services or cybercafés to access the Net and the World Wide Web.

The coming of the new technology has transformed the working lives of writers and researchers, and we are indebted to it. The manufacture of the Xerox photocopying machine several decades ago liberated us from the tedious task of copying long texts by hand; today we are able, thanks to the computer, to benefit almost instantaneously from recent research anywhere in the world. The present generation cannot conceive how in the meantime any of us got by without photocopy and microfilm, let alone without CD-ROM and email. I do however question whether some of these seemingly miraculous techniques, in banishing the tedium, may not also have shed a good deal of the 'magic' along the way? Is it possible that bringing up a text on screen can genuinely match the thrill of holding in one's own hands a medieval charter complete with original seal or the handwritten letter of, say, Queen Victoria or Winston Churchill? Perhaps accessing a database the other side of the globe generates its own particular brand of magic. If so, I have yet to experience it. Speaking for myself, I shall always be thankful that I was able to do the bulk of my professional researching at a time when nearly always you were entrusted with the original newspaper, the original document. Today, understandably, in the interest of preservation of our national heritage, 80 per cent of the time the closest you get is a microfilm.

When I prepared the last edition in 1995 I was somewhat in the dark as to the proportion of my readers who used the new technology and those who, for financial or other reasons, did not. I still am. Once again therefore I should like to reassure those who remain addicted to pen, paper and typewriter. Clearly, for a long time to come a great many researchers and writers are going to carry on using the traditional methods and sources outlined in this book. The computer may give you speedier access to up-to-date information, and may lighten your task in other ways, but it cannot and will not do all your work for you. Thus, for many years yet you will continue to do the bulk of your research in the library and the archive centre. Books and journals will continue to be published in printed form. For many readers of my generation who were brought up to research on the printed page, taking a volume from the bookshelf and leafing through the pages may still seem quicker than loading a CD-ROM and scrolling up and down on screen. Take heart. The old techniques of note-taking and face-to-face interviewing will still be practised. Those of you who have tried to use a computer and decided it is not for you – yet – will not be outlawed overnight. Nor will any sane editor reject a well researched, well-written work purely because it is submitted on A4 paper (now called 'hard copy') rather than on disk. 'Books do not seem likely to be replaced by personal computers,' wrote Lord Rees-Mogg in *The Times*, reassuringly, on 18 May 1998, 'reading from a screen is work, but reading from a page is pleasure.' However much my younger readers may protest – and they have a right to do so, for theirs has been a totally different education – that is a sentiment I heartily applaud.

Mark Twain, the first writer known to have delivered a book to his publisher in typescript, purchased one of the early Remington typewriters in 1874. Five generations on, in 1999, some bestselling authors still choose to write in longhand and to pay a professional typist. The message is clear: the age of electronic authorship – and, it follows, electronic research – may have arrived, but you are still free to suit yourself.

One of the problems I have had to resolve in compiling this new edition is to judge which of the older titles to drop in order to make room for more recent works. Inevitably, with so much new material to hand, some have had to go. I am of course only too well aware that in the present economic climate libraries are having to cut down on the renewal and purchase of their reference stocks, which means that researchers without easy access to a copyright or university library may be at a disadvantage. To this end I have taken the middle road, discarding what I personally consider to be 'dead wood' (titles that have been superseded by more up-to-date, improved works), while retaining as many as space permits of the well-established or one-off reference books that still rank among the best on their subject. If this time round I have inadvertently axed one or two of my readers' favourites, I ask their forgiveness. May I suggest that before they chuck out the earlier edition they make use of the blank pages provided at the back of this one to keep a note of such titles?

As before, publications mentioned in the text are listed alphabetically by title at the end of the relevant chapter rather than in one long bibliography at the end. (Listing by title rather than by author runs contrary to recognised bibliographic practice. Its continuance in this edition is, I hope, justified for reasons of quick reference: the works themselves are referred to first by title in the text and users of earlier editions will have become familiar with this method.) Database files mentioned in the text are not listed in the bibliographies. Microform and CD-ROM editions have been included where most relevant. Publication on film, fiche and CD being such a fast-growing industry, to have attempted more would have been at best incomplete. It would also have added considerably to the bulk (and thus the cost) of this book. A researcher who is 'on the ball' will ask at the library information counter; even if he does not, the competent librarian or archivist will usually bring such editions to his attention. Regrettably, it is not possible always to indicate those books which are out of print, as the situation changes constantly and reprints or new editions may become available during the lifetime of this book. Most of the out-of-print titles mentioned will be found in the larger public libraries or may be borrowed through the public library lending service; but researchers needing to use such books over a long period are recommended to 'shop around' for them in secondhand and antiquarian bookshops (and even jumble sales), or to ask a book finding service to try to locate them (see page 52).

The need to deliver my revised text some months before publication makes it impossible to be fully up to date, but readers who follow my guidelines for using library catalogues and bibliographies should have little difficulty in tracing recently published material or new editions of existing works. Addresses and telephone numbers are a different matter, changing as they do, it seems, with unpredictable and infuriating frequency. (See the note on page xiii about the new area codes and prefixes to be introduced in April 2000 for London, some provincial cities and Northern Ireland.) This means that, depending on the month of publication, even annual guides may be to some extent out of date by the time they appear. This aspect – or hazard, if you like – of modern living is one we simply have to learn to accept. In this edition, as well as fax numbers for most libraries and other sources, I have included a few Websites of use to the researcher. To have added email addresses for every source mentioned would have considerably lengthened the book and increased its cost: as a compromise, those for the major libraries and other sources have been included in Appendix I. It is suggested that readers compile their own individual Websites/email address book.

I should like to take this opportunity to express my gratitude to the many librarians, archivists, curators, press and public relations officers, publishers and others who have so efficiently and courteously dealt with my enquiries on a multitude of subjects over the years, and most especially to the staff of the British Library. I am also indebted to several fellow writers, research colleagues and librarians who made constructive comments on the first five editions, some of whose suggestions are now incorporated. This time round I am especially grateful to Duncan Alexander, Gwynneth Ashby, Nicolas Branden, Geoffrey Copus, Idina Le Geyt, Peter Reynolds and A.P. Woolrich. I have also much appreciated the patience and understanding of my editor at A & C Black, Tesni Hollands, over the unforeseen delays in my producing this revised text. When the book went out of print in the autumn of 1998, this was the first time since its initial publication (1975). Finally, and by no means least of all, I wish to thank my copy-editor, Lynn Bresler, for her meticulous work on this and the last edition.

My mail-bag since the appearance of the first edition makes it clear that *Research for Writers* has been of use not only to the novice researcher and writer for whom it was intended – and even on occasion to those who make a hobby of entering competitions – but also to the more experienced 'diggers' who, so they tell me, suffer occasionally from extraordinary lapses of memory or mental blocks that result in their wasting precious time searching for information which in fact may be close at hand in their own reference collection or in a local library. To all these people I dedicate this sixth edition. In return, the greatest compliment they can pay me will be to *use the book as a working tool, to annotate it profusely, and to update it as their research requires*. For this purpose my publishers have again been persuaded to include a few blank pages at the end for personal notes. If, by the time these pages are filled, the book is starting to come apart at the spine through constant usage, hopefully there may be a seventh edition in the pipeline. As before, comments and suggestions for future editions will be most gratefully received.

A.H.
London, 1999

# 1

## The Writer as Researcher

Every writer, unless he is creating a work of pure fantasy, has to do research. The nature and depth of that research will vary enormously, according to the subject of the work, the field of writing (factual article, novel, biography, history, thesis, children's story, etc.) and whether it is intended for the academic, popular or juvenile market. Whereas the scholar may have comparatively unlimited time (and probably also a research grant) which allows him to follow up pretty well every relevant line of enquiry in detail, the journalist's 'copy' must be on the sub-editor's desk at a given hour, and he is always pressed for time. Both texts must be correct, up to date and original – in other words, properly researched and well written.

In the end-product the academic work, with its notes and references, bibliography and index, may look to be the more meticulously researched, but this can be a deception: the thousand-word newspaper or magazine article, in order to present its data in a convincing, accurate and readable way and to show that its author is fully conversant with the latest events and/or published studies on the subject, may well involve as much, and sometimes more, research in proportion to its length. Whatever the field of authorship, the writer has to know a great deal more than he actually puts into words if what he writes is to ring true – and this applies as strictly to fiction writers as to journalists and historians and biographers. Ernest Hemingway, in an interview published in *Paris Review* (Spring 1958), put this very well. 'I always try to write on the principle of the iceberg,' he said. 'There is seven-eighths of it under water for every part that shows. Anything you know you can eliminate and it only strengthens your iceberg. It is the part that doesn't show. If the writer omits something because he does not know it, then there is a hole in the story.'*

*The same author, in *Death in the Afternoon*, expounds on this theme at greater length in a memorable passage worthy of framing and hanging above every writer's desk. It will be found at the end of chapter 16, in the paperback edition (Arrow Books, 1994), at pages 168–9.

In ideal circumstances an author would write only of what he knows. No one, however, can have first-hand knowledge of every trade or profession in which he wishes to place his characters; few can afford to visit all those far-off lands that they are tempted to use as 'local colour' in their work. In most short stories or novels or plays, therefore, there are bound to be some people, some situations and some settings that are beyond the personal experience of the writer, and for which he must rely to some extent at least on second-hand material – that is to say, on what others before him have observed and recorded, on printed statistics and factual data, and often on the recollections of third parties. The writer of history or historical fiction has no choice but to rely on documentary sources, either in print or in manuscript. In all these instances the research done must be thorough and, as far as possible, undertaken *in the round* (i.e. from more than one angle, avoiding reliance on any one source), or the result will be cardboard people, cardboard backgrounds and a loss of credibility in what may otherwise be an excellent piece of writing.

The prime importance of researching thoroughly before going into print cannot be over-stressed. Once his reader's confidence has been lost, the author will have an uphill battle to regain it. All too often a disillusioned reader or bright schoolchild will write and tell him where he has gone wrong, or – which is worse – may write and tell his editor or publisher, which in turn destroys their confidence and is likely to influence their attitude to the author's future work.

It is dangerous to rely on only one source for a given piece of information, however authoritative that source may seem to be. Mistakes occur all too frequently in even the most erudite book. They may not be the original author's fault at all, but the result of slipshod proof-reading in the editor's office or a printer's error that occurred at a later stage, such as when the typesetter re-sets a line to incorporate the author's or publisher's corrections. The sad thing is that once they are in print, mistakes are bound to be copied in good faith by someone else, and that person's work in turn may well be used as source material by another, and so on, so that even if a correction is made in subsequent editions of the original work, the misprint in that first edition may be perpetuated *ad infinitum*. By 'misprints' in this context is meant the mis-spelling of a proper name, a mis-quotation or a wrong figure – the sort of error that would not necessarily be spotted by a reader. The other kind of mistake, known as a 'literal' in publishing and printing, which may be a character set up in the wrong fount, or upside down, or two characters transposed, and the more obvious spelling mistake are more likely to be spotted at proof-reading stage.

Such are the hazards of authorship that the writer of non-fiction would do well to keep constantly in his mind's eye as he works the image of future trusting generations of students and researchers relying on his text as an authoritative source.

For most modern writers time is a precious commodity. Gone for ever are those halcyon days when Samuel Johnson could speak of a man turning over half a library to make one book; since his day millions more books have been written and published, and our libraries, archive collections and record repositories now house a bewildering and ever-increasing conglomeration of printed, manuscript, microfilmed, recorded and electronically produced material; there are also vast databases worldwide. More than ever before has it become essential for the writer/researcher to organise his working hours to the best advantage. He must know where and how to get at the information he requires in the quickest, as well as the most efficient and economical, way. As the great Dr Johnson also said: 'Knowledge is of two kinds. We know a subject ourselves, or we know where we can find information upon it.' While the specialist must know his pet subject inside out, there is no question but that for the general writer the knowledge of *where to go* to find what he needs is of the greater value. Quite apart from the fact that no one would want to become a walking encyclopaedia, even if it were humanly possible to carry a mass of information on a variety of subjects in one's head all the time, most professional writers would agree that a sound knowledge of available sources (or, failing that, a reliable researcher on whose services they can call) allows them more time to concentrate on the creative activity. Nothing can be more distracting or more paralysing to the flow of ideas and their shaping into words than a nagging worry, 'Where on earth am I going to be able to find out about *that*?'

Seeking information implies curiosity, a characteristic inborn not only in the feline species but in the whole human race. We have all been researchers since we were in the cradle. Long before he can speak or read or write, a baby is obsessed by the desire to find out about the things around him. Attracted by the colour of an unknown object, he reaches out to touch it and, having seized it and found it pleasing to hold, usually puts it into his mouth. What does it feel like? Does it taste good? What is it made of? *What is* it? He has taken the first step along a path of discovery and enchantment that will last a lifetime. From that first childish desire to learn about objects, he progresses to curiosity about himself and his body, and then to other people and animals; from the happenings he observes in his immediate circle to those of history; through history to religion, and then to science and speculation about the future. He will never know

3

it all, but if as he grows older he keeps alive his youthful sense of curiosity he will – especially if he becomes a writer – have endless resources on which to draw, and he will never be bored.

It is a well-known saying that a writer may be angry, disgusted, amused, uplifted or almost anything in between, and his work will be the better for it, but if he is bored it will be reflected in his writing. Robert Louis Stevenson held that life would be only a very dull and ill-directed theatre unless we had some interests in the piece. 'It is in virtue of his own desires and curiosities that any man continues to exist with even patience,' he wrote, 'that he is charmed by the look of things and people, and that he wakens every morning with a renewed appetite for work and pleasure. Desire and curiosity are the two eyes through which he sees the world in the most enchanted colours: it is they that make women beautiful or fossils interesting ...'*

Because a writer's raw material is derived principally from a study of other human beings, their complex relationships, their strengths and weaknesses and idiosyncrasies, as well as their history, he can probably get away with being more openly curious than any other group of people – provided always that he does not offend by his looking or probing. The arts of observation without seeming to observe and of probing without seeming to probe are skills that can – and should – be acquired.

While most writers are also researchers, not all researchers are talented as writers. The prime function of the researcher is to seek information; that of the writer is more complicated, for his duty is both to impart knowledge and to give pleasure – in other words, to entertain as well as to instruct his reader. And just as a factual book can give pleasure to the reader by the manner in which it is written, so the most absorbing and entertaining of stories can impart knowledge. The one thing a writer must never do, under any circumstances, however, is to distort the truth for the sake of a good story.

*Everything* that comes within the writer's own experience is grist to the mill and should be stored away, ideally in note form or on tape or computer, for future use. Ideas, an unusual turn of phrase, a gesture, a conversation overheard, brief descriptions of people or places, on-the-spot reports of events, even pain suffered (you think at the time you will always remember how it felt, but you rarely do): these will be of immense value, provided that they are kept in such a way that they can be turned up quickly when required. (Some practical suggestions for filing and storage are discussed on pages

*From the essay 'El Dorado' in *Virginibus Puerisque*.

18–23.) Naturally it is not possible to predict years in advance what you are going to need, so that how much or how little is noted and filed must be a decision for the individual writer, but it is a fact of life that once you throw something away, you need it. The Preface to Somerset Maugham's *A Writer's Notebook*, first published in 1949, makes interesting reading on this score, for the author admits that there were many years in which he made no notes at all, that he kept no record of his meetings with famous people. 'I never made a note of anything that I did not think would be useful to me at one time or another in my work,' he states, 'and though, especially in the early notebooks, I jotted down all kinds of thoughts and emotions of a personal nature, it was only with the intention of ascribing them sooner or later to the creatures of my invention. I meant my note-books to be a storehouse of materials for future use and nothing else.' So spoke the short story writer and novelist. It would be unthinkable for a diarist or biographer to fail to record his meetings with famous people.

In the course of his researching life a writer will be faced with a variety of tasks. These may range from the simple checking of facts (dates, quotations, spellings, statistics) to the tracing of a contemporary account of some historical event, or the more complicated unravelling of someone's ancestry, or an authentic setting for a novel or play. The best-selling author Frederick Forsyth reckons to divide his research into four categories: *geographical* (which necessitates visits to places); *historical* (checkable in source material); *procedural* (which involves contacting and talking to 'inside' people); and *technical* (checkable facts). It will be obvious that there are wide differences, both of skill and approach, between the four, and that some of the categories overlap or merge.

In *factual research* (statistical, historical and technical), the enquirer knows precisely what he is looking for and what he expects to find, so that, provided he knows where to go for the information, he should encounter no great difficulty. Knowing where to go is the key here.

In pure *historical research* the scope is much wider, as regards both the material available and the use that is made of it. As no two writers, given the same plot and the same set of characters, will come up with an identical story, so no two researchers, confronted with the same documentary sources, will use those sources in an identical way. The basic facts – the skeleton – will be similar, of course, but whereas one researcher will explore a certain avenue in more detail than another and quote extensively from a document that in the eyes of his colleague merits no more than a passing reference, the second may be less selective on one aspect of the search but obsessive about detail on another, depending upon the angle from which their respective works are to be written and on the market for which they are intended.

*Background research* (which includes the geographical and procedural), usually required for a work of fiction, modern or historical, generally demands less discipline but, as a result, may lead the enquirer down some unforeseen channels and possibly end by radically changing the shape or character of his story.

Thus both historical and background research fall into the category of *creative*, as opposed to *factual*, research. In these fields the researcher, not knowing beforehand what he is going to find, must be alive to each and every clue he comes across, any one of which could lead to some vital discovery that could bring his work to life in an exciting and original way.

In general, an article or thesis will require either factual or historical research, or both, whereas most books will demand a mixture of all three types of research, in varying proportions according to their subject and what the writer already knows. In a biography, for example, some factual research will be necessary to substantiate a quotation from a letter or diary of a certain date; historical research to fill in the detail of an event in which the subject of the biography played a leading part; background research to permit the author to describe, say, the environment in which that person grew up. In an historical novel, dates and names and events must be factually correct, while background research will be important in order to bring it to life, to add accurate details of costume, food, manners, etc. of the relevant period. In a modern short story or play, the setting must be authentic and the characters must speak the right language (slang, dialect or technical idiom related to their occupations and age). Some of the problems and pitfalls, as well as the sources of information appropriate to each of these categories of research, are outlined in later sections of this book.

Whatever the subject or nature of the search, the procedure is roughly the same. You may begin with one solid fact or several – this may be a date, or an event, or a name, or sometimes merely an idea – and you build up your dossier rather like the Criminal Intelligence Service officer tracks down his suspect: with patience, persistence, and (hopefully) the occasional lucky break. You make full use of modern technological aids but do not eschew the conventional methods. It may take you months to ferret out one vital clue, or you may chance upon it straight away. Often it is just when you have returned despondently to square one from yet another in a series of blind alleys that you stumble on the missing link – and curse yourself for following up so many red herrings on the way. All professional researchers know the elation such an unexpected discovery produces. Nowhere is it more aptly described than by the university professor quoted in Dr A.L. Rowse's *A Cornish Childhood* as saying, '... I felt that curious thrill, the authentic sensation of the researcher ... It is as if you were to sit down and find you have sat on the cat. The thing comes alive in your hand ...' Peter Fleming, discussing the art of research with the late Joan St George Saunders of Writers' and Speakers' Research, the first professional research service in this country (there are several others now), likened it to fox hunting: 'The horns sound, one races for the first covert – then a halt while the hounds snuffle around in the undergrowth. Here the cunning hunter circles around the wood and knows instinctively which way the hounds will break. Off you go again and by the end of the day you are still there – perhaps to be blooded with success!'*

One of the researcher's greatest problems lies in deciding when to call it a day. It is always possible – and tempting – to go on delving just a little further – provided, of course, that time and adequate funds are available. But he must keep in mind the terms of reference of his work and discipline himself accordingly. Only experience will enable him to acquire the 'feel' of the job, to know when he should follow his hunch and go off at a tangent, when to replace the reference books on the shelf and pick up his pen. The temptation will nearly always be there to continue researching 'for a little while longer'. All too easily the writer can slip into the comfortable routine of a perpetual student.

It is a bad thing to postpone indefinitely the real creative process. Indeed, to prolong researching unduly is regarded by some academics as an indication of a fear of the actual writing. Therefore once a certain stage in the research has been reached, it is best to press on with a first draft. A modest amount of further research will almost certainly be necessary, and possible, at a later stage, when you will know more precisely what you need or in order to up-date, to fill in any gaps or to explore aspects of your subject which you may have ignored at the outset but now wish to include. Very often an editor or agent, after a first reading of the author's typescript, will suggest modifications or additions; in the case of a book, it will be the copy editor who will query with the author certain spellings or statements, some of which may involve extra research.

Modern society is constantly on the move, new studies appear every week, and since it now takes an average of between nine and twelve months from delivery of manuscript to the date of publication of a book, unless a writer is submitting an article of topical interest

*Letter to the author from Mrs St George Saunders, 15 August 1975. Quoted by kind permission of Sir Alan Urwick.

for almost instant publication in a newspaper or journal, it will be impossible for his work to be fully up to date. Modern typesetting procedures and the current practice of going straight into page proofs instead of first into galleys and then into page have made it prohibitively expensive for any but the most essential corrections and up-datings to be incorporated at this stage – apart, of course, from printer's errors and 'literals'. You should not allow this to worry you unduly: it is the same for everyone, and a well-researched, well-written work will always achieve recognition as such.

In the fulfilment of his work, whether it be long or short, fiction or non-fiction, the author will surely have experienced the deep sense of satisfaction that is the reward of a thorough job of research. If it has not been altogether too traumatic an exercise, he may even go along with the view of the poet Robert Herrick:

> Attempt the end, and never stand to doubt;
> Nothing's so hard, but search will find it out.

# 2

# Organisation and Method

The writer's first task, when embarking on a new project, is to survey and organise the material already in his possession. By the time you have done this, you will have a pretty good idea of how much additional research needs to be done. Then, and only then – and always bearing in mind the intended length and complexity of the end-product, as well as the time and funds available – are you ready to move on to tap other sources.

At this stage you should make a preliminary list of everything you need to find out and where you think you will have to go to get it. The key here is to *plan ahead*. This does not apply to research you do on the Internet, to which you have instant access, but at libraries and other information centres the books you want may be in use by other readers, so that you will have to wait a few weeks for them. The people you hope to interview may be busy or away. Information you send for may take longer than you anticipate to arrive. You will be surprised also at how much time and money you will save by taking the trouble to write down all those people and places you envisage having to visit: with the aid of a good map and gazetteer you can plan itineraries that take in several assignments on each trip.

Just as it is false economy to skip the amount of time necessary for a thorough study of basic material and sources, so it is foolish to neglect to give proper thought to setting up a system for the storage and easy retrieval of that material, remembering always to make suitable provision for material still to be acquired. Since both these operations cost money as well as time (time = money being a constant theme throughout this book), this is an appropriate place in which to outline some of the financial aspects of research.

## Costs of Research

The first thing to remember is that it will always cost more than you expect. Leaving aside the question of working time, outgoings will include stationery and equipment, travelling and motor expenses, search fees (charged by some private libraries and by clergy for inspection of parish registers), the purchase of books, periodicals and newspapers, photocopying, photography, computer and fax supplies, telephone and postal expenses (these can be unexpectedly heavy), and, if you have one, the monthly subscription to your Internet service provider (ISP). Meals away from home when researching can be expensive, and you should not forget the lighting, heating and cleaning of a room used as office or study, since over the years this too can mount up – and if you are making an income from writing most of such outgoings can be included as legitimate expenses to set against tax. The fees of a professional researcher, if employed, will be another major item, as will those of an indexer, and, at the end of the day, unless you are a good typist, you should allow for the cost of producing the final typescript in two or more copies. Computer-owners should remember to include the cost of the print-out from disk.

It is an excellent idea to make a list of every conceivable expense you think you are going to incur – and then double it. Costs are rising all the time, and if a book takes four years to complete instead of the eighteen months you envisaged at the outset, this will play havoc with your budget. However, you will not have to fork out the total amount in one go, but as you proceed.

If you are fortunate enough to have a book or article commissioned, explain to the publisher or editor before you negotiate the contract or settle the fee just how much research expenditure is likely to be involved, and, in the case of a book, try to negotiate an adequate advance against royalties; this will probably be payable in instalments. Journalists may be able to arrange their assignments on an expenses-paid basis. In all cases, it is wise to keep a record of every item of expenditure, from a packet of paper clips to the hotel bill, and to ask for receipts for all major payments: you may not be a published writer when you start out, but if you end up as the author of a bestseller or even a writer with a modest regular income from his work, you will need to justify your expenses to the tax inspector.

It is always dangerous to state prices in print, especially in these days of inflation. As a guideline to the uninitiated, however, it should be borne in mind that at the time of going to press (summer 1999) freelance researchers and record agents are charging between £15 and £30 an hour, depending on the special skills involved. Typing costs vary: most agencies and home typists now offer a word processing service, with inkjet or laser printing. (Consult advertisements on the back page of *The Author*.) If you type your own work, remember that paper, ribbons, floppy disks, and ink or toner cartridges for the printer are not cheap. (Members of the Society of Authors may order stationery through their fringe benefit scheme – provided they can collect the goods from the Society's office in Kensington.) By shopping around locally you may find an outlet selling office and computer supplies at discount prices. Do not overlook the need for servicing your equipment from time to time: keeping even the faithful old manual typewriter up to scratch can cost in excess of £50 a year.

Photocopying varies from as little as 5p to 50p a sheet, according to size, to as much as £2.00 for A2 size copies from newspaper pages. The cheapest are those you make yourself on a coin-operated machine. 'Enhanced' photocopies and copies from microfiche or microfilm are more expensive. Bear in mind that applications by post not only cost more, but may also be subject to a minimum charge and handling fee. Some libraries offer an express service at additional cost. Genealogists and family historians constantly bemoan the fact that photocopies of birth, marriage and death certificates now cost £6.50 apiece if applied for in person or between £9.00 and £12.00 when ordered by post (see chapter 7, pages 141–2).

One major expense so often overlooked by a writer is the cost of quoting from copyright material: fees are liable to be charged for anything more than a few lines, although in practice some agents and publishers will be content, in the case of a short passage, with a suitable acknowledgment or possibly a free copy of the book. Reproduction fees for illustrative material, on the other hand, vary according to the size of the reproduction and the nature of the rights sought (i.e. British Commonwealth rights, world rights, etc.), but are normally not payable until the date of publication. Sometimes a publisher is willing to bear all or part of such expenses, and an author wishing to quote extensively from copyright material or to use pictures from private photographers, picture agencies or libraries would be well advised to ascertain the costs in advance and to discuss the financial division of responsibilities prior to the contract being drawn up for signature.

'Hidden' expenses will include the number of free copies an author is expected to hand out. Normally he will receive six free copies of his book and may buy additional copies at a substantial discount. It is courteous to give signed copies to those who have helped to prepare the book for the press, such as the professional researcher, translator, indexer or proof-reader (where these are not taken care of by the publisher), and to the typist; copies should also be presented to anyone who has provided a substantial amount of material or granted the author access to private papers. The publisher is responsible for sending out review copies.

# Equipment

No one would dream of taking up a sports or leisure activity without the proper equipment; nor should a writer or journalist embark on his researches lacking the few essential tools of the trade. It is true that pen and paper, the rudiments of shorthand or speed-writing, access to a good library, and an unlimited amount of time were once all that was needed, and although one might still 'get by' with these, today, when time is money (a recurrent theme of this book, for which I make no apology), it is both sensible and practical to make full use of all that modern technology provides to help us obtain the information we seek as speedily and as inexpensively as possible.

The basic equipment required can be divided into three groups: 1) the tools you take with you in briefcase or car when researching outside the home; 2) equipment for use in the writer's study; and 3) equipment that is 'desirable' (i.e. where funds permit) or for special assignments.

The suggested items are (excluding normal stationery):

**To take out 'on the job'**
Large briefcase and/or shoulder bag
Portable PC (laptop, palmtop or PDA) or alternatively a micro cassette
Recorder/pocket memo/electronic note-taker, with plenty of spare cassettes and batteries (take twice as many as you *think* you will need)
Tape recorder (with or without detachable microphone), good supply of tapes, preferably C90s, and batteries
Camera (if the job requires it), with generous supply of film, flashbulbs and batteries. N.B. The 'instant' or disk camera is quite adequate if pictures are for research, but a good SLR at least is essential if for reproduction
Mobile phone/BT or Mercury chargecard and/or Phonecard
Filofax/personal organiser, or failing that a pocket diary/telephone and address book
Clipboard (useful for writing on as you walk around or when interviewing)
Plenty of notepads
Pocket magnifier
Mini-stapler
Plenty of ballpoints and *pencils*, with sharpener and rubber. (Local record offices and most manuscript departments of libraries permit note-taking only in pencil.)
Ruler
Envelopes and stamps (Royal Mail ready-stamped envelopes are useful.)

Map of area to be visited
Local bus/rail time-tables
Small cash book (for noting tax-deductible expenses)
Spare pair of reading glasses (if used)
Torch
Loose cash (coins), for cloakroom lockers and self-operated photocopying machines (also useful for tea and coffee vending machines)
N.B. For security reasons many libraries and record offices require visitors to deposit briefcases or bulky packages before entering the search rooms. (Ladies are at an advantage here, if they have the kind of briefcase that doubles as a handbag – but there may be restrictions as to size!) If you have to empty your bag, be sure that all your papers are securely fastened or in document folders so that you do not scatter them along the corridor on the way to the search room.

**For the study**
Word processor/personal computer (preferably with hard disk, CD-ROM drive and modem)
Printer (preferably inkjet or laser), with spare inkjet or laser toner cartridge
Fax machine
Good desk lamp
Transcriber for cassette recorder, with foot pedal
Filing cabinet or other storage system
Card index system
Large magnifying glass
Stapler/punch (better than paper clips for fastening notes)
Paper guillotine (for trimming half-used sheets of paper and enabling you to use offcuts for notes and/or bookmarks)
Letter scales, leaflet with current postal rates and good stock of stamps in varying denominations (to save queueing at post office)
Highlighter felt pens in different colours
Soft pencils
Generous stock of yellow 'Post-it' notepads/coloured index flags

**For the professional researcher and those on special assignments** (in addition to the above list)
Sophisticated type of tape recorder, as used by most radio and TV reporters (essential if interviews or recordings are to be broadcast)
Telephone answering machine
Video recorder
Paper shredder (essential if you handle confidential documents)

Photocopier capable of copying from bound volumes

Microform reader (to enable you to use microfiche/microfilm at home)

Modem for connecting to Internet and other databases, plus all the necessary cables and software

*N.B.* It is wise to have a back-up computer in case your main one goes down (if this should happen, it will invariably be at the most critical moment). Keep your old one when you up-grade or buy a secondhand one cheap. Make sure it is compatible. Alternatively stow your old typewriter away in a cupboard or attic for emergencies.

## Computers

Most professional writers and a high percentage of as yet unpublished writers now use word processors or personal computers (PCs). Journalists and researchers in all parts of the globe, no matter how remote, use their computers to access the Internet and the World Wide Web (WWW), which is the fastest growing information resource in the world, and to send and receive email. On the other hand, very many writers still buy computers purely for the word-processing facility.

It does not fall within the scope of this book to discuss the finer points of word processing or to recommend any particular brand of equipment. It would be irresponsible of me to do so. The new technology advances at such a pace that anything I write today is more than likely to be out of date by the time this edition is published. However, a few basic guidelines may not be out of place:

Never rush into a purchase. There are many interesting packages and discounts on offer, both on desktop PCs and portables, and it makes sense to shop around. Visit local dealers, browse through the latest computer magazines, talk to knowledgeable friends, preferably writers. At the end of the day the best advice you can get will undoubtedly come from a fellow author or journalist.

Buy the best system you can afford, preferably a multimedia computer, with a CD-ROM drive, and speakers. You may not need all the equipment now, but when later on you decide to go online and want to download chunks of data, or to run some of the more sophisticated programs on the market, or to go into self-publishing, you will be glad of it. The same goes for a printer, the inkjet or laser models giving the best results. Colour printers are fun, but not really necessary for the general writer, unless you intend to embark on desktop publishing.

The more powerful the processor, the faster it will work. The greater the capacity of hard disk and RAM, the more data that can be stored and the more programs run. Hard disk capacity today is up to ten times what it was five years ago, which is some indication of the rate at which the technology continues to advance. Most systems can be upgraded later, to some extent, but do remember that the new software coming onto the market is increasingly greedy for disk and memory space. Think ahead.

Computers are sold by department stores, stationers, specialist dealers and by mail order. I personally would always go for the specialist dealer or mail order company. Most dealers however seem to be notoriously indifferent to the special needs of writers: in their eyes spreadsheets, computer games and graphics all take precedence over word processing. Do your homework before you commit yourself.

Be sure to tell the dealer precisely what you intend to use the computer for. Insofar as word-processing software is concerned, most writers get along well with Microsoft Word or Wordperfect. It is worth emphasising here that it is definitely NOT a good idea to share your computer with the family, not least because games software is so much more demanding than word-processing software.

If buying locally, insist on a one-to-one 'hands-on' demonstration. Draw up a list, however long, of everything you expect from your word-processing package (it may be line spacing, footnotes, page numbering, a search and replace facility, a word count, or just moving text from one page to another); ask to be shown how to carry out all these operations, and *make notes*. (The manuals supplied never seem to contain the very instructions you yourself need, and when you get home you will not remember.) Another thing to take into account is that you are going to be spending a good deal of time at work on the computer, so be sure to choose a keyboard and screen that you personally feel comfortable with. One of the advantages of buying from a local dealer is that he will set the whole system up for you and hopefully be around to deal with any teething problems that arise, and to upgrade it, if required, at a later date. If you purchase by mail order, the computer will be delivered with the software pre-loaded, but you will have to set it up yourself, with help from the manual or tutorial disk that accompanies the system; you will be given a technical support telephone number to ring whenever you need assistance.

Up to a few years ago when the book and magazine world was divided in its preference between IBM-compatible PCs and Macs (Apple Macintosh), writers were often influenced in their choice of computer by their editors or publishers. Macs run the Macintosh operating system and can read or convert PC disks; PCs run the DOS and Windows systems. Today, thanks to conversion software, most major word-processing packages usually work on both, so this is no longer a factor; nevertheless, it is wise to check both with your publisher and your dealer before you part with your money. For the purposes of desktop publishing Macintosh is the most favoured, on account of its graphics performance.

Many computer systems are now 'multimedia', and come with internal CD-ROM drives and stereo speakers. You must have a CD-ROM drive if you want to make use of the rapidly increasing number of reference works now being published in electronic form. A bonus for music lovers is that you will be able to listen to your favourite CDs as you work; for those who find computers stressful, soothing music could avert potential 'computer rage'. For advice on how writers can make the best use of multimedia, send for a copy of the Society of Authors *Information Sheet*, 'Multimedia for Authors'.

To go online you will need a 'modem', a device which enables your computer to communicate with other computers via the telephone. This may or may not come pre-loaded, or as a 'package' with the system, together with the necessary connecting cables and software. What you will almost certainly receive with a new computer is a large bundle of assorted software. Unfortunately, in order to get the sophisticated facilities that you do need, you may have to take on board all sorts of other options that, in your writing life, you will never use. It is a good idea to sort through these carefully at the outset and stow out of sight anything that does not relate to your work. In this way you will avoid the temptation of experimenting and thus wasting valuable creative time.

Portable computers – 'laptops', 'notebooks' and to some extent 'palmtops' and 'personal digital assistants' (PDAs) – are widely used by journalists and writers on the move. Points to watch when purchasing this type of equipment include compatibility with your desktop PC, battery life, and the size of screen and keyboard. A very small keyboard does not suit everyone, and you may prefer the type on which you write with a stylus on plastic. The more expensive portables are multimedia and have built-in modems enabling the user to send email and faxes, and to access the Internet. Handheld ('palmtop') models are useful for on-the-spot note-taking and have the advantage of fitting into a pocket or handbag. New on the market as I write are 'micro-computers' small enough to be slotted onto a belt. If you already have a PC at home, and need something just to make brief notes on as you work in the library or archive centre, or out on the job, a PDA or handheld computer may suit your needs. (Bear in mind, however, that the smaller the equipment the more costly repairs are likely to be should it break down after the normal twelve-month guarantee has expired.)

There are other items of equipment and software of special use to writers and researchers:

Those who handle highly sensitive information should ask their dealers about the shredders that safely erase all such material from the hard disk on their computer.

Writers and researchers who frequently need to store on computer large chunks of printed material from books or newspapers may find useful the optical character recognition software (OCR). This is normally sold as a package together with a scanner, at a cost of about £100.

Speech recognition software is also now readily available, enabling the user to dictate to a PC at speeds of between 80 and 160 words a minute. Not only are the spoken words transcribed instantly onto the screen, you can use your voice to command the PC to execute other functions such as formatting and editing text, surfing the Net, or simply to read aloud selected text (a useful timing device for speech writers). It has to be said, however, that sound activated software is not yet perfect.

Very soon we are promised a 'computer pen' that will convert up to ten A4 pages of handwriting, however idiosyncratic, into neatly typed text on screen, in one go. Will this be the ultimate work tool for those among us whose handwriting verges on the illegible and who begrudge the time spent typing up research notes? Probably not. Other 'miracles' are sure to follow. (Watch this space in the next edition.)

## Photocopiers

Unless you do a great deal of photocopying, it is not really worth while purchasing a machine. Some of the cheaper desk-top models copy only from loose sheets, and not all those that take bound books give satisfactory results, especially if the volume to be copied is thick or tightly bound. Eager salesmen may promise copies at a fraction of the commercial cost, which can be tempting, but when you take into account the cost of materials, electricity, servicing charges, annual depreciation of the machine *and* operating – your valuable working time – there may not be a great saving. The value of having a photocopier at hand is the *convenience* of being able to run off copies instantly, without the need to make a special trip into town. Much depends, therefore, on how close you live to the nearest copy shop. Remember that you can use a fax machine to make a working copy of the odd sheet, but that this is not a permanent copy (it will fade after about six months). Some of the latest plain paper fax machines do double as photocopiers.

# Organisation of Material

There are few hard and fast rules in research, but it is wise to establish at the outset, and to adhere to, some systematic method of note-taking and data storage. There is little point in accumulating a mass of notes, press cuttings and other material unless you also devise a fairly foolproof system which will enable you either to bring up on screen or manually locate what you want *when you want it*. Those who store manually should get into the habit of replacing any documents they have extracted immediately after use so that they can find them again later. (This will take only a minute or two at the time. It could take two hours, or more, if the document has been mislaid.)

Storage methods will differ according to individual circumstances and taste, and according to the type of material involved. Computer owners who set up personal databases will find them ideal for the storage of research notes and other information. The rest of us, soldiering on manually, divide into two camps: those who favour card indexes, and those who prefer notebooks, pads or loose sheets of paper, with a filing cabinet or cupboard large enough to house them.

## Electronic storage

Building and maintaining a database on your PC is not difficult with the aid of your manual and the appropriate bibliographic software. Follow instructions, and try to keep it as simple as possible. Remember that the object of the exercise is to be able to access speedily everything you store. Remember too that in order to keep your database up to date you must regularly key in your research. This is not a problem if you use a portable PC when out on the job: you simply load the data onto your desktop when you get home. But if you have to copy your notes onto the word processor and you do this when you are tired after a day's concentrated work, you may well make errors of transcription (we are all human). With a manual system you could have filed that same material, in note form, on paper, within minutes of getting home.

Always keep at least one back-up copy of your database on floppy disk. It is a good idea to get into the habit of doing this each time you key in new data – it will take a few minutes at most and, in the unfortunate event of a crash, you will have lost nothing. You should of course always make a back-up copy of your current writing, after each session.

No one storage system is ever perfect. There is the added problem, if you are storing electronically, of what to do with the accumulation of photocopies, newspaper clippings, photographs, and correspondence. Or, for that matter, your original notes (which you must keep, in case you need to double-check something). The ideal solution is clearly a compromise: a database *and* a filing cabinet. (You will of course create a key index, suitably cross-referenced and regularly updated.)

## Card indexes

The principal advantages of a card index are its flexibility and portability. It need not be expensive. All sorts of cartons, from shoe boxes to cereal packets, can if necessary be converted into filing receptacles; and for the one-off job a local printer may be persuaded into supplying slips of paper cut to size, which you can use instead of cards (but they must not be *too* flimsy). For permanent filing I recommend the commercially manufactured type of box in metal or plastic. You should buy only the kind of guide cards which have plastic or reinforced alphabetical tabs, as the cheaper variety will not stand up to hard wear. Record cards (ruled or plain) will withstand constant fingering better than slips. (For real economy, the researcher can always do what some professional indexers do, and once a particular job is finished, re-use the cards or slips by writing on the other side – preferably using a different coloured ballpoint so that there is no danger of confusion should the odd one be accidentally turned over.)

Cards or slips may be carried to and from the reference library or other place of research, as required, either in envelopes (clearly marked in subjects or whatever divisions best fit the job in hand) or in small packs secured by rubber bands. They can be sorted into alphabetical, subject or chronological order, either in one continuous series or per chapter and, if necessary, re-grouped as the work proceeds; coloured cards and coloured stickers (available in various shapes) may be used to denote different subjects or periods within each main division, and slips bearing brief cross references can be inserted as appropriate. The value of such a system is that its permutations are so great.

## Loose sheets and notebooks

Many writers prefer to make their notes on larger sheets of paper. For them the shorthand reporter type of notebook is recommended, or there are various sizes of ruled pads, with or without punched holes, for fitting into loose-leaf ring binders or spring binders. Keeping notes in exercise books is not a good idea, unless a separate book is used for each section of the research, and even then it is advisable to number the pages and make a simple index in the front of the book, otherwise it may be difficult to locate the exact subject-matter when it is required.

For filing purposes it is best, when using sheets of paper rather than cards or slips, to note each item on a separate sheet or at least to leave a good gap between each item so that the notes can be cut up at home and each one slotted individually into its right folder or envelope. Although this may sound extravagant, writing on both sides of the sheet, unless it is on the same subject and clearly indicated by a bold 'PTO' or arrow at the bottom right-hand corner of the first side, is false economy – much valuable material has been 'lost' in this way. It is all too easy to gather up notes and file them without checking to see what is written on the back; nothing is more frustrating to the writer than to *know* that he has made a note of some vital fact or quotation or source – but *where*? It is also a good plan to get into the habit of putting material away as soon as possible after returning from the library, or after use. Otherwise the telephone may ring, there is nothing else handy on which to jot down a message, so the sheets lying on the desk are turned over, scribbled on – inevitably, sooner or later, something will go astray.

## Working chronologies

Some writers engaged on an historical study or biography find it helpful to make themselves a working chronology to keep at their elbow while they work. This can be a straightforward listing of events or, in the case of a biography, may consist of a loose-leaf ring binder with the sheets arranged so that when the book is open the left-hand page lists the happenings in the life of the biographee and his family, while the right-hand page lists outside events of approx-imately the same date. Ample space should be left between dates for subsequent insertions as research proceeds, to avoid the necessity of retyping pages. The time spent on the preparation of this simple working tool will be amply repaid by the ease with which the writer will be able to see his subject in perspective as he works.

Another useful system for the non-fiction writer is a small card index containing, on separate cards, a brief note of all the important points that must be covered, chapter by chapter. Before starting each chapter the writer can cast his eye over the cards and re-group them in the order in which he intends to deal with them, and when that chapter is finished anything that needs to be mentioned again later can be transferred on to the relevant section, so that he will not lose sight of it when the time comes.

## Filing

If the documentation is not vast, the most convenient form of storage may be in large manila envelopes, clear plastic or multi-coloured document wallets, numbered or clearly marked as to subject or content; some researchers prefer the 'concertina' type of file or the folders secured with elastic that have up to nine divisions. For all but the simplest research collections, however, a steel filing cabinet will be a worthwhile investment. There are some small trolley-type cabinets on castors, which will suit the writer who likes to have his material at his elbow, at desk or armchair, wherever he works; otherwise the single- or multi-drawer cabinet, with or without suspension filing, is the best buy. As each book or writing project is completed, the material can be cleared out, parcelled up and stored elsewhere to make space for the next assignment.

So far as the storage of used material is concerned, the cardboard cartons obtainable free from wine shops and supermarkets are most useful; but photographs and manuscripts are best kept dust-free and flat in the kind of boxes still supplied with top-quality typing papers. For the perfectionist, or the writer who envisages the need to have quick access to his old material, there are excellent lightweight storage containers, ranging from collapsible box files to the more rigid corrugated board storage cabinet complete with drawers. Simple parcels wrapped in brown paper and clearly labelled may be adequate. It is worth remembering that cardboard and brown paper allow documents to 'breathe', whereas metal does not; valuable archive material (e.g. original letters) should not be kept for any length of time in a closed filing cabinet.

Whatever system you adopt, there are two essentials that will prove their worth over and over again: the establishment of a key for quick reference, either on disk or on paper, and a system of clear labelling. Notebooks with alphabetical divisions or the most compact of desk-top card indexes are recommended for the former, a supply of labels and felt marker pens in various colours for the latter. The card index, which may be kept in a box or in a rotary filing unit, should be as simple as possible, containing just sufficient information – either names and telephone numbers, or titles of books and periodicals, with page references and/or dates, or any suitable code of reference numbers – to send the user directly to the required source material.

A word of advice now to those who are setting up a new storage system – THINK BIG! As work progresses, you are bound to accumulate at least twice as much material as you planned for. Bear in mind, too, that a four-drawer filing cabinet takes up no more floor space than the single-drawer model. Few writers will be like the well-known historian and biographer who has admitted to having taken four years to decide to buy a proper filing cabinet and another four years to fill it – but those who do find themselves with empty drawers at the outset can always put them to good use. (Think of the peace of mind it will give you when you go away to research or on holiday to know that the one and only copy of your unfinished manuscript is securely stowed away, comparatively fireproof and out of the reach of vandals!)

The same goes for original material loaned to the writer. This is a big responsibility, and it is advisable always to make a point of photocopying or taking notes of what you need and returning the originals to their owners without delay. If this is absolutely not possible, at least keep the material in a safe place. Newspaper cuttings will go brown if kept in daylight for any length of time, and photographs can be easily damaged and rendered unsuitable for reproduction if left lying around on the desk. Some picture agencies require the borrower to pay substantial costs for the loss or damage of negatives or transparencies.

Books should always be treated with special care, whether they are loaned by private individuals or borrowed from the library. If they are to be handled a great deal, it is a good idea to cover them with plastic film or brown paper. *Never* write in the margins or turn down corners to mark a reference (unless of course the book belongs to you and you regard it as a working copy); and be very careful when photocopying that you do not bend it in such a way as to damage the binding. I now use 'Post-it' Index flags for quick reference; lightweight, in dispensers of fifty, and available in various colours, they can be written on, used over and over again, are easily removed and leave no mark on the page.

Take special care to write on the backs of photographs only with a very soft pencil; anything else can do irreparable damage. It is best to keep all illustrative material in a separate drawer, box file or filing tray, with each print inside a plastic folder or stiffened envelope. Elementary advice, maybe, but it is a fact that many photographs suffer through being left lying about unprotected; even if they are stacked underneath other papers they may sometimes inadvertently be scribbled on, and once that kind of damage is done it cannot be undone.

For those who handle original documents, there is an excellent booklet, *Caring for Books and Documents* by A.D. Baynes-Cope, published by the British Library. A free leaflet, 'The Care of Records: Notes for the Owner or Custodian', is available from the British Records Association, c/o London Metropolitan Archives, 40 North-

ampton Road, London EC1R 0HB (tel. 020 7833 0428); send a
stamped addressed envelope.

Three final tips:

1  Having set up the system that suits you and your project, do make
   an effort to keep the filing up to date, or the whole purpose will
   be defeated. If it is not possible to slot material away as it comes
   in, it is a good idea to keep some kind of 'pending' box or file, or
   a nest of filing baskets, into which you can put it until you have
   the time.
2  Remember that every good filing system has a 'Miscellaneous' file,
   and get into the habit of looking there for anything you cannot
   find instantly. As the 'Miscellaneous' file grows – and it is wise to
   allow plenty of space for it – new subject headings will suggest
   themselves and the appropriate material can be extracted and filed
   separately.
3  NEVER THROW AWAY ANY NOTES without keeping a record
   of the sources.

# Research Methods

Having established your storage system, electronic or manual, or
ideally a combination of both, you are now ready to tackle the actual
research.

If you are online you should make the Net your first port of call,
visiting the Websites relevant to your subject, browsing through
library catalogues and posting questions to appropriate newsgroups.
Armed with the fruits of this initial foray, you will be ready to
embark on more in-depth – or what I now privately call 'terrestial'
as opposed to 'Net' – research. Your starting point here will almost
certainly be a library or archive centre.

## Using the Internet and email

To judge from media publicity and sales talk, one might be forgiven
for assuming that one has only to go online for all one's research
problems to be solved at the press of a few keys, and that hence-
forward you will be able to access everything you need from the
comfort of your study armchair.

This is not so. Realisation of the technologists' dream that one
day – perhaps – a vast online library may be created out there
which will contain the full text of every book that has ever been
published is a long, long way off. (Which is good news for writers

of works in copyright.) For the forseeable future therefore writers and researchers should treat 'the Net' – also known as the 'Information Superhighway' or 'Cyberspace' – simply as the *first*, but never the only, library or information centre that they visit. It is of course the most powerful research tool and source of information yet known to man. So far as research is concerned, the Net's most important component is the World Wide Web (WWW, or simply 'the Web' for short), which consists of millions of linked pages of information on every subject imaginable. It is true that what you find on the Web may be much more up to date than anything available in the conventional library. But do not be fooled: it is not 100 per cent reliable. The sheer volume of material already in Cyberspace and the alarming fact that anyone with a Web page can put pretty well anything they wish on it, true or false, or just misleading, demands that the researcher be on his guard. You should also bear in mind that Web pages are constantly being updated or amended, or may be removed altogether, so that it could prove dangerous, in research terms, to rely on or quote sources other than those you know to be authentic and more or less permanent. As with any other library research you do, never skimp on checking and double-checking and evaluating. Be suspicious of anything that does not come from a known, authoritative source.

One of the greatest advantages for the researcher is that, unlike the library, the Net is open seven days a week, twenty-four hours a day. You do not have to wait when a title is in use by another reader or return a book by a certain date. Whenever the mood takes you, or the need arises, you can access the catalogues of major libraries all over the world. You can visit the Websites of organisations and individuals at will and, when you find the information you want, download it onto your computer. You can post unlimited questions to newsgroups of your particular interests and, by using the email facility, correspond globally with fellow professionals and contacts at mimimal expense. You can also have your own Web page or pages.

The downside is that you may find navigating the Net irritatingly slow, as you scroll endlessly through pages of advertising and irrelevant information in order to get at precisely what you seek. (But isn't it also only too easy to waste a lot of time in libraries?) Then there is the very real danger that unless you are exceptionally disciplined you may become too addicted to the process – at the expense of both your writing time and your purse. You will probably have to cope with receiving masses of time-consuming junk email (known as 'spam'). Worse still, you run the risk of exposing your computer to attack by virus.

That said, the practicalities of going online are not complicated.

Let us assume that your modem is installed. Now you must choose an Internet service provider (ISP). In the past, all ISPs have charged the user a monthly subscription, but due to intense competition the trend now is for the majority of them to offer their basic services free of charge (they get commission from the telephone companies and from advertisers). Those that continue to charge a subscription will be offering additional services. (Check these out before you sign up.) You will of course still have to pay, via your telephone bill, for the time you are online. This is normally charged at a local call rate, but – beware – the costs soon mount up, especially in the early days while you are finding your way around. You may be able to reduce these costs by nominating the ISP's number under one of the discount schemes available, such as BT's 'Family & Friends'. Recently some ISPs have begun offering free telephone access to the Internet at evenings and week-ends, provided you switch your telephone account to them, and this may well become the norm.

Some ISPs offer faster access to the Net than others. There are a number to choose from, including the major telephone companies, BT and Cable & Wireless. Two of the largest, America Online (AOL, which now owns Compuserve) and Netscape Communications merged in November 1998. Pipex, Demon and Virgin are also popular. Shop around, ask other writers for recommendations, read the trade journals. Above all, suit your budget and your particular needs. Do not worry if you find later that you have made the wrong choice: it is easy to switch to a different provider.

Your ISP will supply the necessary software to connect your computer with theirs, through which you can connect to a vast network of computers worldwide. In order to read pages on the Web you need what is known as a 'Web browser' program, such as Microsoft Internet Explorer or Netscape Navigator. With this running, all you have to do to access a page is to type in the appropriate address, known as an URL (Uniform Resource Locator); this normally starts with 'http://www'. There are a number of 'search engines' on the Web which, when you type in a key word or topic, will help you to access the pages you need, the most popular being Altavista, Infoseek, Lycos and Yahoo. The golden rule for trawling the Net is to be as specific as possible at the outset – in other words, narrow down as far as possible the exact information you are seeking, otherwise you will have to wade through a mass of material you do not want. The Deja News site will enable you to find 'Usenet' groups (discussion or newsgroups on over 30,000 different subjects) to whom you can 'post' messages or questions. This facility – and email – may well prove to be the most valuable for the individual researcher and writer.

Highly recommended for all researchers who surf the Net is a recent publication from Helicon, *The Hutchinson Directory of Web Sites*, which comes with two free CD-ROMs and lists over 5,000 Websites, usefully divided into subjects. It also contains a full glossary of Internet terms.

It is of the utmost importance to maintain a record of the sites you visit and of the routes you use to access them. A quick automatic way of being sure to get back to those you regularly use is through the 'Bookmark' facility (on Netscape) or 'favorite' facility (on Microsoft Internet Explorer); but I personally believe that it also pays to draw up your own Website and email address book and keep it at your elbow. No matter how 'comprehensive' the printed lists claim to be, somehow they never seem to include everything that you yourself need.

Going online offers the facility, at no extra cost, to create one or more Web pages of your own, as well as to correspond with other computer users worldwide by electronic mail ('email'). For email purposes you will be given a special 'mailbox' or electronic address, incorporating your name, through which you send and receive messages. Email is both cheaper and faster than using normal postal services (the latter now dubbed 'snail mail'). It is also very easy to operate. For a useful introduction to the subject and its value to writers, read the Society of Authors' *Information Sheet* 'Electronic Mail'.

To the uninitiated all this may appear at first sight as a bewildering, impenetrable maze, not least because of the Net's strange jargon, the addresses that consist of long strings of lower case letters, the unique rules and standards known as 'Protocols' and 'Netiquette'. They should not be unduly alarmed. Like all other worthwhile professional skills, using the Internet has to be learned, and to learn it you must be prepared to practise. Only in this way will you acquire expertise – most probably by trial and error, with or without tuition, and for much of the time with your nose in one or more of the many manuals on the market. You should make full use of the help available on screen. As you would when visiting any library with which you are unfamiliar, allow yourself time to find your way around. Take it one step at a time. Never under any circumstances rely on mastering the skill with a deadline looming and your editor breathing down your neck. If you lack patience or have little time between writing projects, go for some private tuition or enrol for a course at your local adult education centre. It will be money well spent.There are Input Output Centres at a number of the London public libraries and in Birmingham which offer individual flexible training and Internet access at reasonable cost (details are obtainable from Marylebone Library: tel. 020 7486 3161). Ask at your local library for similar training opportunities in your area. For a 'hands on' trial without committing yourself, visit one of the numerous cybercafés that are springing up not only in London but also now in the major provincial cities.

Inevitably in the wake of the Internet and email 'explosion' the market has been deluged with literature on the subject. I cannot recommend too highly *Internet Research: Theory and Practice* by Ned L. Fielden and Maria Garrido. Published in the States, and available in the UK (see bibliography at the end of this chapter), its expressed purpose is 'to make the Internet less forbidding and more comprehensive for researchers'. Practically everything the novice – or, for that matter, the experienced – researcher needs to know is covered, in a clear and reader-friendly style (which is a welcome change from that of some other manuals). The advantages and disadvantages of the Net are discussed; the techniques of online searching and the basic protocols explained; much valuable advice given on specific Net skills and resources. There are separate chapters on the nature of research, Internet tools, information retrieval, and Internet subject resources; and appendices on writing the research paper and citation format. Most importantly, the book teaches good research methods.

It is surprising that among manuals galore there have been few as yet that cater specifically for the needs of writers. Two I have found useful are also American publications, both by Timothy K. Maloy: *The Writer's Internet Handbook* and *The Internet Research Guide*. Although naturally slanted towards the needs of the American writer, these books contain much that will assist all writers and researchers insofar as search techniques and resources are concerned.

Two titles announced for publication in early 2000 promise to address the subject in detail for the benefit of writers in the UK: Jane Dorner's *The Writer's Internet Handbook*, and *A Writer's Guide to the Internet* by Trevor Lockwood and Karen Scott.

In the meanwhile, you will find that most issues of *The Author* carry at least one article on some aspect of the new technology (the Society of Authors no longer publishes its supplement, *The Electronic Author*).There is an informative article on the Internet as a research tool for writers by David Couchman in the current *Writers' & Artists' Yearbook*. Gordon Wells' three titles, *The Book Writer's Handbook*, *The Magazine Writer's Handbook* and, more recently, *The Business of Writing*, all contain sensible advice on word processing and the use of computers. On the Net itself, at http://www.purefiction.com/pages/res1.htm there is a regularly updated guide for writers posted by Charlie Harris entitled *Using the Internet for Research (FAQ)*. ('FAQ' stands for Frequently Asked Questions.)

A good academic introduction to the subject is William J. Martin's *The Global Information Society*. *The Keyguide to Information Sources in Online and CD-ROM Database Searching* by Chris Armstrong is one of the best international guides for professional researchers. Other recommended titles include *Databases in Historical Research* by Charles Harvey and Jon Press; *Going Online, CD-ROM and the Internet*, by Phil Bradley; *Internet Bible* by Brian Underdahl and Edward Willett; *The Rough Guide to the Internet and World Wide Web* by Angus J. Kennedy; *Surfing on the Internet* by J.C. Herz; *Teach Yourself Internet*; and *The Which? Guide to the Internet*.

## Using libraries

Finding your way round the library or libraries where you intend to do the bulk of your research is half the battle for the writer. The first thing to remember is that the librarian's job is to guide the researcher or reader to the right books; he is not paid to do original research for you. It is nevertheless astonishing how much a co-operative, interested librarian will do, and it is always politic to take him into your confidence about the scope of your research and what you are writing. Similarly, it is advisable to contact the librarian of a special library, either by telephone or letter, before making a first visit; provided he is given due notice of your interest, the librarian or one of his assistants will usually then prepare a preliminary selection of titles, and you can begin work without delay. If you do not do this, you may find that the librarians are tied up with other readers when you arrive, and you can easily waste half a day of valuable researching time.

In public libraries, the reference departments of most public libraries and the majority of special and private subscription libraries, you have access to the stacks and are free to browse among the books arranged on the shelves related to your subject; where this is not the case, you should ask a library assistant to explain how the catalogue or subject index is organised and how to order books. Where the catalogue is online, you order books on computer terminals. At the major copyright and university libraries a certain number of reference works are on what is known as 'open access', that is to say on shelves where they may be consulted by the reader or from which they may be taken to the reader's desk (but not of course out of the reading room) and returned after use; all other titles must be applied for in the usual way. Where a library is not computerised you will have to look up the relevant shelf-marks in the general catalogue and fill out a requisition slip for each title.

Ordering by computer has speeded things up dramatically: for example, at the new British Library the waiting time has been cut from up to two hours to about thirty minutes, and you find out immediately whether a book is in use by another reader or unavailable for some other reason. Nevertheless it is wise to order what you need at the earliest moment (some libraries will allow you to reserve books a day or two in advance), and to fill in the short waiting period by using works that are on the open shelves or by consulting the catalogue for the next phase of your research. Because of lack of space, many libraries today 'out-house' selected classes of books; be prepared for these to take twenty-four hours or more to arrive.

Researchers wishing to use the British Library or other copyright libraries, those of the Imperial War Museum, National Maritime Museum, Royal Botanic Gardens and most university and museum libraries must obtain a reader's ticket, and it is advisable to do so in advance of your first visit – although temporary day tickets are normally issued on demand. Write to the Admissions Office of the relevant library for full details and application forms. You will probably be asked to supply two passport-size photographs, one of which will be incorporated into your pass, and in some cases for a letter of introduction.

On your first visit to a library, devote a little time to familiarising yourself with the layout and cataloguing system. Where the catalogue is online, you will be guided every step of the way on screen. You do not need to know the full title of the item you seek, or even the author's name: one key word, be it part title, part author's name or just subject, should produce results.

A word of advice here for the uninitiated who find themselves confronted by an unfamiliar array of new technology equipment. DO NOT PANIC! There is nearly always an instruction manual, probably somewhat dog-eared as a result of frantic searching by other users in need of assistance, and usually pretty incomprehensible to the lay person! (To be fair, they *are* nowadays becoming more 'user friendly'.) This manual will tell you which keys to press and in what order. Once you have pressed the first key, step-by-step instructions will appear on screen to guide you through the next phase, and if you do something wrong a message will appear instantly on screen to that effect, with instructions on how to remedy the error. If all else fails, put yourself in the hands of a trained library assistant, who will do it all for you the first time. (In my experience, far from resenting such demands on their time, librarians are quite keen to show off their newly acquired skills and to play with their 'new toys'; but this attitude will not last for ever. Watch very carefully: you will not be popular if you have to ask for help a second time.)

When you find yourself in a library that is not yet online, you should ask one of the library assistants to explain any unusual features, and how to look up anonymous works, yearbooks and directories, or the proceedings of learned societies. Some libraries display a map showing the layout of the reference shelves, or there may be a printed leaflet available. Most have separate card indexes arranged under authors and subjects, but occasionally you may come across a 'dictionary' type of catalogue which combines author, subject and title in one alphabetical listing. Nowadays the catalogue after a certain date will most likely be maintained on microfiche; the regular updating of these by computer is a godsend to researchers. You should be meticulous in replacing all microfiches in their correct numerical sequence after use, for the sake of subsequent researchers (and long-suffering librarians).

In smaller libraries the catalogue is usually cumulative, but in others there may be separate drawers or cabinets containing cards for acquisitions within a stated period. This 'Recent Acquisitions' section should not be overlooked. The trap here for the inexperienced lies in the word 'acquisitions', for although this section of the catalogue will consist of mainly new titles, it will also include books that have been purchased or otherwise acquired recently – some of which may have been published some years ago. When you fail to find the book you are looking for in the general catalogue, therefore, always turn to this section.

The majority of libraries in the United Kingdom have adopted the Dewey Decimal Classification, which divides human knowledge into ten classes, each sub-divided to accommodate subjects within each class. Try to memorise the main divisions, as follows:

000 General Works
100 Philosophy
200 Religion
300 Social Sciences
400 Languages
500 Science
600 Technology
700 The Arts and Recreations
800 Literature
900 Geography, Biography and History

*The British National Bibliography* (*BNB*) also uses the Dewey classification, and if you are seeking a published work on a certain subject, and do not know the author or precise title, you should go straight to the relevant class listing, as you would do in the library.

## Note-taking

There are three 'golden rules' of researching:

1 *Copy accurately*
   Care must be taken to retain original spellings in quoted matter, using an editorial *sic* in square brackets if necessary. It is a good idea to get into the habit of double-checking all figures, proper names and page references immediately they are written or typed. For example, the date '1943' can so easily be copied as '1934' when one is tired (or more easily, because one's mind is on the year in which one is working, say, '1998' as '1989' or '2001' as '2010'!), and whereas it takes only a few seconds to verify the figure at the time, such a mistake can take hours to correct later – or may not be discovered until the work is in print. Writing unusual proper names and place names in block capitals in the researcher's notes also helps to avoid error and will save a lot of trouble if, several weeks later, the writer is unable to decipher his own hurried scribbles.

2 *Check, double-check and, if in doubt, triple-check all facts*
   Primarily where verbal recollections are given to the researcher by private individuals, but whenever and wherever possible in all other cases, especially if any doubts are entertained as to the accuracy of facts (even if printed facts), these should be verified in another source. Where confirmation of a fact or figure cannot be obtained and the writer remains in doubt, it is best either to avoid using it or, if you must, to state the source or sources relied on. The problem of 'conflicting authorities' is discussed in chapter 4 (page 86).

3 *Keep a note of all sources*
   The importance of keeping full reference notes cannot be over-stressed. Valuable time may be wasted if, for example, when your first draft is written, you wish to examine a particular source in more detail but cannot turn up instantly a note of the author, title, date and relevant page number, and preferably also the shelf-mark of the library where you originally saw it. Even more time will be wasted if you have omitted to follow the recommendation under (1) above to check page references on the spot and, failing to find what you are looking for at, say, page 241, you must thumb through a hefty tome, possibly without the help of an index, only to discover the right passage at page 421 (Whenever this happens, the shortcut is to try first all the permutations for the number

originally written down.) Making brief cards or slips for each reference as you go along will halve the work when it comes to compiling a 'notes and references' section or the bibliography (see chapter 10, 'Preparation for the Press', pages 180–90). Press cuttings and photocopies should be clearly marked with the book title, newspaper or periodical, plus volume number, date, publisher and page number where appropriate. Remember to do this before you hand in the volume or microfilm or replace it on the shelf.

What should you do when you come across an incorrect date or figure in a library book, perhaps a wrong page entry in an index? In the interest of future users, the temptation is to amend the text – in pencil, of course – but is it worth the risk of being expelled from the premises for life? The duty librarian is probably too busy to take much heed. My opinion is that if it is a modern title, provided you have the time and the inclination, you should write to the publisher asking him to make the correction in any reprint or new edition. If it is an old book, sadly there is nothing to be done.

## Photocopying

All reference libraries and most other libraries and record offices operate a photocopy service, subject to the usual copyright restrictions and a ban on old or rare editions that might be damaged in the process. Microfilms and the type of photocopy suitable for reproduction can usually be obtained only from major libraries and record offices, and may take several weeks, but the electrostatic print or 'rapid copy' or 'xerox' as it is sometimes called, which is the most useful to the researcher, is often available while you wait or within twenty-four hours. Some libraries have installed coin-operated machines and expect you to make your own copies.

With material that is out of copyright there is no problem, but unless the copyright owner has given permission in writing, copying of all other printed matter is restricted to one article from any one issue of a newspaper or periodical, at any one time; or to a total of one-tenth of any one book in copyright. In all cases the applicant will be required to sign a statement that he has not before obtained a photocopy of the same extract, that he requires the copy purely for the purposes of research or private study and that he will not use it for any other purpose without the permission of the copyright holder. The cost is modest when one considers the amount of time it takes to copy a text by hand. Another factor to be borne in mind is that the photocopy is an *accurate* copy. When ordering photocopies from a library, it is essential to keep a note of the author, title, date of publication and edition of the source material, since these will not always appear on the photocopied sheets and the originals may not be returned to you; write these on the photocopies as soon as you receive them, and always before filing.

Commercial photocopying services abound in every city and major town these days, with self-operating machines at some railway stations, department stores and supermarkets. The quality of copies varies considerably, as does the cost; some places offer a substantial discount for a large number of copies made at any one time. These 'copy shops' are not usually worried about copyright and will often copy a complete book without demur, although in so doing both they and the purchaser are breaking the law. Anyone planning to copy a large amount of text still in copyright should first apply for permission to the publisher.

Infringement of copyright by reprography is an international problem. The British Copyright Council's booklet *Photocopying from Books and Journals* clarifies the present law.

A recent development has been the launch by the Copyright Licensing Agency of the Digitisation Licensing Scheme, to run from September 1999. Under this scheme scanning licences for individual works or parts of works are to be offered to universities, higher education establishments, pharmaceutical companies and churches. It is envisaged that in due course digitisation will overtake photocopying. For further details write to The Secretary, The Copyright Licensing Agency Ltd, 90 Tottenham Court Road, London W1P 0LP.

## Copyright

Copyright exists to protect the tangible form in which creative people such as writers, artists and musicians set out their original work. The key phrase here is 'tangible form': there is no protection for ideas or plots. Nor is there any copyright in titles, although the use of a title may be restricted where confusion is likely to arise between rival works, or between, say, a book and a film or play. There are special laws regarding composite productions (films, broadcasts, sound recordings, etc.), computer programs and, most recently, databases. The vast amount of in-copyright material now getting onto the Internet and onto pirated videos and CDs presents a major problem that even the new technology may find difficult to solve.

In the United Kingdom copyright exists as soon as the work in question has been set down in any medium. There are no formalities of registration, and it is not necessary for the work to be published. Book writers, scriptwriters, illustrators and translators also benefit from what are known as 'moral rights': these are 1) the right to be identified as the author whenever a work is published, performed or broadcast, called 'the right of paternity'; 2) the right to object to derogatory treatment, called 'the right of integrity'; and 3) the right not to have work falsely attributed to them. While the right of integrity is automatic, the right of paternity must be asserted in writing: this is usually printed beneath the copyright line on the verso title page of a book. Moral rights do not apply to work published in newspapers, periodicals or collective works of reference.

Recently the law on copyright has been harmonised within member states of the European Union, following implementation of EC Directive 93/98. Known as 'the Term Directive', this came into force in the United Kingdom on 1 January 1996. A more recent European Union Directive, concerning databases, has been effective since 1 January 1998. The major amendment affecting writers has been to extend the term of copyright from the previous fifty to seventy years from the end of the calendar year of an author's death. Thus the works of authors who died between 1 January 1925 and 31 December 1944, which had gone out of copyright under the fifty-year rule, are now protected under the new seventy-year rule: this is known as 'revived copyright'. Ownership of that copyright belongs to the person or company who owned it when the original term expired or, if that person has died, or the company no longer exists, to the author's personal representatives. The work of authors who died before 31 December 1924 is now out of copyright.

The current copyright statute of the United Kingdom is the Copyright, Designs and Patents Act 1988, which came into force on 1 August 1989, replacing all previous copyright statutes. International copyright is safeguarded by two separate conventions: the Berne Convention of 1886 and the Universal Copyright Convention of 1952, to which different countries adhere. Both conventions have been revised over the years, most recently in 1971.

In the United States the Copyright Act 1976, which came into force on 1 January 1978, replaced the old Act of 1909. It is important to remember that US copyright law differs from British copyright law in several respects.

For outlines of these various statutes, as well as the new European Union amendments, see the articles on British and US copyright in the current *Writers' & Artists' Yearbook*. Helen Rosenblatt, Legal Adviser of the Authors' Licensing & Collecting Society, has prepared a very clear outline of the current law in a short document entitled 'Unravelling Copyright', which may be obtained from ALCS, Marlborough Court, 14–18 Holborn, London EC1N 2LE. A more detailed and very up-to-date guide to British copyright law, Denis de Freitas' *BCC Guide to the Law of Copyright and Rights in Performances*, is available through bookshops or from the British Copyright Council, Copyright House, 29–33 Berners Street, London W1P 4AA. Other recommended titles include the Society of Authors' *Quick Guides* 'Copyright and Moral Rights', 'The Protection of Titles' and 'Copyright in Artistic Works, including Photographs'; and Raymond A. Wall's *Copyright made easier*. The excellent *Handbook of Copyright in British Publishing Practice* by J.M. Cavendish and Kate Pool contains much good advice, but a new edition is needed to bring it fully up to date. Professional researchers should consult *Copyright for Library and Information Service Professionals* by Paul Pedley.

British copyright law is immensely complicated. The 1988 Act, which replaced all previous statutes and sought to re-state the law of copyright in the United Kingdom, specifically forbids 'unfair dealing' in all works still in copyright. In practice this means that anyone wishing to quote substantially from a work in copyright must obtain permission from the owner of that copyright, normally the writer of the work in question, if he is still alive, or, after his death, his heirs and/or literary executor or person to whom the copyright may have been assigned. Biographers and historians should remember that although a letter *belongs* to the recipient, the copyright in it is vested in the writer of that letter and, after his death, for a period of seventy years, to his estate; this applies also to letters published in the press.

While the quotation of short passages for the purposes of criticism or review is deemed to be 'fair dealing', in all other cases involving more than a short phrase or a couple of lines of poetry it is advisable to obtain formal clearance. Generally speaking, the Society of Authors and the Publishers Association have agreed that the use of up to 400 words of prose (or a series of extracts of up to 300 words each, totalling no more than 800 words) from any one work, or up to a quarter of a poem, may be deemed 'fair dealing', *provided only that the words quoted are for criticism or review*. If you are quoting more than a short phrase from copyright material in any other context, permission should be sought, as the use of a 'substantial' part of a work without permission is an infringement of copyright. It goes without saying that acknowledgment should always be made to the author, title and publisher. The Society of Authors' *Quick Guide* 'Permissions' sets out the position very clearly.

It is important to allow plenty of time for the clearance of material you wish to quote. Write initially to the permissions department of the original publisher. If they do not control the rights, they should pass your request on to the author, his agent, literary executor, or, if relevant, to any subsequent publisher of the work. Foreign rights are frequently controlled by publishers or literary agents abroad, but the

UK publisher should be able to provide a name and address to write to. A fee may be payable, the amount depending on the length of the passage or passages it is intended to quote and on the nature of the rights sought (i.e. British only, or British Commonwealth or world rights).

Advice on the reproduction of Crown copyright material should be sought from The Copyright Unit, Her Majesty's Stationery Office, St Clements House, 2–16 Colegate, Norwich NR3 1BQ (tel. 01603 621000; fax 01603 723000).

Clearing the copyrights on illustrative material is best left to a professional picture researcher or your publisher.

Difficulties sometimes arise in tracing copyright owners, especially in the case of unpublished material such as correspondence. A letter to the press may bring results, or try the WATCH (*Writers and Their Copyright Holders*) project at the University of Reading Library, Whiteknights, PO Box 223, Reading RG6 6AE. This ongoing Anglo-American project began in 1994 and is maintained jointly by the University of Reading and the University of Texas, Austin, USA. Its regularly updated file on the World Wide Web (http://www.lib.utexas.edu/Libs/HRC/WATCH) contains copyright information on almost 3,000 authors, politicians and public figures.

Infringement of copyright can lead to heavy financial penalties. Researchers should be constantly on their guard against plagiarising another writer's text. Although there is no copyright in facts, it is essential to take care when making notes that you differentiate between actual quotations and your own précis. It is all too easy, months later, inadvertently to use the original author's words as your own, and then you may find yourself in trouble.

Writers with many reproductions of copyright material to clear, and who have neither the time nor the inclination to undertake this task themselves, should consider using the services of an agency such as LJC Permission Services, 8 Burstow House, Skipton Way, Horley, Surrey RG6 8LP (tel. 07000 782332; fax 07000 782331). A fixed fee is payable per permission.

## Use of portable equipment in libraries

Most major libraries now set aside a section of their search rooms for those who wish to use laptops, computer notebooks or (more rarely nowadays) portable typewriters. Cassette recorders are permissible only by special arrangement with the librarian – this will depend on whether or not a private room, or part of a room, can be made available so that other readers are not disturbed. Dictating into a recorder undoubtedly saves time and fatigue, in the library, but can create problems of transcription unless proper names are spelled out and punctuation indicated; nothing at all will be saved if, at the end of the day, it proves necessary to go back to the original to check a quotation. The researcher will find a small recorder of real value, however, where a good deal of interviewing or travelling has to be done: even if there are objections to using such a device during an interview, a quick dash to the car or hotel afterwards to record one's impressions while all is fresh in one's mind is very worthwhile, and so is a recorded on-the-spot description of buildings and scenes to be portrayed in a writer's work. For this purpose I have found the small battery-operated hand-held type of machine known as a 'pocket memo' or 'electronic note-taker' to be ideal. (You can speak into this faster than you can type onto a keyboard, and you can do it while walking around.) A larger machine with separate microphone and facility for longer-playing tapes is more suitable for interviewing or sound recording, and here it is best to choose a model which will run both on batteries and on mains. If you intend to transcribe your mini- or micro-cassettes, you will need the appropriate transcriber, with foot pedal; most of the larger machines have a socket for plugging in a pedal (essential for tape transcription).

The use of microform readers (for microfiche and microfilm) baffles some novice researchers. The machines do vary, and it is wise in the first instance to ask a library assistant to show you how to operate one. It is very important never to touch the film with greasy fingers or to get it twisted, and always to re-wind the film onto the original spool before returning it to the issue desk. (Nothing is more exasperating to the next user than to discover that the spool must be rewound!) Similarly, it is most important – for the sake of the next user – to replace all microfiches after use in the box provided *in the correct numerical order*.

In libraries where there are a number of microfilm readers installed, often close together, some people find they cannot do more than an hour or two's work at a time, partly because of the noise of other users constantly winding and re-winding and partly due to eyestrain. Some professional researchers tackle these difficulties by wearing earplugs and/or tinted spectacles.

## Interviewing

Interviewing people, and getting the maximum information out of them, is a skill that is acquired with practice. There are no hard and fast rules, but here are a few tips from personal experience:

Always write or telephone in advance, stating clearly who you are, why you need the information, and precisely what it is you seek.

If time permits, take 'two bites at the cherry'. People are naturally on the defensive at a first interview, but when you go back a second time they already know you and will welcome you as a 'friend'.

Never ask a crucial or controversial question right at the start. If necessary, put the person being interviewed at ease, make some social small talk first. It can be quite productive sometimes to bring out your 'key' question almost at the end of the interview, as though it were an afterthought and not all that important – the interviewee will be relaxed by that time and much more expansive.

Don't assume that you can use a cassette recorder. A lot of people are nervous of being recorded and will 'freeze' if you insist. A good plan is to have your machine tucked away in your briefcase and then, when the interview is well under way, you can say something like, 'This is tremendously good stuff, I can't get it all down accurately in my rusty shorthand... would you mind very much if I put it on tape?'

Offer to let interviewees see anything you intend to quote in print, and ask them how they wish to be acknowledged. And always write afterwards to thank them for sparing the time to talk to you.

The question of how far to trust information given to you from personal recollection is dealt with in the chapter on Biography and Autobiography (see pages 116–36).

Up to a few years ago Eve McLaughlin's *Interviewing Elderly Relatives*, written primarily for the guidance of genealogists and family historians, was the only handbook on the subject in existence in the UK. Now I am able to recommend three further titles. *Interviewing Techniques for Writers and Researchers* by Susan Dunne offers a step-by-step approach, from the research and planning that are necessary beforehand to getting the best out of the interview and (increasingly important nowadays) avoiding libel. Sally-Jayne Wright's *How to Write and Sell Interviews* contains other valuable advice on the technique: how to talk to anyone, from the man-in-the-street to the celebrity; how to ask the questions that get results; body language and telephone manner; even what to wear. *Interviewing for Journalists* by Joan Clayton is equally strong on practical advice.

So much for search procedures and storage of material. Throughout the writing of this chapter I have tried to keep in mind the needs of the novice writer of fiction, the amateur family historian and the biographer. Hopefully I have included one or two tips that may be of use to the more experienced. Students preparing theses and writers embarking for the first time on academic work are recommended to read Roy Preece's *Starting Research*.

Another excellent title aimed at the academic writer is Eileen Kane's recently revised *Doing Your Own Research*. *Lifting the Lid* by David Northmore is a guide to investigative research.

There are many ways of researching. Methods that work for others may not come naturally to you. Members of the younger generation of writers may scorn anything but the electronic. Many of the 'oldies' among us are scared stiff of the new technology, but may be tempted at some stage to give it a go. To them I would say this: yes, do consider storing your notes electronically, setting up your own personal database, surfing the Net. But give it time. Never let yourself be pressurised into taking on board in one go all that IT has to offer, simply to keep up with other writer friends. And *never* when you are already launched into or about to begin a major work. Always, always go for the method of working that you feel most comfortable with, the one that intrudes the least on your creative skills. That way, and only that way, you will save yourself a lot of unnecessary stress – and possibly also an unnecessary overdraft into the bargain.

*The Author*, quarterly journal of the Society of Authors, free to members, £7 per issue to non-members

*BCC Guide to the Law of Copyright and Rights in Performances*, by Denis de Freitas, British Copyright Council (Copyright House, 29–33 Berners Street, London W1P 4AA), London, 2nd edn, 1998

*The Book Writer's Handbook 1996–7*, by Gordon Wells, Allison & Busby, London, 1995

*The Business of Writing*, by Gordon Wells, Allison & Busby, London, 1998

'The Care of Records: Notes for the Owner or Custodian', British Records Association, *Guidelines 1*, 1997, available free (send a stamped addressed envelope) from the BRA, c/o London Metropolitan Archives, 40 Northampton Road, London EC1R 0HB

*Caring for Books and Documents*, by A.D. Baynes-Cope, British Library, London, 2nd edn, 1989

'Copyright and Moral Rights', *Quick Guide No. 1*, Society of Authors, 1997

*Copyright for Library and Information Service Professionals*, by Paul Pedley, Aslib, London, 1998

'Copyright in Artistic Works, including Photographs', *Quick Guide No. 11*, Society of Authors, London, 1997

*Copyright made easier*, by Raymond A. Wall, Aslib, London, 2nd edn, 1998

*Databases in Historical Research*, by Charles Harvey and Jon Press, Macmillan, London, 1995

*Doing Your Own Research*, by Eileen Kane, Marion Boyars, revised edn, 1999

'Electronic Mail', *Information Sheet* compiled by Storm Dunlop, Society of Authors, London, 1995

*The Global Information Society*, by William J. Martin, Aslib, London, 1995

*Going Online, CD-ROM and the Internet*, by Phil Bradley, Aslib, London, 10th edn, 1997; paperback 1998

*Handbook of Copyright in British Publishing Practice*, by J.M. Cavendish and Kate Pool, Cassell, London, 3rd edn, 1993

*How to Write and Sell Interviews*, by Sally-Jayne Wright, Allison & Busby, London, 1995

*The Hutchinson Directory of Web Sites*, Helicon, Oxford, 1999 (with 2 free CD-ROMs)

*The Internet: A Writer's Guide*, by Jane Dorner, A & C Black, London, scheduled for January 2000.

*Internet Bible*, by Brian Underdahl and Edward Willett, IDG Books, USA (distributed in UK by Transworld), 1998 (with free CD-ROM)

*Internet Research: Theory and Practice*, by Ned L. Fielden and Maria Garrido, McFarland, Jefferson, N. Carolina, 1998 (available in the UK from Shelwing Ltd, 4 Pleydell Gardens, Folkestone, Kent CT20 2DN; tel. 01303 850501; fax 01303 850162)

*The Internet Research Guide*, by Timothy K. Maloy, Allworth Press, New York, 2nd edn, 1999

*Interviewing Elderly Relatives*, by Eve McLaughlin, Federation of Family History Societies, 3rd edn, 1993; originally published by the FFHS, now available from *Family Tree Magazine*, 61 Great Whyte, Ramsey, Huntingdon, Cambs. PE17 1HL

*Interviewing for Journalists*, by Joan Clayton, Piatkus Books, London, 1994

*Interviewing Techniques for Writers and Researchers*, by Susan Dunne, A & C Black, London, 1995

*Keyguide to Information Sources in Online and CD-ROM Database Searching*, by Chris Armstrong, Mansell, London, 2nd edn, 1995

*Lifting the Lid: A Guide to Investigative Research*, by David Northmore, Cassell, London, 1996

*The Magazine Writer's Handbook, Millennium edition*, by Gordon Wells, Allison & Busby, London, 1999

'Multimedia for Authors', *Information Sheet* compiled by Storm Dunlop, Society of Authors, London, 1995

'Permissions', *Quick Guide No. 10*, Society of Authors, London, 1997

*Photocopying from Books and Journals: A Guide for All Users of Copyright Literary Works*, by Charles Clark, British Copyright Council, London, 1993

'The Protection of Titles', *Quick Guide No. 2*, Society of Authors, London, 1997

*The Rough Guide to the Internet and World Wide Web*, by Angus J. Kennedy, Rough Guides Ltd, London, 4th edn, 1998

*Starting Research: An Introduction to Academic Research and Dissertation Writing*, by Roy Preece, Pinter Publishers (Mansell), London, 1994

*Surfing on the Internet*, by J.C. Herz, Little, Brown, London, 1995; paperback 1996, reprinted 1998

*Teach Yourself Internet*, by Mac Bride, Hodder Headline, London, 3rd edn, 1998

'Unravelling Copyright', by Helen Rosenblatt, available from the Authors' Licensing & Collecting Society, Marlborough Court, 14–18 Holborn, London EC1N 2LE

*Using the Internet for Research (FAQ)*, by Charlie Harris, on the Web at http://www.purefiction.com/pages/res1.htm, 1996–98, updated monthly

*The Which? Guide to the Internet*, by Richard Wentk, Which? Books, London, 1997

*Writers' & Artists' Yearbook*, published annually by A & C Black, London; articles on word processing and on British and US copyright

*Writers and Their Copyright Holders* (WATCH), joint project run by the University of Texas Harry Ransom Humanities Research Center and the University of Reading; online at http://www.lib.utexas.edu/Libs/HRC/WATCH

*A Writer's Guide to the Internet*, by Trevor Lockwood and Karen Scott, Allison & Busby, London, scheduled for spring 2000

*The Writer's Internet Handbook*, by Timothy K. Maloy, Allworth Press, New York, 1997

*Note:* The *Information Sheets* published by the Society of Authors are free to members (with s.a.e.) or otherwise obtainable at £1.00 each, post free, from the Publications Department, Society of Authors, 84 Drayton Gardens, London SW10 9SB. The *Quick Guides* published by the Society are also free to members (with s.a.e.) or to non-members at £2.00 each, post free, from the same address. Allworth Press books are distributed in the UK by Windsor Books International, The Boundary, Wheatley Road, Garsington, Oxford, OX44 9EJ (tel. 01865 361122; fax 01865 361133).

# 3

# Basic Sources of Information and their Location

A writer's raw material will normally be derived from a combination of the following sources: personal knowledge, experience and observation; printed, microfilmed or electronically-stored material (books, newspapers, periodicals, etc.); unpublished documentary, recorded or filmed sources (manuscripts, family papers, theses, archive collections, tapes, photographs, etc.); and other people's knowledge, experience and observation. Of these the most important must be the first-mentioned, since it is a writer's own viewpoint, drawn from his personal knowledge, experience and observation, that above all else puts a stamp of originality upon his work and distinguishes it from the work of every other writer.

Except where the work in hand is one of pure reminiscence and even then certain statements will probably need to be substantiated by fact – it is however not enough to rely solely upon your own knowledge. As soon as your original material has been studied and sorted according to the shape of the projected piece of writing, you must consider what are the other sources of information to be tapped.

## Printed Sources

### Books

Printed books and information about books are obtainable primarily from bookshops, publishers and libraries. When you are engaged on a specific project, you will always find it worthwhile to acquire copies of the standard works on your subject, which you can keep at your elbow and either annotate in the margins or interleave with narrow strips of paper or markers on which you write some basic headings or other indications. It goes without saying that library books and books belonging to other people should *never* be marked in any way; but 'working copies' are a writer's essential reference tools and should be used to the best advantage.

New books may be purchased from booksellers or, in case of difficulty, direct from the publishers. A good bookseller will be aware of what has been published recently on a particular subject and, through *The Bookseller* and other trade papers, and his contact with publishers' representatives, of forthcoming titles. He will look these up for a customer in one of the Whitaker bibliographies, normally *BookBank* or *BookBank Global*, which are updated monthly on CD-ROM, or on *BookBank OP* (which covers UK and Europe and English-language books which have gone out of print since 1970). Some smaller booksellers use the microfiche or hardback editions of *Whitaker's Books in Print*. If the title is not in stock, delivery may take a couple of weeks or more, depending on the publisher, and it is sometimes quicker to telephone one of the larger bookshops in London or one of the big provincial cities rather than wait for your local shop to obtain a copy. You can also order books online through the Internet Book Shop (at http://www.bookshop.co.uk or www.bol.com) or major booksellers, all of whom are online.

A most useful and inexpensive publication for the book-buyer is Peter Marcan's *Outlets for Specialist New Books in the UK*, which lists not only bookshops and mail order businesses, but practically every book supply source in the country; it also contains a great deal of other related information. There is also an up-to-date edition of *Bookshops of London* by Michael Collins.

You will probably be able to obtain most of the books you need for your research through your local public library or, if you are a member, a private subscription library or institution library. If you want to obtain a new title reasonably quickly, be sure to put in an application as soon as you see it announced in the press. A modest reservation fee is payable at the public library, and normally you will not be allowed to retain a new book after its initial borrowing period if it has been requested by another reader. However, two weeks or so should give you ample time to make some notes and to decide whether or not you need to buy the book. At other libraries you may be able to retain the book until someone else asks for it.

So far as not-so-new titles are concerned, if your public library does not stock what you need, you should be able to borrow them through the inter-library lending scheme. The British Library Document Supply Centre at Boston Spa, Wetherby, West Yorkshire LS23 7BQ, will loan books, film, fiche and other types of documentation from its own collection; it also supplies photocopies. Requests for such material should whenever possible be channelled via the local library or the British Library in London; but if this is not possible occasional users may use the easy order LEXICON service direct (tel. 01937 546599; fax 01937 546210). For full details of a wide range of services available from the Centre, contact the Customer Service (tel. 01937 546060). There is a special arrangement for British Library readers, who may search the DSC Monograph Catalogue on the Online Public Access Catalogue (OPAC) terminals in the reading rooms and order material on a 'next-day delivery' service from Boston Spa. Items supplied in this way cannot however be taken out of the reading room; material required on loan for use at home must be applied for as outlined above. You can obtain free access to the DSC catalogues via the online British Library catalogue at http.//opac97.bl.uk or on the DSC home page on www.bl.uk.

It happens sometimes that you cannot afford to wait even a few days for material – you may need it for one chapter before you can proceed to the next – and then it may be worth the expense of travelling to your nearest copyright library or other major reference library. Remember, however, that you cannot count on seeing a very recent title there: acquisition and cataloguing processes take time. Sadly, due to cutbacks in spending many libraries cannot renew reference titles as frequently as in the past, and except in the larger libraries you may not always find the latest edition of the directory or yearbook you seek.

## Copyright and reference libraries

Under the provisions of various Copyright Acts that have been passed since 1709, certain libraries are entitled to receive one free copy of every book published in the United Kingdom. These are: the British Library (London); the Bodleian Library (Oxford); the Cambridge University Library (Cambridge); the National Library of Wales (Aberystwyth); the National Library of Scotland (Edinburgh); and Trinity College Library (Dublin).

In all these libraries the researcher can be confident of finding everything he needs that has been published from the 18th century onwards, and also much earlier material (collections that have been bequeathed or titles purchased over the years in the sale room). A small percentage of stock may have been destroyed during the last war or otherwise mislaid.

Graduates and other *bona fide* researchers and students are able to use the various well-stocked university libraries, of which the University of London Library, the John Rylands University Library of Manchester and the Sydney Jones Library of Liverpool University are excellent examples. There are also libraries at all the great London museums: the Imperial War Museum, the Caird Library at the National Maritime Museum (the largest maritime reference library in the world), the Natural History Museum, the Science Museum and the Royal Botanic Gardens at Kew.

Among the major reference libraries open to the general public is the Westminster Reference Library just behind Trafalgar Square, London; some of the others are listed on pages 204–5. A visit to the nearest of these and to other reference libraries in the provinces may well fulfil your needs and save you the expense of travelling farther afield.

The headquarters of the British Library – the UK's national library, and the richest and most comprehensive in the world – has recently moved from Bloomsbury to purpose-built premises in the Euston Road, in north London, next door to St Pancras railway station. This move, the biggest in library history, consisting of over 150 million items, was spread over two and a half years as, starting with the Humanities, one by one all the London collections (except the Newspaper Library) were transferred to the new building and the former reading rooms closed. Mid-1999 saw the opening of the Science reading rooms, and since then the Library has operated from only three sites: St Pancras, where the main collections are now housed; Colindale, in north London, the home of the British Library Newspaper Library; and Boston Spa, at Wetherby, West Yorkshire, the base of the inter-library lending and document supply service.

At St Pancras there are eleven reading areas, on three levels: Humanities 1, Humanities 2 (which includes the Library and Information Sciences Service and the Recorded Sound Information Service), Rare Books and Music (where you can use the Listening and Viewing Service of the National Sound Archive), Manuscripts, the Oriental and India Office, Maps, and Science 1, 2 and 3 (spread over five reading rooms). Each has a staffed enquiry desk and a selection of informative leaflets describing its particular collections and services. At the core of the complex is a six-storey glass-walled tower housing the King's Library (the 65,000-volume collection of George III, presented to the nation by his son, George IV in 1823). As you would expect from a purpose-built new library, the facilities are excellent: easy disabled access, desks wired for personal computer use, computer terminals for online catalogue searching linked to an automated book request system, and much else.

British Library readers who for years have been familiar with the layout of open access reference works in the Round Reading Room may find themselves at a loss when first visiting the new Library. As when using any other library or archive centre for the first time, you must allow yourself time to find your way around. There are two ring binders near the enquiry desk in the Humanities 1 reading room entitled 'Humanities 1 and 2 Title List', which will help. Or you might join one of the free 'Reader Training Sessions' organised by the new Reader Education Service. These last for about an hour and can be booked by telephone on 020 7412 7733.

Admissions to the British Library, some other copyright libraries and most major libraries is free. The Bodleian Library, Oxford, and Cambridge University Library charge a fee (according to status; details from their Admission offices). Some reading rooms are open to all without formality, but others require a reader's pass. These are issued on personal application only and are for those who need to see material not readily available elsewhere or whose work requires the facilities of a large research library. You will be asked to state the subject of your research and to have your application signed by a university tutor or someone of authority who will vouch for you; a membership card of the Society of Authors or Writers' Guild may be sufficient. Take a couple of passport-size photographs with you (one will be incorporated into the pass).

Holders of public library tickets in their home town may use them to gain admission to the special reference collections of all London public libraries and to borrow books from the lending branches. Tickets may also be used at other libraries by arrangement with the librarian.

Many libraries are open late on certain evenings in the week. At the British Library, the larger St Pancras reading rooms are open to 8 p.m. from Monday to Thursday; the Central Reference Library in Westminster is open until 8 p.m. from Monday to Friday. Some public libraries now open on Sundays. If you have to travel some distance, you would do well to plan your schedule to make the maximum use of the longest possible working day. Books usually have to be handed in well before closing time, and photocopying orders will not be accepted after a certain time, so that it is important not only to allow for any necessary last-minute note-taking, but also for ordering, and paying for, photocopies.

For those who can afford it, a subscription to the London Library, 14 St James's Square, London SW1Y 4LG (tel. 020 7930 7705; fax 020 7766 4766), will prove very worthwhile. Members may take out ten books at a time (fifteen for country members, who may also borrow by post but have to pay the postage in both directions). Subscribers have access to the stacks and the use of a comfortable reading room, equipped with CD-ROM readers and free access to the Internet. The computerised catalogue is accessible via the World Wide Web (at webpac.londonlibrary.co.uk), and copies of the printed catalogue covering earlier holdings are available for purchase, a boon to those who live in remote areas and wish to order by post, fax or email. The annual subscription, currently £130.00, may be set against a professional writer's tax; short-term subscriptions are available, without borrowing facilities (apply to the Membership Administrator for details).

Another London subscription library is the Highgate Literary and Scientific Institution Library, 11 South Grove, Highgate Village, London N6 6BS (tel. 020 8340 3343); the subscription there is £40.00 for one person, £63.00 for a family. Among the nineteen other surviving independent libraries in the provinces are those of Birmingham, Exeter, Leeds, Newcastle-upon-Tyne and Plymouth (see Appendix I, page 205).

## Special libraries

The use of libraries in general has been discussed in the previous chapter. The questions that now arise concern location: how to find out about the special libraries that are likely to help you in your particular field, and how to locate in those libraries the particular books you need.

The first place to look is in the *Aslib Directory of Information Sources in the United Kingdom*. This gives a comprehensive listing of practically every library and source of information in this country; it contains a subject index, details such as opening hours and the facilities available; it is brought up to date biennially; and all libraries possess the latest edition – ask for it at the enquiry desk. The Library Association's *Libraries in the United Kingdom and the Republic of Ireland* lists addresses, telephone numbers and names of librarians. Valerie McBurney's *Guide to Libraries in London*, which focuses on research collections in all types of library, includes subject and organisation indexes and maps enabling the user to locate libraries. The Aslib *Directory of Museum and Special Collections in the United Kingdom* and the Aslib *Directory of Literary and Historical Collections in the United Kingdom* are also excellent, containing details of lesser known as well as the well-known collections. The *Guide to Libraries and Information Units* concentrates on government libraries and those of official and public bodies.

The best guides to libraries and research institutions internationally are *The World of Learning*, the *World Guide to Libraries* and the *World Guide to Special Libraries*. Specifically for Europe there are the *Guide to Libraries in Western Europe*, the *Guide to Libraries in Central and Eastern Europe* and the *Directory of Special Collections in Western Europe*.

Regrettably, space does not permit the mention here of more than a few individual libraries, named in the text under the various subjects of research discussed. A selective list of UK libraries is printed in Appendix I under subject headings and of foreign libraries in chapter 9, 'Information from and about Foreign Countries'.

## Catalogues and guides

Many libraries now catalogue their collections electronically, or, if not online, on CD-ROM or on microfiche. Rarely nowadays will you be confronted with a card index system. At the British Library, for example, if you are using the Open Access Catalogue (OPAC) you have only to key in the name of the author, a title or merely a key word, in order to find the material you seek (if you are on the Internet, remember that you can access this catalogue at http://opac97.bl.uk). Within the OPAC the three catalogues of most use to the general researcher are the Humanities and Social Sciences Books and Periodicals Catalogue (from 1975); the Humanities and Social Sciences and Periodicals Catalogue (to 1975); and the Humanities Open Access Material Catalogue. You can of course also use the old printed catalogues. For example, the *British Library General Catalogue of Printed Books to 1975* is out of print but is still on many library shelves.

If, on your first visit, you are unsure how to proceed, don't waste precious researching time: ask for assistance at the reader's enquiry desk; it will be given readily. In most libraries free leaflets are available explaining how to search the catalogues. Be prepared to wait to do an online or CD-ROM search, as the terminals are in much demand.

Often you may need information at the library on a subject about which you know next to nothing, let alone the name of any author or title; here, unless you have access to an online catalogue you must use the subject catalogue or a bibliography (see below). You can also consult *Walford's Guide to Reference Material*, which has an excellent subject index. *The Reference Sources Handbook* (formerly published as *Printed Reference Material and Related Information Sources*), written for librarians, is a first-class evaluation of reference books for research. British Library readers will appreciate R.C. Alston's *Handlist of Unpublished Finding Aids to the London Collections of the British Library*. Members of the Institute of Historical Research may use the *Guide to IHR-Info: Hypertext Internet Server*, part 2 of which is a guide to the library.

At the British Library the OPAC catalogue is linked to an automated book request system (ABRS) which enables the user to request or reserve any catalogued item; confirmation appears on screen that the item requested has been ordered or if for any reason it is unavailable. You return to your desk, where a light flashes when the book or journal can be collected at the issue desk, usually within half an hour. Compared to the old system, this saves the researcher a great deal of working time.

## Bibliographies

If a bibliography has been published on the particular subject or person you are interested in, you should find a copy on the reference shelves together with other source books related to that subject. You can check whether a bibliography exists by looking at the *Bibliographic Index*, which is available in most major libraries in printed form and (since November 1984) online. *The World Bibliography of Bibliographies*, compiled by a great 20th-century bibliographer, Theodore Besterman, is comprehensive only up to the mid-1970s. For more recent bibliographies you should check the subject index of the *British National Bibliography* (*BNB*). The bibliographies of other countries are listed in volume 3 of *Walford's Guide to Reference Material* mentioned above, under 'National Bibliographies'. *The World Bibliographical Series* launched in 1977 by Clio Press aims to provide a uniform collection of bibliographies covering every country in the world, at the rate of about fifteen volumes per year.

The Library Association, 7 Ridgmount Street, London WC1E 7AE has published bibliographies on a variety of subjects over the years; these will be found in most reference libraries. For information, write to or telephone Library Association Publishing at the above address (tel. 020 7636 7543; fax 020 7636 3627).

Readers unfamiliar with bibliographic practice should remember that the numbers given in the index are entry numbers, *not* page numbers.

## Electronic and other book information services

The use of the computer to access bibliographical data has transformed dramatically the researcher's routine. Most professional researchers are now skilled in online searching, at home as well as in the library, but if you are a beginner and are baffled, even frightened, by the new machines and the new jargon, do not despair. Help is readily available, both on screen and in the form of trained library assistants who will guide the uninitiated through the complexities.

If you cannot access the database yourself and a computer search service is on offer, this will be done for you by a qualified member of staff, after consultation with you, and preferably in your presence. It will be charged according to staff time, the time connected to the computer and the cost of printing out the material retrieved, and may vary from database to database. You will have the choice of collecting the print-out a few days later or paying for the references to be printed immediately. There is a minimum charge, and a deposit is usually payable. Ask at the library enquiry desk for details. If the cost seems high, remember that the computer file will be more up to date than the printed equivalent and may contain additional information; the computer search will also be very much quicker than a manual search through many volumes.

Space does not permit a list of all the databases worldwide accessible by UK researchers, as these are now so numerous and vary from library to library. Your library enquiry desk should be able to supply a full listing.

The British Library's Automated Information Service, BLAISE (the United Kingdom's first bibliographic database, launched in 1977), provides access to 21 databases containing over 19 million bibliographic records in the humanities and social sciences fields, regularly updated. These include a comprehensive range of British Library London Collections catalogues: the British Library Catalogue, c. 1450–1975; the British Library Humanities and Social Sciences Catalogue, 1975 to date; the Science Reference & Information Service Catalogue, 1975 to date; the British Library Maps Catalogue, 1974 to date; the British Library Music Catalogue, 1980 to date. Among other files on BLAISE are *The British National Bibliography*, 1950 to date; *British Books in Print*, c. 1965 to date; *Library of Congress* bibliographic records 1968 to date; the *English Short Title Catalogue*, 1475–1800; *Grey Literature in Europe (SIGLE)*,* 1980 to date; and *Serials*, c. 1700 to date. (Some of these can be accessed for free via OPAC97.) There is a choice of 'pay-as-you-go' or fixed price service annual subscriptions to Blaise Line or Blaise Web, open to libraries, institutions and individuals. For details contact the British Library National Bibliographic Service, Boston Spa, Wetherby, West Yorkshire LS23 7BQ (tel. 01937 546585; fax 01937 546586). If you are online you will find guides to BLAISE on the British Library's Web server (http://www.bl.uk).

On a totally different level, the Book Trust (Book House, 45 East Hill, Wandsworth, London SW18 2QZ (tel. 020 8516 2977; fax 020 8516 2978) operates a Book Information Service for members and non-members (charges on request). It is always worth asking if they have a printed booklist on a particular subject.

---

*Literature not normally available through bookselling channels and thus difficult for the lay person to find.

## Tracing books

Often you want to trace a particular book whose exact title and author you do not remember. Provided you have a vague idea of these, or the approximate date of publication, it is no longer difficult. Whereas in the past this might have involved a lengthy search, nowadays you should be able to trace the item instantly by its keyword, via OPAC.

The earliest listing in this country is the *London Catalogue of Books*, covering the period 1700–1855. *The English Catalogue of Books*, volume 1 of which covers the period 1801–36 and later volumes (variously at three- and five-year intervals), continues until 1968. *Whitaker's Cumulative Book List* (from 1924) used to be published quarterly, with annual and five-year cumulations; in 1984 it was re-titled *Whitaker's Book List*. As mentioned earlier in this chapter, there is now a Whitaker file available for online searching on BLAISE. All libraries and booksellers subscribe to one or more of the Whitaker bibliographic compilations on CD-ROM or microfiche. The current printed volumes of *Books in Print*, although obviously not quite so up to date, are usually available to readers for quick reference at the library enquiry desk.

So far as American titles are concerned, the *National Union Catalog* is especially useful as it gives authors' dates; from 1968 onwards it is on BLAISE, and may also be accessed online at www.lib.ncsu.edu. For further reference look at the *American Book Publishing Record, Books in Print* (US), the *Cumulative Book Index* and the *Subject Guide to Books in Print*.

*International Books in Print* and the *Guide to Microforms in Print*, both from Saur, are worldwide in coverage.

It is worth remembering that the weekly trade paper, *The Bookseller*, publishes bumper spring and autumn issues (available as a separate subscription) containing details of forthcoming books for the next six months. Another tip, if you wish to keep fully up to date, is to put yourself on the mailing lists of those firms who publish in your particular field or fields of interest. Use *Whitaker's Directory of Publishers* or the *Cassell Directory of Publishing* to find out where to reach them. And keep an eagle eye open for reviews and advertisements in the national press. It goes without saying that you will be an avid browser in your local bookshop!

## Obtaining out-of-print books

If you want to acquire titles that are out of print, either for your own reference collection or for work on a specific project, you should make a point of informing your local antiquarian or secondhand bookseller of your special interest. He will then let you know when suitable books come in and will advertise for them through the trade, probably in *Bookdealer*; there is no charge for this service and no obligation to buy when a quotation is forthcoming, subject to the book or books remaining unsold in the meantime; but the process may take several weeks. *Cole's Register of British Antiquarian and Secondhand Bookdealers* (*The Clique*) and *Sheppard's Book Dealers in Europe* are the handbooks most used by the trade; another recommended title is the *Skoob Directory of Secondhand Bookshops in the British Isles*. You should also look at the *Book and Magazine Collector*.

Another way to obtain an out-of-print title is to use a specialist bookfinding service. Leading UK booksellers who offer customers this service include Blackwell's (Oxford), Hatchard's (Cambridge), and Heywood Hill and Maggs Bros. in London. Dillons booksearch service is based in Durham (tel. 0191 384 2095; fax 0191 386 0430), and that of Waterstone's in Tunbridge Wells (tel. 01892 522700; fax 01892 521400). There are a large number of individual bookfinding specialists spread throughout the UK, and many of them are listed, by county, in a *Register of British Bookfinders*, available from C.A. Winder Publications, Toronto House, 11 Mayfield Grove, Harrogate, N. Yorks HG1 5HG (tel. 01423 521187). From the same source you can obtain a *Register of British Bookdealers' Specialities*, arranged under subject. Some bookfinders advertise regularly in the national and literary press. Recommended well-established specialists include Bookfinders (18 Hawthorndene Road, Bromley, Kent BR2 7DY; tel/fax 020 8462 7331); Melrose Books (35 Dornden Drive, Langton Green, Tunbridge Wells, Kent TN3 0AE; tel. 01892 862078) and Twiggers Ltd (17 Mullins Path, Mortlake, London SW14 8EZ (tel. 020 8878 8644; fax 020 8878 7826). There are many others. It is a good idea to find one locally whom you can trust and keep him informed of your requirements. You may be asked for a modest search fee in advance. For example, Twiggers, mentioned above, will search for four titles free of charge; if they have not been successful after a month, you may opt for an extended search for up to three months on payment of £3.00 per title. Their fee for advertising in trade journals in the United States is also £3.00 per title.

Obtaining out-of-print books from abroad is much quicker than it used to be, thanks to the Internet and payment by credit card, but it has to be remembered that tracing all out-of-print titles takes time, whether in the UK or elsewhere. (See chapter 9, page 163 for further information on firms importing foreign titles.)

The *Books on Demand* programme of paper facsimile repro-ductions marketed by University Microfilms International (The Old

Hospital, Ardingly Road, Cuckfield, West Sussex RH17 5JR (tel. 01444 445000; fax 01444 445050) includes some 132,000 out-of-print titles ranging from the 15th century to the present day.

# Newspapers and Periodicals

The major holding in this country of national and foreign papers and periodicals is at the British Library: newspapers, fortnightlies, weeklies and some monthlies at the British Library Newspaper Library, Colindale Avenue, London NW9 5HE (tel. 020 7412 7353; fax 020 7412 7379), opposite Colindale Underground Station; all other periodicals at the main Library at St Pancras (96 Euston Road, London NW1 2DB). The major exceptions to this broad division are the pre-1801 London newspapers (the Burney and Thomason collections) and the Oriental and India Office collections, all of which are now at St Pancras (96 Euston Road, London NW1 2DB). British Library ticket holders are admitted to the Newspaper Library without formality; for others short-term tickets will be issued on application in person to the main reading room, subject to proof of identity bearing a signature.

There is a card-index catalogue at Colindale (with a duplicate at St Pancras) listing alphabetically by title all the papers held, with dates. The researcher using this index should remember that where there are several papers or magazines of the same title, the cards are arranged within the title alphabetically under the place of publication. An eight-volume printed *Catalogue of the Newspaper Library, Colindale*, was published in 1975. It is planned to provide readers with a complete catalogue, retrospectively converted to machine-readable form, in the near future.

For some years now the Newspaper Library has been systematically microfilming its entire collection, so as to preserve the original newsprint from decay through constant handling. Most foreign newspapers are purchased on microfilm and since 1986 all UK newspapers are microfilmed on receipt. This is a great convenience both to the reader and to the library staff, as in many cases up to a year's run of a paper or journal can be housed on one spool, thus eliminating the handling of bulky volumes and conserving storage space. Microfilms of newspapers and journals are currently on sale (prices on application). Photocopies from microfilm and microfiche, as well as print-outs from CD-ROM and the Internet may be made on a self-service machine at the Library at a very reasonable 35p–70p per page, depending on size; photocopies from original newspapers, made by staff, cost from 50p–£2.00 per page (enhanced photocopies from £10.00–£17.50 per page). Postal applications are subject to a minimum charge (currently £12.00). An express reading room service is available at extra cost (full details on application). All photo-copying is subject to the usual copyright regulations (only one article from any one issue of a paper or periodical at any one time).

## Tracing newspapers and periodicals

The researcher wishing to trace an early English-language newspaper will find all those published in Great Britain and Ireland in the period up to 1900 listed in the *British Library General Catalogue of Printed Books*. *Willing's Press Guide*, first published in 1871 as *Frederick May's London Press Directory*, and now issued annually, is one of the best quick reference guides to modern newspapers and periodicals in the United Kingdom; recent editions also cover publications overseas. A complete set of *Willing's*, together with several earlier newspaper press directories dating from 1846, is on the open shelves at Colindale; it contains an A–Z list, a list of publications under subjects, and (until recently) a list under English counties and towns. *The Newspaper Press in Britain: An Annotated Bibliography* edited by David Linton and Ray Boston, which contains a useful chronology of British newspaper history 1476–1986 and a location listing of papers and other archives, is highly recommended, together with its more recent companion volume, *The Twentieth-Century Newspaper Press in Britain*. Also very useful is the *Encyclopedia of the British Press 1422–1992*, edited by Dennis Griffiths. Forthcoming from the same editor will be the *Encyclopedia of the World Press*, scheduled for the year 2001. The British Library's own *Bibliography of British Newspapers* has been in progress since 1982, one or two counties per volume.

So far as foreign newspapers are concerned, *The Europa World Year Book* gives details of the press of each country; and volume 3 of *Walford's Guide to Reference Material* lists the various national source books under each country in both the 'Newspapers' and 'Periodicals' sections.

*Benn's Media* (formerly *Benn's Media Directory*) covers the whole world and is the oldest-established media guide: now in three volumes and published annually, it is directly descended from *Mitchell's Newspaper Press Directory*, which was first published in 1846. It covers newspapers, periodicals, house journals and much other related information on embassies and high commissions, news agencies, broadcasting and all aspects of the media including cable and satellite. A handy paperback reference and contacts guide to the media is the paperback *The Media Guide*.

In the general catalogue at the British Library periodicals are entered in a series of volumes filed under 'P' and headed 'Periodical Publications'; the titles are arranged alphabetically under the place of publication. The transactions or proceedings of most learned societies are not here, but catalogued under the name of the society. It is necessary, therefore, first to look in the general catalogue under the title of the periodical, which will give either a finding reference to 'Periodical Publications' (i.e. the place of publication) or to the name of the relevant society, which may be catalogued under a particular country, town or university. This sounds more complicated than it is in practice, and you will very quickly get into the swing of it. (If you are using OPAC this does not apply, as all you need to do is key in the title of the periodical or just its key word.) Note that periodicals which are not catalogued may be at the British Library Document Supply Centre; see pages 43–4.

There are two invaluable finding aids for international periodicals: the *ISSN Register*, issued quarterly, listing periodicals from 180 countries, and *Ulrich's International Periodicals Directory*, published in hardback and CD-ROM, and also online.

So far as British newspapers and periodicals are concerned, *Serials in the British Library*, which has replaced the earlier *British Union-Catalogue*, is the standard guide. Cynthia L. White's *Women's Magazines 1693–1968* is a classic in its field; a more recent study is *Women's Magazines: The First Three Hundred Years* by Brian Braithwaite, which has a useful 'births, marriages and deaths' section listing the successes, mergers and failures over the years. A new online product launched by Primary Source Media is a collection of *International Women's Periodicals*, spanning the 18th to early 20th century. David Reed's *The Popular Magazine in Britain and the United States of America 1880–1960* covers most aspect of magazine publishing in the period. Finally, use should be made of the microfiche *Keyword Index to Serial Titles (KIST)*, which lists all significant words in serial holdings of the British Library, the Science Museum Library and Cambridge University Library.

Now that *The Times* is on microfilm, you should have no difficulty in finding a library locally where you may have access to the complete run, starting with the first issue of 1 January 1785. Other papers may not be so easy to find in the provinces, but lists of newspapers (worldwide) that are available on microfilm, CD-ROM and online may be obtained from Primary Source Media (The Gale Group), 50 Milford Road, Reading RG1 8LJ (tel. 0118 957 7213; fax 0118 939 4334) and from Chadwyck-Healey Ltd, The Quorum, Barnwell Road, Cambridge CB5 8SW (tel. 01223 215512; fax 01223 215514). Primary Source Media have recently embarked on the ambitious project of putting online all complete issues of *The Times* from 1785 to 1990. They also have in progress an ongoing series of Early English Newspapers on microfilm.

A huge preservation programme is under way to save some 3,500 fragile local and regional newspapers dating from 1800 to 1950. This *Local Newspapers in Peril* initiative, co-ordinated by Newsplan, a panel of the Library and Information Co-operation Council, has been made possible by a substantial Heritage Lottery Fund grant, the balance to be raised from the newspaper industry, suppliers and the library sector. Newsplan intends to microfilm and digitise all those items most at risk and will install 800 microfilm readers, with disability access, in libraries throughout the UK. Information on library newspaper holdings will also be made available on the Internet.

## Indexes to newspapers

The most valuable of British newspaper indexes to the researcher is the *The Times Index*. The official index has been published since 1906, and an earlier, slightly less accurate version, known as *Palmer's Index to The Times*, from 1790 to June 1941. The *Index* is now published monthly, with annual cumulations; since 1973 it has included references to the *Sunday Times, Times Literary Supplement, Educational Supplement* and *Higher Education Supplement*. Other newspapers in the United Kingdom which publish or have at one time published indexes are the *Financial Times* (May 1912–20, and more recently from 1981), the *Glasgow Herald* (annually from 1906) and *The Guardian* (from 1986). All these indexes are on the open shelves at Colindale, together with indexes to several American papers such as the *New York Times, Washington Post, Chicago Tribune* and *Los Angeles Times*, and indexes to a few Commonwealth and foreign newspapers. Microfilms of indexes to a number of British and continental newspapers are published by Primary Source Media (The Gale Group) (formerly Research Publications International) of Reading. Others are now online.

A major research tool for the 1990s is the *British Newspaper Index (BNI)* on CD-ROM. This covers fifteen newspaper titles: *The Times, The Sunday Times, Financial Times, The Guardian, The Observer, The Independent, Independent on Sunday, The Daily Telegraph, The Sunday Telegraph, Daily Mail, The Mail on Sunday, The Times Literary Supplement, The Times Higher Educational Supplement, The Times Educational Supplement* and *The Times Educational Supplement (Scotland)*. University Microfilms Inc., The Old Hospital, Ardingly Road, Cuckfield, West Sussex RH17 5JR (tel. 01444 445000; fax 01444 445050) offers a number of abstracting and indexing databases including *Newspapers*, which provides access to the *New York Times*, *The Washington Post*, *The Wall Street Journal* and other US newspapers.

## Indexes to periodicals

The earliest index to periodicals is *Poole's Index to Periodical Literature*, which covers the period 1802–1906; its comparatively recent author index is extremely useful. The *Reader's Guide to Periodical Literature* is an American publication that dates from 1900; its English equivalent, the *Subject Index to Periodicals*, first published in 1915, changed its name to the *British Humanities Index* in 1962. Some of the more specialised indexes of interest to the researcher are the *Wellesley Index to Victorian Periodicals, 1824–1900*, the *Abstracts in New Technologies and Engineering* (*ANTE*), which has replaced the *Current Technology Index*, the *British Education Index* and a series published by H.W. Wilson of New York, of which the *Art Index*, the *Biography Index*, the *Business Periodicals Index*, the *Humanities Index*, the *Index to Legal Periodicals* and the *Social Sciences Index* (the last two formerly published as one index 1965–74, and before that date as the *International Index*) are the most likely to be of interest to the UK writer/researcher. *Library and Information Science Abstracts* (*LISA*) is an important database which is international in coverage. The electronic *Periodicals Contents Index*, first published in 1990, covers periodicals in the humanities and social sciences published since 1770.

Among the indexes to particular magazines which are of immense value to researchers are those to the *Gentleman's Magazine*: the printed index volumes cover the period 1731–1819, with separate indexes to the biographical and obituary notices. *Notes & Queries* carries indexes to each volume and cumulated indexes for every twelve volumes. Both of these publications are excellent sources of information on a variety of subjects. Among recent indexing projects has been the index compiled by Geraldine Beare to the *Strand Magazine* 1891–1950, also of great value.

The majority of modern periodicals carry volume indexes, which are a great help in tracing material quickly. Where there are no such printed indexes, it is necessary to skim through the contents page of each issue to find a particular paper or feature, or the researcher can apply to the editorial office of the publication concerned, if this is still in existence, where an index may be held on computer or on a card index.

Most public libraries keep long runs of local newspapers, county magazines and publications of their local historical and archaeological societies; these will also be found on the shelves of county record offices.

The British Library Science, Technology and Business Service houses a vast number of scientific and technical periodicals, including those formerly at the Patent Office Library.

The researcher wishing to trace a medical paper should do so in the *Index Medicus*, to which most medical libraries subscribe.

## Press cuttings

Press cuttings have a value, as a starting point, in all research but (in my opinion) should be used with care and never as a substitute for original research. A collection of cuttings is only as reliable and comprehensive as the person or persons assembling the cuttings were (or are) reliable and conscientious.

The major exception to this has to be the admirable press cuttings library of the Royal Institute of International Affairs at Chatham House, 10 St James's Square, London SW1Y 4LE (tel. 020 7957 5723/020 7314 2783; fax 020 7957 5710), which contains much material of value to researchers on foreign and Commonwealth matters. The collection prior to 1940 is on microfilm, that of the period 1940–70 has been transferred to the British Library Newspaper Library at Colindale (indexes at Chatham House), and the present library collection runs from 1971.

The Press Association News Library, at 292 Vauxhall Bridge Road, London SW1V 1AE (tel. 020 7963 7012; fax 020 7963 7065), has a collection of some 15 million cuttings from 1928 onwards, as well as a photo bank of five million pictures. This archive is open to the general public seven days a week (Monday to Friday 8 a.m. to 8 p.m.; Saturday, 8 a.m. to 6 p.m; Sunday, 9 a.m. to 5 p.m.). Alternatively, research is undertaken by in-house staff on a commercial basis (rates on application). A photocopying service is available.

Many newspapers, libraries, trade associations and other professional bodies hold cuttings collections, and it is always worth asking what they have and having a look at them: you may well pick up leads for further research in this way.

# Official Publications

Most British official publications are available at the main reference libraries and public libraries. The former British Library Official Publications Library collection has been re-named the Social Policy Information Service and will be found at the new British Library in St

Pancras in the Science 2 North reading room (tel. 020 7412 7536; fax 020 7412 7761). It includes government publications of all countries, publications of the European Commission, the United Nations and other international and intergovernmental bodies. British Parliamentary papers, complete sets of *Hansard* and the *London Gazette*, current UK electoral registers and all the main statistical yearbooks are among a large number of reference books on the open shelves.

The definitive source for UK material is the Chadwyck-Healey series, *Great Britain: Stationery Office Catalogues of Government Publications, 1894–1970* (*Annual Catalogues of British Official and Parliamentary Publications*, 1894–1919 on microfiche, later volumes clothbound under the title *Annual Catalogues of Government Publications*, including, as vol 1, *Seven Quinquennial Consolidated Indexes to Government Publications, 1936–1970*). *The Catalogue of United Kingdom Official Publications on CD-ROM* (*UKOP*) lists both the publications of Her Majesty's Stationery Office and other organisations since 1980. Also useful is the *Catalogue of British Official Publications Not Published by HMSO*.

A vast amount of United Nations bibliographic information will be found on the CD-ROM *UNIBIS Plus*, which is retrospective to 1979 and now issued quarterly. You can also obtain information on the UN and its specialised agencies from the United Nations Information Centre, Millbank Tower (21st floor), 21/24 Millbank, London SW1P 4QH (tel. 020 7630 1981; fax 020 7976 6478).

On the European Union the best source is the bi-monthly *European Access*, available online weekly from October 1999 at http://www.europeanaccess.co.uk. *EUROCAT*, published quarterly on CD-ROM, is a complete catalogue of EU publications and documents. There is also the *European Union Information Directory of UK Sources*. As an up-to-date introduction you cannot better Timothy Bainbridge's *The Penguin Companion to the European Union*. *Bona fide* researchers (but not students) may use the Library and Information Unit at the European Commission, Jean Monnet House, 8 Storey's Gate, London SW1P 3AT (tel. 020 7973 1992; fax 020 7976 6478). Westminster Reference Library, 35 St Martin's Street, London WC2H 7HP (tel. 020 7641 4634; fax 020 7641 4606) is one of the UK's three EU depository libraries.

# Miscellaneous

The *Essay and General Literature Index*, covering work published since 1900, is the best place to look for miscellaneous articles and reviews. The *English Short Title Catalogue* (*ESTC*), now available on

CD-ROM as well as online (BLAISE), is a unique source for books, lists, advertisements, song catalogues and much other printed matter; the material dates from 1473, but is chiefly of the 18th century.

Quotations may be checked in numerous compilations available in every reference library and online. Full use should also be made of concordances to the Bible, to Shakespeare, Tennyson and other major writers; people tend to forget just how time-saving these can be when one is reasonably sure of the author and when one has a major word or phrase to go on. *Granger's Index to Poetry*, with its title, first line, author and subject indexes, is indispensable. The *Song Index* and its supplement are useful sources for songs up to 1934, and there is also the *Song Catalogue* section of the *BBC Music Library Catalogue of Holdings*; the *Popular Song Index* and its supplements bring the catalogues up to the present time. For music bibliographies and catalogues of printed music, see volume 3 of *Walford's Guide to Reference Material*, under 'Music', and the *British Catalogue of Music*. The *International Index to Music Periodicals* from Chadwyck-Healey is on CD-ROM and online; there is an ongoing 'Full Text' database online to which current and retrospective articles are constantly being added.

If you need to check on any particular kind of literature or printed matter – for example, hymns or nursery rhymes – you should always look in the subject index of the reference library first, to find out the standard work.

## Translations

The best source is the *Index Translationum*, which has been published since 1932. Since 1949 it has been issued annually by UNESCO, but is now only on CD-ROM in a cumulated annual edition. It should be available in major reference libraries.

## Street and telephone directories

The Guildhall Library in London has a collection of street directories from the late 18th century, available on microfilm; many have been published by the Society of Genealogists on microfiche. There are two useful bibliographies: the *Guide to the National and Provincial Directories of England and Wales, excluding London, published before 1856*, by Jane E. Norton, and P.J. Atkins' *The Directories of London 1677–1977*. For present-day publications consult *Current British Directories* and *Current European Directories*. Most county record offices have sets of their local directories. These are extremely useful for checking addresses and names of neighbours, in biographical and family history research, as are the court guides (for the aristocracy) which also date from the late 18th century. The yellow pages of modern telephone directories may help you to find experts in a particular field.

## Maps

The British Library's collection of maps (manuscript and printed) is one of the most important cartographic repositories in the world. The Maps Reading Room is on level 3 of the British Library, where there is a Map Reference Enquiry Desk to assist readers. The map catalogue is on CD-ROM and is separate from the British Library main online catalogue. The Public Record Office, most local record offices and some libraries, such as the Royal Geographical Society Library and Birmingham Central Library, also hold special historical collections. Volume 3 of the *Catalogue of the National Maritime Museum Library* is another good source-guide. A recent title from Phillimore, *Maps for Historians*, by Paul Hindle, is a practical guide and source of information.

Stanford's, at 12–14 Long Acre, London WC2E 2LP (tel. 020 7836 1321; fax 020 7836 0189), sells antique and modern maps and atlases covering the world. The first edition of the Ordnance Survey has been reprinted, and the historical series is still available; the modern editions, in various scales, may be purchased from the main Ordnance Survey agents, the National Map Centre, 22–24 Caxton Street, London SW1H 0QU (tel. 020 7222 2466; fax 020 7222 2619), or ordered from most booksellers.

# Unpublished Sources

## Manuscripts and private papers

The major source of manuscripts in England is the British Library Department of Manuscripts. There is a Manuscripts reading room at St Pancras, for access to which you need a supplementary pass in addition to the normal reader's ticket; a letter of recommendation is required. There is a ten-volume Index of *Manuscripts in the British Library*, listing in one alphabetical sequence the holdings to 1950; more recent acquisitions, catalogued as Add. MSS, will be found in a series of volumes on open access. A good quick reference guide is *The British Library Guide to the Catalogues and Indexes of the Department of Manuscripts*. This useful booklet also lists the reference books on open access in the Manuscripts reading room and the catalogues available there of MSS holdings in other libraries.

If you wish to trace the location of other MSS or to ascertain whether any private papers exist, or to find out if such papers have been deposited or registered, you should first get in touch with the Royal Commission on Historical Manuscripts, Quality House, Quality Court, Chancery Lane, London WC2A 1HP. The Commission maintains a National Register of Archives, consisting of more than 40,000 unpublished lists and catalogues of manuscript collections (privately owned records and those held in repositories other than the Public Record Office, in the UK and abroad). The NRA database is available on the Internet at http://www.hmc.gov.uk or via Telnet at public.hmc.gov.uk. Publications of the Commission include a *Guide to Sources for British History* series and an ongoing set of *National Register of Archives Information Sheets* (for titles, see bibliography at end of this chapter). Their *Surveys of Historical Manuscripts in the United Kingdom* is a select bibliography which lists completed surveys (published and unpublished) and those known to be in progress.

The search room at Quality House is open to the public. A limited amount of specific enquiries can be handled by post or fax (020 7831 3550). Telephone enquiries are *not* accepted. The Commission's Web site is http://www.hmc.gov.uk. Search facilities include the use of computerised indexes: Personal, Business and Subject, as well as a Repositories File containing up-to-date details of record offices. A valuable research tool, published jointly by the Commission and the Institute of Historical Research, is R.J. Olney's *Manuscript Sources for British History: their Nature, Location and Use.*

So far as literary manuscripts are concerned, you should look at the *Location Register of English Literary Manuscripts and Letters* and at the *Index of English Literary Manuscripts*, covering the period 1450–1900. Sadly, publication of the latter has been suspended beyond 1900 letter 'P' (see bibliography p. 73).

An excellent finding aid to unpublished material is the Chadwyck-Healey *National Inventory of Documentary Sources in the United Kingdom and Ireland* (*NIDS*), on microfiche, updated eight times a year and also on CD-ROM. Most major libraries subscribe, and there are useful leaflets explaining how to use the inventory. *British Archives: A Guide to Archive Resources in the United Kingdom and Ireland*, by Janet Foster and Julia Sheppard, is another indispensable reference tool, listing archive collections by town, by county and alphabetically; the introduction contains useful advice to the first-time user of archival material. David Iredale's award-winning *Enjoying Archives* is both practical and entertaining.

Researchers handling documentary source material for the first time will find extremely helpful Frank G. Burke's *Research and the*

*Manuscript Tradition*; although written from the American perspective, it contains much practical advice of value to everyone working in this field. The British Records Association publishes a useful 'Archives and the User' series, regularly updated and reprinted (details from the BRA, 40 Northampton Road, London EC1R 0HB).

## Public records

The Public Record Office (PRO) – the national archive of the United Kingdom – holds official documents going back to the 11th century. Nowadays all government records are automatically deposited within thirty years and (with certain exceptions) are open to the public thirty years after their creation.

Formerly in Chancery Lane, central London, in recent years virtually all the records have been transferred to a purpose-built complex at Kew, where there are no less than 96 miles of shelving. (Census returns, non-parochial registers and PCC Wills have been sent to the Family Records Centre, see pages 141–2). The old building in Chancery Lane is closed.

Admission to the PRO is free, but you must have a reader's ticket. On your first visit take with you some formal proof of identity bearing your signature (a driving licence or cheque card) and a ticket will be issued to you. Those who are not British citizens should present their passport or national identity card.

In recent years academics and researchers have welcomed the extended opening hours at Kew, with two late evenings to 7 p.m. and Saturday opening (last document ordering 2.30 p.m.); see page 192 for full details. Provided you know the exact references, you may order documents in advance of your visit (tel. 020 8392 5261).

The reading rooms at Kew include a Research Enquiries Room, a Map and Large Document Room and a Microfilm Reading Room (where the microfilms are on self-service). In most rooms there are separate areas where you may use your PC, typewriter or tape recorder. Documents requests are made on computer terminals, and readers are issued with bleepers keyed to their seat number which let them know when they can collect from the issue desk. There are self-service printers for copying from microfilm and fiche, and an efficient reprographic service for ordering other copies. As documents are classified by department or ministry rather than by subject, you must first ascertain to which class the files you need belong. In the class lists you can then look chronologically to find the piece number(s) you need to order. It is not as complicated as it sounds. There are several 'Introduction to Archive Materials' pamphlets available free of charge from the PRO bookshop, and qualified staff are on hand to deal with enquiries and to help first-time users to operate the computer terminals. The current *Guide to the Public Record Office* is currently available only on microfiche.

A recent development has been the opening to readers of the staff research library containing some 150,000 titles on all aspects of British history. This library is located off the Microfilm Reading Room.

Looking to the future, the Archives Direct 2001 Programme plans to provide online access to the current *Guide to the Public Record Office*, as well as a range of other Internet services.

Parliamentary records from 1497 are at the House of Lords Record Office, and records of British rule in India to 1947 at the British Library, in the Oriental and India Office Collections reading room. The Imperial War Museum, Lambeth Road, London SE1 6HZ, houses documentary and illustrative material on the two World Wars, and the Churchill Archives Centre at Churchill College, Cambridge CB3 0DS, is collecting papers of 20th-century politicians, scientists and both military and naval commanders; however not all of these are yet open to the public.

At the Guildhall Library in London you will find records relating to the City from medieval times, including those of many of the City livery companies (although some of these perished in the Great Fire of 1666). Consult the *Guide to Archives and Manuscripts at Guildhall Library*.

The National Library of Scotland possesses a priceless collection of manuscripts, ranging from early monastic writings to modern political papers; there are printed and manuscript indexes. Also in Edinburgh are the Scottish Record Office and the National Register of Archives (Scotland).

The National Library of Ireland and Trinity College Library, both in Dublin, house many Irish records. You should also contact the Public Record Office of Northern Ireland in Belfast. When the old Public Record Office in Dublin was destroyed in 1922 most, but not all, of the records perished.

The addresses, telephone and fax numbers of all national and provincial record offices will be found in the Royal Commission on Historical Manuscripts booklet, *Record Repositories in Great Britain*. See also Appendix I of this book (pages 192–201).

## Theses

It is always worthwhile checking on dissertations, as these can be a most valuable source of information. Aslib has since 1950 published an *Index to Theses accepted for Higher Degrees in the Universities of Great Britain and Ireland*; it is now published under the title *Index to Theses with Abstracts*. The universities of Oxford, Cambridge and London publish separate annual lists. There are *Abstracts of Dissertations* for Oxford and Cambridge going back to 1925, and lists for London in the University Calendar 1930–40, as well as *Subjects of Dissertations, Theses etc. for Higher Degrees* covering 1937–51. The Institute of Historical Research has published annual lists since 1901. Issued in May each year, *History Theses* consists of two parts: 'Theses completed' and 'Theses in progress'. You can also check on work in progress in *Current Research in Britain*; there are separate volumes for the Humanities, Social Sciences, Biological Sciences and Physical Sciences.

For North American doctoral dissertations and master theses consult the UMI *Dissertation Abstracts*, available in paperback or on CD-ROM. UMI also offers a Datrix Direct customised title search for a nominal fee. A wide range of reproductions is available on paper and microform. Ask for details: University Microfilms Inc., The Old Hospital, Ardingly Road, Cuckfield, West Sussex RH17 5JR (tel. 01444 445000; fax 01444 445050).

## Broadcast and televised material

There have been many changes in the worlds of radio and television in the wake of the Broadcasting Act 1990. While these changes do not much affect the researcher into historical material, if you are seeking current information you should contact the relevant radio or television company direct. Barrie Macdonald's *Broadcasting in the United Kingdom: A Guide to Information Sources* is an essential reference tool. *The Media Guide* contains addresses and telephone/fax numbers of the various companies, as well as a list of independent producers (with telephone numbers). The Spotlight publication *Contacts* is also very useful in this respect.

Most sizeable reference libraries possess the Chadwyck-Healey microfiche editions of *BBC Radio: Author and Title Catalogues of Transmitted Drama, Poetry and Features, 1929–1975* and *BBC Television: Author and Title Catalogues of Transmitted Drama and Features, 1936–1975, with Chronological List of Transmitted Plays*. Also available on microfiche are the *Radio Times*, from 1923, *The Listener*, from 1929, and the *BBC Home Service: Nine O'Clock News 1939–1945* (60,000 pages of newsreaders' typescripts).

The BBC Written Archives Centre, Peppard Road, Caversham Park, Reading RG4 8TZ (tel. 0118 946 9280/1/2; fax 0118 946 1145) is open to *bona fide* researchers by appointment only. The BBC Sound Archives are not open to the public but may be accessed through the British Library National Sound Archive (NSA), which has now moved from South Kensington to the new British Library, 96 Euston Road, London NW1 2DB.

One of the largest and most diverse sound archives in the world, the National Sound Archive contains broadcasts and published recordings, and also a unique collection of unpublished recordings, dating from 1890 to the present day. Its online catalogue, CADENSA, which includes more than one and a half million entries, may be consulted at two special terminals in the Humanities 2 reading room at the new British Library. The Library and Information Service of the NSA is on open access, but if you wish to use the Listening and Viewing Service (located in the Rare Books and Music reading room at the British Library), you must make an appointment in advance. You will need a British Library reader's pass (see page 46). There is also a Northern Listening Service at the British Library's premises in Boston Spa, near Wetherby, West Yorkshire.

Under the terms of the new Broadcasting Act the National Film Archive is to maintain a national television archive. It is now the National Film and Television Archive (NFTA).

## Filmed and recorded material

The researcher interested in filmed material and the history of the cinema should contact the British Film Institute (BFI) at 21 Stephen Street, London W1P 1PL (tel. 020 7255 1444; fax 020 7436 7950). The BFI National Library houses the world's largest collection of information on the cinema and television; it is open to non-members for reference (day membership available). The National Film and Television Archive, a division of the BFI, is administered from the same address, but the films themselves are stored at Berkhamsted. A viewing service is available for *bona fide* researchers.

If you need newsreel material, contact the British Universities Film and Video Council (BUFVC) at 77 Wells Street, London W1P 3RE (tel. 020 7393 1500; fax 020 7393 1555), where academic or other *bona fide* researchers may access the computerised British Universities Newsreel Project. This database contains records of all British cinema newsreels from 1910 to 1979. You will not be able to see the actual footage there, but will be directed to the relevant source, probably British Pathé or British Movietone. Some newsreels are available on video.

There are two recently published indispensable guides for the researcher: *Film and Television Collections in Europe: The Map-TV Guide* ('Map' meaning the Mercury Archive Programme, Strasbourg), which contains detailed information on 1,900 film and television collections in 40 different countries, and *The Film Researcher's Handbook*, which is a guide to sources in Africa, Asia, Australasia, North America and South America.

*Halliwell's Film and Video Guide* and the *BFI Film & Television Handbook* are standard reference tools. Among a wealth of other titles I recommend the Cassell/BFI *Companion to Cinema* series, the *International Dictionary of Film and Filmmakers* and *International Film Index*. For the early period of cinema, there is the mammoth *History of the Cinema 1895–1940*, a collection of 3,574 microfiches plus printed guide and index from Chadwyck-Healey. The same firm publishes the *Film Index International*, which is updated annually.

## Oral history collections

Although the term 'oral history' is a fairly recent one, in fact this was the very first kind of history, as Paul Thompson has pointed out in *The Voice of the Past*. The growth of oral history study groups today reflects an interest in and awareness of the value of this field of research, which demands quite different skills from those of the historian who handles only documentation.

Researchers interested in the subject should consider joining the Oral History Society; membership includes a subscription to the Society's journal, *Oral History*. Contact the Society direct at the Department of Sociology, University of Essex, Colchester, Essex CO4 3SQ (tel. 01206 873333; fax 01206 873410), or through the National Sound Archive. The best introduction to the subject, apart from the Thompson title above-mentioned, is *Oral History: Talking about the Past*, by Robert Perks; the same author has compiled *Oral History: An Annotated Bibliography 1945–1989*. A new and practical title has recently been published by Sutton in their *History Handbooks* series: *Oral History*, by Ken Howarth.

The *National Life Story Collection*, a National Sound Archive project currently in progress, is bringing together recordings of 20th-century people from all walks of life; this is bound to prove a valuable source for researchers.

It is a sobering thought that already less than 50 per cent of all records exist on paper, as opposed to film, tape and computer storage systems. This means that researchers are going to spend an increasingly greater proportion of their working time looking and listening instead of poring over the printed or handwritten page in library and record office. Whether we like it or not, the revolution is under way, and we are going to have to get used to it, so the sensible thing to do is to prepare ourselves by acquiring the necessary new skills.

*Abstracts in New Technologies and Engineering* (*ANTE*), formerly the *Current Technology Index* (*CTI*), bi-monthly by Bowker-Saur, East Grinstead; also as *ANTE Plus*, quarterly on CD-ROM, and online

*Abstracts of Dissertations approved for the PhD, MSc and MLitt Degrees 1925/6–1956/7*, Cambridge University Press, 1927–59

*Abstracts of Dissertations for the Degree of Doctor of Philosophy 1925–40*, Oxford University Press, 12 vols, 1928–47 (BLitt and BSc theses are included in vols 10 and 12)

*American Book Publishing Record*, published weekly and monthly, with annual and 5-year cumulative volumes, by Bowker, New Providence, N.J. There are sets of cumulative volumes covering the period 1950–84 and an earlier volume for the years 1876–1949

'Archives and the User' series, the British Records Association, 40 Northampton Road, London EC1R 0HB

*Art Index*, published quarterly since 1929 by H.W. Wilson, New York; now monthly by annual subscription, printed, CD-ROM, magnetic tape and online

*Aslib Directory of Information Sources in the United Kingdom*, published biennially by Aslib, London and regularly updated, 2 vols, 10th edn, eds K.W. Reynard and J.M.E. Reynard, 1998; also on CD-ROM

*Aslib Directory of Literary and Historical Collections in the United Kingdom*, ed. K.W. Reynard, Aslib, London, 1993

*BBC Home Service: Nine O'Clock News, 1939–1945*, microfiche, Chadwyck-Healey, Cambridge

*BBC Radio: Author and Title Catalogues of Transmitted Drama, Poetry and Features, 1929–1975*, microfiche, Chadwyck-Healey, Cambridge

*BBC Television: Author and Title Catalogues of Transmitted Drama and Features, 1936–1975, with Chronological List of Transmitted Plays*, microfiche, Chadwyck-Healey, Cambridge

*Benn's Media* (formerly *Benn's Media Directory*), 3 vols, published annually by Miller Freeman PLC, Tonbridge

*BFI Film & Television Handbook*, published annually by the British Film Institute, London

*Bibliographic Index*, published since 1938 by H.W. Wilson, New York; now three times a year in paperback with annual cumulation volumes

*Bibliography of British Newspapers*, British Library, London, in progress, 6 vols to date, 1982–

*Biography Index*, published since 1946 by H.W. Wilson, New York; now quarterly on CD-ROM, magnetic tape and in print, updated monthly online

*Book and Magazine Collector*, published monthly since March 1984, London

*BookBank*, published on CD-ROM by Whitaker, London, available on annual subscription and updated monthly

*BookBank Global*, published on CD-ROM by Whitaker, London, available on annual subscription and updated monthly

*BookBank OP*, published on CD-ROM by Whitaker, London, available on annual subscription and updated quarterly

*Bookdealer*, published weekly since 1971 by Werner Shaw, London

*Books in Print* (UK and European), see *Whitaker's Books in Print*

*Books in Print* (US), published annually by Bowker, New Providence, N.J., 10 vols; also on fiche, CD-ROM and online; also *Books in Print Plus*, *Books in Print with Book Reviews Plus*, *Books Out-of-Print with Book Reviews Plus*

*The Bookseller*, published weekly by Whitaker, London; special 'Buyer's Guides', spring and autumn

*Bookshops of London*, by Michael Collins, Two Heads Publishing, London, 1999

*British Archives: A Guide to Archive Resources in the United Kingdom and Ireland*, by Janet Foster and Julia Sheppard, Macmillan, London, 4th edn, 1998

*British Catalogue of Music*, published three times a year by Bowker-Saur, East Grinstead

*British Education Index*, first issued 1954, now published by Leeds University Press, Leeds; 4 part issues plus one annual cumulation

*British Humanities Index*, published quarterly since 1963, with annual cumulations, by the Library Association, London; since January 1990 by Bowker-Saur, East Grinstead; also as *BHI Plus*, on CD-ROM by annual subscription, updated quarterly

*British Library General Catalogue of Printed Books*: original edition to 1975 out of print; reprinted, with supplements, to 1989, by Saur, Munich, 1980–88; CD-ROM by Saztec Europe, distributed in UK by Chadwyck-Healey, Cambridge; microfiche edition, updated regularly, British Library, London, 1986–; also online via BLAISE-LINE

*The British Library Guide to the Catalogues and Indexes of the Department of Manuscripts*, by M.A.E. Nickson, British Library, London, 3rd edn, revised by J. Conway, 1998

*British National Bibliography* (*BNB*), weekly since 1950, with cumulative monthly, annual and some 5-yearly volumes; now published by British Library National Bibliographic Service, Wetherby, on various subscription options (printed, microfiche and CD-ROM); there is a complete set from 1950 on two CD-ROMs, also two cumulations on microfiche, 1950–1984 and 1981–1992. There is a complete *BNB* file on BLAISE

*British Newspaper Index (BNI)*, from 1990, updated quarterly on CD-ROM, Primary Source Media (The Gale Group), Reading

*British Union-Catalogue of Periodicals*, originally published in 4 vols by Butterworth, London, 1955–58; some supplementary vols; replaced in 1981 by *Serials in the British Library*, *q.v.*

*Broadcasting in the United Kingdom: A Guide to Information Sources*, by Barrie Macdonald, Mansell, London, 2nd rev. edn, 1993; new edition in preparation

*Business Periodicals Index*, published since 1958 by H.W. Wilson, New York, now monthly on CD-ROM, magnetic tape and in print; updated weekly online

*Cassell Directory of Publishing: UK, Commonwealth and Overseas*, published annually by Cassell and The Publishers Association

*Catalogue of British Official Publications Not Published by HMSO* (now *TSO*), published bi-monthly, updated every two months, and annual cumulation, Chadwyck-Healey, Cambridge

*Catalogue of the National Maritime Museum Library*, vol. 3, *Atlases and Cartography*, HMSO, London, 1971

*Catalogue of the Newspaper Library, Colindale*, compiled by P.E. Allen, 8 vols, British Library, London, 1975

*The Catalogue of United Kingdom Official Publications (UKOP)*, on CD-ROM, retrospective to 1980, now updated every two months on CD-ROM and monthly on the World Wide Web, published jointly by The Stationery Office, London and Chadwyck-Healey, Cambridge

*Cole's Register of British Antiquarian and Secondhand Bookdealers*, published annually by Michael Cole (The Clique), 7 Pulleyn Drive, York YO24 1DY

*Companion to Cinema* series, published by Cassell/BFI, London, various dates

*Contacts*, published annually (November) by Spotlight, available on mail order from them at 7 Leicester Place, London WC2H 7BP (tel. 020 7437 7631)

*Cumulative Book Index*, published annually since 1928 by H.W. Wilson, New York; now quarterly, in print, on CD-ROM, magnetic tape and online

*Current British Directories*, CBD Research, Beckenham, 12th edn, 1993

*Current European Directories*, CBD Research, Beckenham, 3rd edn, 1994

*Current Research in Britain*, 4 vols annually, formerly published by British Library, now by Community of Science, Baltimore, USA (details not to hand at time of going to press)

*The Directories of London 1677–1977*, by P.J. Atkins, Cassell, London, 1990

*Directory of Museum and Special Collections in the United Kingdom*, ed. Peter Dale, Aslib, London, 2nd edn, 1996

*Directory of Special Collections in Western Europe*, ed. Alison Gallico, Bowker-Saur, East Grinstead, 1993

*Dissertation Abstracts*, from 1861, paperback and CD-ROM, University Microfilms Inc., Cuckfield, West Sussex

*Encyclopedia of the British Press 1422–1992*, ed. Dennis Griffiths, Macmillan, London, 1992

*Encyclopedia of the World Press*, ed. Dennis Griffiths, Fitzroy Dearborn, London, scheduled for publication 2001

*The English Catalogue of Books*: first vol. 1801–36 and subsequent 3- and 5-year cumulations; discontinued (last vol. published 1969)

*English Short Title Catalogue 1473–1800*, on CD-ROM, British Library, London, 1998

*Enjoying Archives*, by David Iredale, Phillimore, Chichester, 1985

*Essay and General Literature Index*, published since 1934 by H.W. Wilson, New York; now twice a year with annual and five-year cumulations; also on CD-ROM and online, updated annually

*EUROCAT: The Complete Catalogue of EU Publications and Documents*, quarterly on CD-ROM, Chadwyck-Healey, Cambridge

*The Europa World Year Book*, 2 vols, published annually by Europa Publications, London

*European Access*, ed. Ian Thomson, published bi-monthly, by Chadwyck-Healey, Cambridge, in association with the UK offices of the European Commission; online weekly from October 1999

*European Union Information Directory of UK Sources*, published by the European Commission, London, 2nd edn, 1998; updated regularly on the Internet (http://www.cec.org.uk)

*Film and Television Collections in Europe: The Map-TV Guide*, Blueprint, London, 1995; CD-ROM in preparation

*Film Index International*, on CD-ROM, updated annually, Chadwyck-Healey, Cambridge

*The Film Researcher's Handbook*, compiled by Jenny Morgan, Blueprint, London, 1995

*Financial Times Index*, from 1981, monthly with annual cumulations, Primary Source Media (The Gale Group), Reading

*Gentleman's Magazine: General Index to the first 56 volumes (1731–86)*, 2 vols; *General Index... 1787–1819, Index to the Biographical and Obituary Notices, 1731–1780 and 1781–1819*, 2 vols: 1st vol, British Record Society, London, 2nd vol, Garland, New York and London

*Glasgow Herald* (now *The Herald*) *Index*, in printed form 1906–1988; since 1989 by Scottish Media Newspapers, Glasgow, online only

*Granger's Index to Poetry*, first published 1904; 8th edn, ed. W.E. Bernhardt, Columbia University Press, New York, 1986

*Great Britain: Stationery Office Catalogues of Government Publications*, 1894–1970 (*Annual Catalogues of British Official and Parliamentary Publications*, 1894–1919, on microfiche; *Annual Catalogues of Government Publications*, 1921–1970, 5 vols, clothbound), Chadwyck-Healey, Cambridge

*The Guardian Index*, from 1986, microform, monthly with annual cumulations, University Microfilms Inc., Cuckfield, West Sussex

*Guide to Archives and Manuscripts at Guildhall Library*, Guildhall Library, London, 1989

*Guide to IHR-Info: Hypertext Internet Server*, ed. Glen Segell, Institute of Historical Research, London, 1995

*Guide to Libraries and Information Units*, ed. Peter Dale, British Library, London, 33rd edn, 1998

*Guide to Libraries in Central and Eastern Europe*, compiled by Maria Hughes, British Library, London, 1992

*Guide to Libraries in London*, compiled by Valerie McBurney, British Library, London, 1995

*Guide to Libraries in Western Europe*, ed. Peter Dale, British Library, London, 2nd edn, 1994

*Guide to Microforms in Print*, published in 2 vols annually by Saur, Munich; also *Subject Guide to Microforms in Print* and supplement on CD-ROM

*Guide to the National and Provincial Directories of England and Wales, excluding London, published before 1856*, by Jane E. Norton, Royal Historical Society, London, 1950; reprinted with corrections, 1984

*Guide to Reference Material*, ed. A.J. Walford; see below under *Walford's Guide to Reference Material*

*Guide to Sources for British History*: 1, *Papers of British cabinet ministers 1782–1900*; 2, *The manuscript papers of British scientists 1600–1940*; 3, *Guide to the location of collections described in the Reports and Calendars series 1870–1980*; 4, *Private papers of British diplomats 1782–1900*; 5, *Private papers of British colonial governors 1782–1900*; 6, *Papers of British churchmen 1780–1940*; 7, *Papers of British politicians 1782–1900*; 8, *Records of British business and industry 1760–1914: textiles and leather*; 9, *Records of British business and industry 1760–1914: metal processing and engineering*; 10, *Principal family and estate collections: family names A–K*; 11, *Principal family and estate collections: family names L–Y*, Royal Commission on Historical Manuscripts, London, 1982–1999

*Guide to the Public Record Office*, current edn on microfiche, 1999

*Halliwell's Film and Video Guide*, published annually by Harper-Collins, 14th edn, 1998

*Handlist of Unpublished Finding Aids to the London Collections of the British Library*, by R.C. Alston, British Library, London, 1991

*Hansard: Parliamentary Debates*, 1803 onwards; now published daily during sessions by The Stationery Office (formerly HMSO), London. Chadwyck-Healey, Cambridge, publishes various series of Parliamentary Papers from 1715, in microform

*History of the Cinema 1895–1940*, 3,574 microfiches plus printed guide and index, Chadwyck-Healey, Cambridge

*History Theses*, 3 vols, covering the period 1901–1990, Institute of Historical Research, London, 1976, 1984, 1994

*Humanities Index*, published since 1974 by H.W. Wilson, New York; now by annual subscription; also monthly on CD-ROM and magnetic tape; updated weekly online

*Index of English Literary Manuscripts, covering the period 1450–1900*, 4 vols to date, Mansell, London, 1980–97. (Vol. 4, 1800–1900, ends with Part 3 at 'Patmore'. No further vols scheduled.)

*Index to Legal Periodicals*, published since 1952 by H.W. Wilson, New York, now monthly; online and CD-ROM from August 1981

*Index of Manuscripts in the British Library*, 10 vols, Chadwyck-Healey, Cambridge, 1985

*Index Medicus*, published monthly since 1960 by National Library of Medicine, Washington

*Index to Theses with Abstracts* (continuing series *Index to Theses* published since 1950), now published by Expert Information Ltd, for Aslib, London, 5 issues per year; also online

*Index Translationum*, published quarterly 1932–40, and annually since 1949 by UNESCO, Paris; now only on CD-ROM (annual cumulated edition)

*International Books in Print*, 2 vols, published annually by Saur, Munich; also on CD-ROM as *International Books in Print Plus*, annually

*International Dictionary of Film and Filmmakers*, ed. Christopher Lyon, 3 vols, Macmillan, London, 1987–91

*International Film Index 1895–1990*, ed. Alan Goble, 2 vols, Saur, Munich, 1992

*International Index to Music Periodicals*, Chadwyck-Healey, Cambridge; on CD-ROM and online; 'Full Text' online

*International Women's Periodicals*, online at www.womensperiodicals. psmedia.com, Primary Source Media (The Gale Group), Reading

'Introduction to Archive Materials' series of pamphlets, available free at the Public Record Office, Kew

*ISSN Register* (formerly *ISDS Register*), published quarterly on magnetic tape and CD-ROM by the ISSN International Centre, Paris

*Keyword Index to Serial Titles* (*KIST*), quarterly on microfiche, by annual subscription, or annual volume, British Library National Bibliographic Service, Wetherby

*Libraries in the United Kingdom and the Republic of Ireland*, published annually by the Library Association, London, 25th edn, 1998

*Library and Information Science Abstracts* (*LISA*), published monthly by Bowker-Saur, East Grinstead; also *LISA Plus*, updated quarterly, on CD-ROM, and *LISA Online*, updated monthly

*The Listener*, weekly, 1929–1991, BBC, London; microform edition, Chadwyck-Healey, Cambridge (1929–1979 on microfilm; 1980–1991 on microfiche)

*Location Register of English Literary Manuscripts and Letters*, ed. David Sutton, 4 vols, British Library, London, 1988–95: *18th and 19th Centuries*, 2 vols, 1995; *20th Century*, 2 vols, 1988

*London Catalogue of Books*, series of overlapping catalogues covering the years 1700–1855 (first vol., Bent, 1773)

*London Directories from the Guildhall Library, 1677–1855*, on microfilm, Primary Source Media (The Gale Group), Reading

*London Gazette*, published since 1665; now daily, Monday to Friday, The Stationery Office (formerly HMSO), London

*Manuscript Sources for British History: their Nature, Location and Use*, by R.J. Olney, Institute of Historical Research/Royal Commission on Historical Manuscripts, London, 1995

*Maps for Historians*, by Paul Hindle, Phillimore, Chichester, 1998

*The Media Guide*, ed. Steve Peak and Paul Fisher, published annually by Fourth Estate, London (a *Guardian Book*)

*Mitchell's Newspaper Press Directory*, first published 1846; now *Benn's Media, q.v.*

*National Inventory of Documentary Sources in the United Kingdom and Ireland* (*NIDS*), by subscription (8 units per year) from Chadwyck-Healey, Cambridge; also on CD-ROM

*National Life Story Collection*, in progress at the British Library National Sound Archive, London

*National Register of Archives Information Sheets: Sources* for 1, *Labour History*; 2, *Colonial History*; 3, *History of Women*; 4, *History of Education*; 5, *Business History*; 6, *Family History*; 7, *History of Film, Theatre and Television*; 8, *History of the Armed Forces*; 9, *Criminal and Legal History*; 10, *Newspaper History*; 11, *Architectural and Garden History*; 12, *Merchant Shipping and Seamen*; 13, *Fine Art and Artists*, available from the Royal Commission on Historical Manuscripts, London

*National Union Catalog* (US), Library of Congress, Washington: printed vols to 1982; on microfiche from 1983; may be accessed via BLAISE and on www.lib.ncsu.edu

*The Newspaper Press in Britain: An Annotated Bibliography*, eds David Linton and Ray Boston, Mansell, London, 1987

*Notes & Queries*, published since 1849 by Oxford University Press, Oxford, with various index vols and cumulated indexes; now quarterly

*Oral History*, by Ken Howarth, Sutton Publishing, Thrupp, Glos., 1999

*Oral History*, journal of the Oral History Society, 1969–; published twice a year

*Oral History: An Annotated Bibliography 1945–1989*, compiled by Robert Perks, British Library, London, 1990

*Oral History: Talking about the Past*, by Robert Perks, Historical Association, London, 1992

*Outlets for Specialist New Books in the UK* (formerly *Directory of Specialist Bookdealers in the UK Handling Mainly New Books*), Peter Marcan, London, 6th edn, 1995

*Palmer's Index to The Times*, 1791–1941; see under *The Times Index*

*The Penguin Companion to the European Union*, by Timothy Bainbridge, Penguin Press, London, 1998

*Periodicals Contents Index*, on CD-ROM and the World Wide Web, by annual subscription from Chadwyck-Healey, Cambridge

*Poole's Index to Periodical Literature, 1802–1906*, Boston, Mass., reprinted 1938, 1969; *Cumulative Author Index*, Pierian Press, Ann Arbor, Michigan, 1971

*The Popular Magazine in Britain and the United States of America 1880–1960*, by David Reed, British Library, London, 1997

*Popular Song Index*, by Patricia P. Havlice, Scarecrow Press, Lanham, Maryland, 1975; supplements, 1978, 1984, 1989

*Radio Times*, weekly, BBC Worldwide Publishing, London; on microfilm 1923–79 and microfiche 1980–1994, both Chadwyck-Healey, Cambridge

*Reader's Guide to Periodical Literature*, published since 1900 by H.W. Wilson, New York; now by subscription monthly, in print, on CD-ROM and magnetic tape, and online

*Record Repositories in Great Britain*, Royal Commission on Historical Manuscripts/PRO Publications, London; updated regularly (latest, 11th edn, 1999)

*Reference Sources Handbook*, eds. P.W. Lea and A. Day, Library Association, London, 4th edn, 1996 (formerly published under the title *Printed Reference Material and Related Information Sources*)

*Register of British Bookdealers' Specialities*, C.A. Winder Publications, Harrogate

*Register of British Bookfinders*, C.A. Winder Publications, Harrogate

*Research and the Manuscript Tradition*, by Frank G. Burke, co-published by Scarecrow Press, Lanham, Maryland, and the Society of American Archivists, 1997

*The Royal Commission on Historical Manuscripts Information Sheets*, see *National Register of Archives Information Sheets*

*Serials in the British Library*, microfiche, quarterly with annual cumulations, British Library National Bibliographic Service, Wetherby, since 1981; *Serials in the British Library 1976–86*, microfiche cumulation, British Library National Bibliographic Service, Wetherby, 1988

*Sheppard's Book Dealers in Europe*, published annually by Richard Joseph Publishers, Farnham

*Skoob Directory of Secondhand Bookshops in the British Isles*, Skoob, London, 6th edn, 1996; new edition in preparation

*Social Sciences Index*, published since 1974 by H.W. Wilson, New York, now by annual subscription, also on CD-ROM, magnetic tape and online, updated monthly

*Song Catalogue*, in *BBC Music Library Catalogue of Holdings*, 4 vols, BBC, London, 1966

*Song Index*, by M.E. Sears and P. Crawford, H.W. Wilson, New York, 1926; supplement, 1934

*Strand Magazine: Index 1891–1950*, by Geraldine Beare, Greenwood, Westport, Conn./London, 1982

*Subject Guide to Books in Print*, published annually since 1957 by Bowker, New Providence, N.J.; now also on microfiche, CD-ROM and online

*Subject Index to Periodicals*, published annually 1915–53, then quarterly with annual cumulations, 1954–61; now the *British Humanities Index*, *q.v.*

*Subjects of Dissertations, Theses and Published Work presented by Successful Candidates at Examinations for Higher Degrees*, covering the period 1937–51, University of London Library, London

*Surveys of Historical Manuscripts in the United Kingdom: A Select Bibliography*, Royal Commission on Historical Manuscripts, London, 2nd edn, 1994

*The Times*, microfilm edition 1785 to present day, by subscription (update delivered every three weeks), Primary Source Media (The Gale Group), Reading; online edition in progress

*The Times Index*, 1785 to present day, currently by subscription monthly with annual cumulative volume, Primary Source Media

(The Gale Group), Reading; also on microfilm for years 1906–76. Also *Palmer's Index to The Times, 1790–June 1941* (out of print) but on CD-ROM 1790–1905, Chadwyck-Healey, Cambridge

*The Twentieth-Century Newspaper Press in Britain: An Annotated Bibliography*, compiled by David Linton, Mansell, London, 1994

*Ulrich's International Periodicals Directory*, published annually in 5 vols, by Bowker, New Providence, N.J.; also on CD-ROM as *Ulrich's on Disc* (annual subscription with quarterly updates), and online

*UNIBIS Plus*, databases of the United Nations Bibliographic Information System, on CD-ROM quarterly (one retrospective disk to 1992), Chadwyck-Healey, Cambridge

*The Voice of the Past*, by Paul Thompson, Oxford University Press, Oxford, 2nd edn, 1988; reprinted 1989

*Walford's Guide to Reference Material*, 3 vols: 1, *Science and Technology*, eds M. Mullay and P. Schlicke, 8th edn, 1999; 2, *Social and Historical Sciences, Philosophy and Religion*, eds A. Day and M. Walsh, 7th edn, 1997; 3, *Generalia, Language and Literature, The Arts*, eds A. Chalcraft, R. Prytherch and S. Willis, 7th edn, 1998. Each volume updated every few years

*Wellesley Index to Victorian Periodicals, 1824–1900*, ed. W.E. Houghton, 3 vols, University of Toronto Press/Routledge, London, 1966–79

*Whitaker's* bibliographic services, see under *BookBank, BookBank Global, BookBank OP, The Bookseller*

*Whitaker's Books in Print*, published on microfiche by Whitaker, London, available on annual subscription and updated monthly; also in printed form, 5 vols, annually

*Whitaker's Cumulative Book List* 1924–83 (re-titled *Whitaker's Book List* in 1984), Whitaker, London

*Whitaker's Directory of Publishers*, published annually by Whitaker, London

*Willing's Press Guide* (first published in 1871 as *Frederick May's London Press Directory*), now annually by Hollis Directories, Teddington, Mddx; also on CD-ROM

*Women's Magazines 1693–1968*, by Cynthia L. White, Michael Joseph, London, 1970

*Women's Magazines: The First Three Hundred Years*, by Brian Braithwaite, Peter Owen, London, 1995

*World Bibliographical Series*, Clio Press, Oxford, in progress, 1977–

*World Bibliography of Bibliographies*, compiled by T. Besterman, 4th edn, 4 vols + index, Societas Bibliographica, Lausanne, 1965, 1966; *Supplement 1964–1974*, ed. Alice Toomey, 2 vols, Bowker, New York, 1977

*World Guide to Libraries*, Saur, Munich, 14th edn, 1999
*World Guide to Special Libraries*, Saur, Munich, 4th edn, 1998; both
   these guides, together with the *American Library Directory* are
   available online as *World Guide to Libraries* and *World Guide to
   Libraries Plus*, by annual subscription, Saur, Munich
*The World of Learning*, published annually by Europa Publications,
   London

*Note:* Bowker-Saur are part of Reed Business Information Ltd. Their
titles are distributed in the UK by Bowker-Saur Ltd, Windsor Court,
East Grinstead House, East Grinstead, West Sussex RH19 1XA (tel.
01342 326972; fax 01342 336198). Scarecrow Press Inc. (formerly
of Metuchen, N.J., now Lanham, Maryland, USA) titles are
distributed in the UK by Shelwing Ltd, 127 Sandgate Road,
Folkestone, Kent CT20 2BL (tel. 01303 850501; fax 01303
850162), and H.W. Wilson titles by Thompson Henry Ltd, London
Road, Sunningdale, Berks SL5 0EP (tel. 01344 624615; fax 01344
626120).

# 4

# Factual and Historical Research

The more research you undertake, the more you learn about sources. If you keep a careful note of every reliable source used, either on computer or manually (I find a card index filed under subjects is the best for quick reference), you can build up for yourself not only a unique and valuable research tool, but one that will save you hours of searching whenever a similar problem crops up in your work. It will prove its worth time and time again.

So much is in print these days that there can be scarcely any subject from, say, animated cartoons to Zimbabwe, on which you are not going to find some 'standard' work or encyclopedia; nor any trade, profession, ethnic or religious group for which there is no recognised association, biographical dictionary or 'Who's Who' – all essential sources for the researcher. Obviously it is impossible in one short chapter to deal exhaustively with particular sources. Some starting points only are suggested here, therefore, under the two headings 'Factual' and 'Historical' research, together with a warning of some of the pitfalls that lie in the path of the unwary. In all research you have to begin by consulting first one authoritative source, which leads you to the next, and that in turn to another, and so on, until you have satisfied yourself that you have found out all that you need to know. Patience and persistence are the essential qualities. Remember, too, that a negative result in research may have value.

## Factual Research

The major difficulty here has always been that topical facts and figures are usually out of date by the time they are published. The same applies to all writing on modern society, for nothing stands still in the world, which is developing and changing with every day that passes. To some extent, from the researcher's viewpoint, online cataloguing and access to the Internet has made it easier to get at more up-to-date information than was previously the case. Even so, a book, once it has gone to the typesetter, may be only lightly corrected at proof stage. That said, it is sometimes possible, if you are expecting some vital new facts or statistics to be released between delivery of your typescript and the day it actually goes to press, to indicate to your editor at the outset that you may wish to update specific points at the very last moment, either in the text or (which may be easier) by way of an explanatory footnote. If the editor is willing, then you will have the opportunity of accessing the relevant database or telephoning the source from which your original information came and asking for the most recent facts and figures. All such updatings to your text must be kept to the absolute minimum, however, as anything above an agreed percentage will be charged to the author and will eat into your royalties.

Another problem is that the bases used for the calculation of statistics vary from one subject to another, and from one organisation to another, so that comparison can be, at worst, highly dangerous, and at best, misleading; often, also, you may find it impossible to obtain the precise breakdown you seek. Without expert help and knowledge it is unwise to meddle with statistics: where these do not exactly fit the context, the best solution is to quote them as they are presented and to add a footnote to this effect.

## Sources of factual information

Use of the computer search services on offer at major libraries is becoming widespread, and many writers have purchased the necessary software and subscribe to one or more databases, which they can access from home. However, not all writers or researchers are able or wish to use these electronic facilities. In any case, much factual research must still be done from printed sources and by personal contact with experts in the field. Ideally, a combination of both produces the best results.

So far as printed sources are concerned, encyclopedias and yearbooks are an excellent starting point, especially the latter if you subscribe and can access the latest articles online. You can find out what yearbooks exist on a given subject by consulting *Current British Directories* or *Current European Directories*, both of which have detailed subject indexes, or *Ulrich's International Periodicals Directory* (which includes the former *Irregular Serials and Annuals*). Other publications most useful to the English writer for quick reference are *Whitaker's Almanack*, *The Statesman's Year-Book*, *The Annual Register of World Events*, *The Europa World Year Book* and *Britain: An Official Handbook*. New in this field is *The Hutchinson Almanac 1999*.

*The Times* newspaper is the best source for recent events; its *Index* is now published monthly, with annual cumulations. From 1990 there is the *British Newspaper Index* on CD-ROM (see page 56). Keesing's *Record of World Events*, which started in July 1931 as a weekly publication, *Keesing's Contemporary Archives*, is now published eleven times a year (July/August being a double issue); it has an excellent reputation, and most reference libraries subscribe to it. You can also rely on its US equivalent, *The Facts on File Weekly World News Digest*.

So far as UK statistics are concerned, the Office for National Statistics issues a *Monthly Digest of Statistics* and an *Annual Abstract of Statistics*. There is a great deal more information available, both in printed and in electronic form, and researchers are recommended to contact the National Statistics Information and Library Service, Office for National Statistics, 1 Drummond Gate, London SW1V 2QQ (tel. 020 7533 6262; fax 020 7533 6261). There is also the Library of the Royal Statistical Society at the DMS Watson Building, University College London, Gower Street, London WC1E 6BT (tel. 020 7387 7050 ext. 2628). For Europe a useful publication, regularly updated, is *Statistics Europe*. The historical aspect is well covered by *British Historical Statistics* and by *European Historical Statistics 1750–1975*. The statistical masterfiles of the Congressional Information Service of the United States are held on CD-ROM at the British Library, in the Science reading room (Social Policy Information Service).

On facts in general the most up-to-date compilations at the time of writing (spring 1999) include the *Chambers Book of Facts*, *The Cambridge Factfinder*, *The Hutchinson Factfinder* and the *Larousse Desk Reference Encyclopedia*. Depending on your subject, it is also well worth looking at the various titles in the *Chambers Compact Reference* series. *The Guinness Book of Records* is a classic, and both *The New Shell Book of Firsts* and the *Penguin Book of Firsts* are crammed with useful information. No one writing about Britain should be without a copy of Bamber Gascoigne's *Encyclopedia of Britain*.

The use of bibliographies, concordances, books of quotations and other reference tools has been discussed in the previous chapter. The researcher keen on tracking down factual information should be able to get at what he needs without any problem. Sometimes, however, professional help may be necessary, especially if time is an important factor.

The Information Bureau (51 The Business Centre, 103 Lavender Hill, London SW11 5QL; tel. 020 7924 4414/fax 020 7924 4456), formerly the *Daily Telegraph* Information Bureau, offers a general research and information service on a subscription or *ad hoc* basis, using printed and online resources, a vast press cuttings collection, and business and media contacts built up over many years. For non-account subscribers requiring quick checking of dates, facts and figures, or names to contact in associations, there is a minimum charge (valid spring 1999) of £10.00 + VAT (hourly rate £70.00 + VAT).

The former Science Reference and Information Service of the British Library (SRIS), has become the Science, Technology and Business Service (STB), which is now installed in the Science reading rooms at the new British Library at St Pancras. The reading rooms at Kean Street, Chancery House and Southampton Buildings are closed. The STB offers an unrivalled service to those who seek information on science and technology, business and industry, and patents. Much of the material in these collections is on open access, spread over five reading rooms (see page 218). Note that whereas previously the SRIS was open to the general public, you must have a British Library reader's pass to use the STB. Basic services are free, but enquiries that require much staff time and use of resources, including the many databases available, are priced. A detailed information pack will be sent on demand; write to Press and Public Relations, The British Library, 96 Euston Road, London NW1 2DB.

The Business Collections are housed in the Science 3 reading room, where much of the printed material is on open access. There is a quick information telephone enquiry point, partly funded by Lloyds Bank, available free of charge. This British Library–Lloyds Bank Business Line (020 7412 7454/020 7412 7977) is open Monday to Friday from 9 to 5. If you wish to use the electronic sources of information, you should ring this line in advance of your visit, in order to book a work station (no charge). The British Library Business Information Research Service, with its team of experienced researchers, will carry out in-depth research on a fee-paying basis, using a wide range of printed and electronic sources (tel. 020 7412 7457; fax 020 7412 7453). Quotations will be provided before the work is undertaken.

This may sound rather complicated to the new researcher seeking information in the field of business or science, but you will find the STB staff very helpful. There are several invaluable reference tools available in the Science reading rooms for those doing their own research, primarily the SCICAT (catalogue of the former SRIS (now STB) books and journals from 1968) and the British Library *How to Find* and *Key Resource* series of guides on a wide range of subjects, including chemistry, medicine and biology; company information; library sources; patents; and trade marks. (Some specific titles are mentioned elsewhere in this book under the relevant subject.)

*The New York Public Library Science Desk Reference* is a gold-mine of information divided into thirteen areas of interest, with cross references and lists that guide the user to sources for further research. For the history of technology you cannot beat *The Timetables of Technology*, a chronology of people and events from c. 3700 BC to 1993. The *Biographical Dictionary of the History of Technology* is also recommended.

## Getting hold of experts

You may sometimes find yourself at a loss as to how to contact experts on particular subjects when there is no one in your immed-iate circle who can help. Here the best advice to be given is, 'Do not be shy. Go straight to the horse's mouth' – in other words, look up the professional or trade association concerned (or it may be an international company, a bank, or almost any other kind of group), and either write or telephone to the general secretary, press or public relations officer. Remember that all these people have a vested interest in being portrayed correctly, and also that the expert is always flattered to be consulted. If the person you approach is too busy or unable for some other reason to give you what you want, he will usually be able to put you in touch with someone else.

The best way to find out if there is a relevant association is to look in an up-to-date *Directory of British Associations* or the equivalent volumes for Europe, the *Directory of European Industrial & Trade Associations* and the *Directory of European Professional & Learned Societies*. Another very useful source, and fully up to date, is the *Hollis Press & Public Relations Annual*, which lists an enormous number of press contacts (with addresses and telephone numbers) in virtually every field of professional, industrial and commercial life, as well as official and public information sources, PR consultancies and much other invaluable data. The same firm now publishes a similar directory for Europe, *Hollis Europe*. There is also a list of societies and institutions in *Whitaker's Almanack*, but this is not so infor-mative, nor is it as comprehensive as the two publications mentioned above. The researcher concerned with making contacts in the arts or the media will find *The Media Guide* and *The Marcan Handbook of Arts Organisations* indispensable. Information and press officers in government departments are listed in the *IPO Directory*. Lastly, do not overlook your local 'yellow pages' directory: there may be some contact on your own doorstep.

The *NUJ Freelance Directory* is a computerised catalogue of free-lance journalists in Britain and Ireland (and some overseas), listed alphabetically, geographically and by subject speciality. It is available at modest cost to non-members and has a useful role to play in the finding of local contacts.

# Historical Research

History itself does not change, but the interpretation of history changes constantly as new material comes to light. There will always therefore be a demand for writing that offers a new slant – a reappraisal of events and of people – based on the latest research. This applies almost as much to the history of, say, the 'Dark Ages' as to that of the present day. There are also 'fashions' in historical writing: recently the medieval period has been much explored, especially by social historians of the European countries. Insofar as the 20th century is concerned, in the United Kingdom official papers are released for public examination after thirty years. Every January the Public Record Office braces itself for an onslaught of historians, journalists and researchers who descend sleuth-like upon Kew from all over the world, intent on scrutinising every memo or minute or other scrap of paper emanating from the Cabinet Office, the Foreign and Commonwealth Office and the various ministerial departments. Nearly every year something is pounced upon that makes a headline in the national press. But the bulk of the raw material gathered filters only very gradually into print.

When you go to the reference library to look up an historical fact, you will find that the titles are usually grouped in the following manner: history generally, then world history, British history, European history, and (if the collection is large enough) history country by country. In the general section there are all the great standard works published by the Cambridge and Oxford university presses, cheek by jowl with less weightier more modern volumes. It is advisable to go first to the modern works, to get the benefit of recent research; the 'standard histories' are updated but, being rather learned tomes, not very frequently. Use them for corroborative, in-depth research.

One of the best ways of keeping abreast of the latest research is to read the journals and other publications of the major historical societies. If you have time, join one and attend its lectures and conferences. You may like to know that a subscription to the Historical Association's *The Historian* includes membership of a local branch. Contact the Secretary at 59a Kennington Park Road, London SE11 4JH (tel. 020 7735 3901; fax 020 7582 4989) and ask for details, including a catalogue of the Association's current publications. You should also look at the *Transactions* and other serial publications of the Royal Historical Society. The *Writings on British History* series, now called the *Annual Bibliography of British and Irish History*, is a useful tool, and the Society also publishes a number of handbooks and guides for students and scholars. If you are a graduate you will be able to join and use the Institute of Historical Research library at Senate House, London. The Institute maintains a database – HISTORY – of resources for historians on the Internet.

It is impossible in one short chapter to do more than touch on a few of the problems that confront the novice setting out to find historical information. There is one point I should like to stress: in this current age of obsession with electronic access to information, we should not lose sight of the value of the original document. A database is only as good as the information fed into it and is subject to human error of transcription. The original document must always be the primary source.

So far as titles are concerned, obviously every writer will purchase to keep at his elbow as many of the major works on his subject as he can afford. Outstanding among several recent compilations is Charles Arnold-Baker's *The Companion to British History*, a very readable, reliable, if occasionally idiosyncratic, single-volume encyclopedia crammed with information not only on the history of this country, but also on a wide range of other subjects.

For general reference on British history I recommend *The Cambridge Historical Encyclopedia of Great Britain and Ireland*. The *English Historical Documents* series covers the period from c. 500 to 1914. There is also the Macmillan *Historical Facts* series, covering the period 1485–1985, and *British Political Facts 1900–94* in the same publisher's *Historical and Political Facts* series. Winston S. Churchill's *A History of the English-Speaking Peoples* is a classic. There are many others.

Some recent social histories of Europe are mentioned in chapter 5 (pages 96–7). *International Historical Statistics: Europe 1750–1993* and *European Political Facts 1900–1996* are very useful (there are also volumes in the *International Historical Statistics* series for the Americas and for Africa, Asia, Oceania; see bibliography). Recommended general studies include the four-volume series by Eric Hobsbawm: *The Age of Revolution 1789–1848*, *The Age of Capital 1848–1875*, *The Age of Empire 1875–1914* and *Age of Extremes: The Short Twentieth Century 1914–1991*; also Martin Gilbert's *History of the Twentieth Century*.

For quick reference on world history, a recommended work is the *Chambers Dictionary of World History*. Space does not permit here the inclusion of sources for the history of individual countries, but some titles are recommended in chapter 9 (pages 162–79). Look also at *Walford's Guide to Reference Material*, volume 2, under 'Ancient',

'Medieval' or 'Modern' history and the area of the world (or country), as appropriate.

## Conflicting authorities

One of the main problems that you must be prepared to encounter in historical research is that of conflicting authorities. Inevitably at some stage in your work you will come across two, if not three, or more, different dates or interpretations of the same event. How do you know which one to trust?

Wherever possible, you should yourself go back to the original, contemporary source. If this is not feasible, you have the choice of either weighing up the theories advanced by the various historians and coming down firmly on one side – and sticking to it – or, if you have the space and the inclination, of giving an account of the conflicting views and your reasons for preferring one to all others.

## Dates

The different reckonings of dates in historical documents often confuse the beginner. Under the Julian calendar, which was in universal use throughout the Middle Ages and in some countries, such as England and Russia, until as late as the 18th and early 20th centuries respectively, the year began on 25 March. The Gregorian calendar, in which 1 January was reckoned as the beginning of each year, was introduced on the Continent in 1582, when ten days were cut out of that year in order to take care of accumulated errors of reckoning. This new calendar was not adopted in England until 1752, although for some years prior to that date a double indication was normally given in official documents (and in some private papers) for dates falling between 1 January and 24 March, as, for example, '24 February 1655/6'. The trap is that during the period 1582–1752 a traveller could leave, say, Italy, on one date and arrive in England several days earlier, because of the discrepancy in the calendar. From the end of the 16th century most English official correspondence with foreign powers carries either both dates, i.e. '12/22 December 1635', or an indication of the reckoning used, i.e. 'O.S.' (Old Style) or 'N.S.' (New Style).

The practice followed by most modern historians is to take the beginning of the historical year as 1 January. All dates between 1 January and 24 March are thus written as, for example, '22 February 1559' rather than '22 February 1558/9', except in quoted matter, where the date should always be copied faithfully as in the original text and an explanatory 'O.S.' or 'N.S.' added in square brackets if necessary. For a full discussion of this whole question, see

C.R. Cheney's *Handbook of Dates for Students of English History*. This useful book contains, among other information, tables of regnal years, Easter days and calendars for all possible dates of Easter from AD 500 to the year 2000, which will enable the researcher to avoid the most common errors of dating in historical work. (A new edition is in preparation for use after the year 2000.) Another standard reference work on the subject is the *Handbook of British Chronology*. *Whitaker's Almanack* contains a 'Calendar for Any Year' from 1770 to 2030.

Dates in private papers sometimes cause the researcher a headache. Letter-writers not infrequently give an incomplete date or omit it altogether, and another trap to watch out for is that at the new year people through the ages have tended to forget, writing, for example, '5 January 1888' when they meant '5 January 1889'. Where neither contents nor letterheading provide the answer, and the date does not become clear as research progresses, you will have to choose between doing without that particular document and hazarding an intelligent guess – in which case you should make it clear that the original is undated. The Society of Genealogists has published a useful booklet on dating systems of the past, to aid family historians in the interpretation of references: *Dates and calendars for the genealogist*. It will be of use to all who do historical research, as will Lionel Munby's *Dates and Time: A Handbook for Local Historians*.

## The use of periodicals in historical research

Periodicals of interest to the historical researcher include *Historical Research*, formerly the *Bulletin of the Institute of Historical Research*; the *English Historical Review*; the Historical Association's *History*, which is a digest of historical research, and its quarterly magazine *The Historian*; and *History Today*. Check them all – not forgetting back issues – for articles on your subject. Women's magazines and newspapers are an excellent source for fashion, prices and entertainments at a particular date, while *The Tatler* and *Illustrated London News* contain useful background information on the social scene. Cartoons, from the national press, *Punch* and other sources, may also be of value to the researcher. Advertisements sometimes yield as much information as textual material.

*The Age of Revolution 1789–1848, The Age of Capital 1848–1875, The Age of Empire 1875–1914*, by Eric Hobsbawm, Cardinal Books, 1988–89; *Age of Extremes: The Short Twentieth Century 1914–1991*, by the same author, Michael Joseph, London, 1994; reprinted 1995

*Annual Abstract of Statistics*, Office for National Statistics, published by The Stationery Office (formerly HMSO), London

*Annual Bibliography of British and Irish History* (previously *Writings on British History*), published by Oxford University Press for the Royal Historical Society

*The Annual Register of World Events*, first published 1758; now by Keesings Worldwide, Washington D.C. (UK office: 69A Lensfield Road, Cambridge CB2 1EN; tel. 01223 508050)

*Biographical Dictionary of the History of Technology*, ed. Lance Day and Ian McNeil, Routledge, London, 1998

*Britain: An Official Handbook*, The Stationery Office (formerly HMSO), London, annually

*British Historical Statistics*, by B.R. Mitchell, Cambridge University Press, Cambridge, 1988

*British Newspaper Index* (*The Times* and other major national papers from 1990), on CD-ROM, Primary Source Media (The Gale Group), Reading, updated quarterly

*British Political Facts 1900–94*, eds David Butler and Gareth Butler, *Historical and Political Facts* series, Macmillan, London, 7th edn, 1994

*The Cambridge Factfinder*, ed. David Crystal, Cambridge University Press, Cambridge, 3rd edn, 1998

*The Cambridge Historical Encyclopedia of Great Britain and Ireland*, ed. Christopher Haigh, Cambridge University Press, Cambridge, 1985; paperback edn, 1990

*Chambers Book of Facts*, Chambers (Larousse PLC), London, new edn, 1998

*Chambers Compact Reference* series, Chambers (Larousse PLC), London, in progress

*Chambers Dictionary of World History*, Chambers (Larousse PLC), London, 1993; rev. edn, 1994

*The Companion to British History*, by Charles Arnold-Baker, Longcross Press, Tunbridge Wells, 1996

*Current British Directories*, published by CBD Research, Beckenham, 12th edn, 1993

*Current European Directories*, published by CBD Research, Beckenham, 3rd edn, 1994

*Dates and calendars for the genealogist*, by Clifford Webb, Society of Genealogists, London, 1998

*Dates and Time: A Handbook for Local Historians*, by Lionel Munby, Phillimore, Chichester, 1997

*Directory of British Associations 1998/99*, published by CBD Research, Beckenham, 14th edn, 1998; also on CD-ROM

*Directory of European Industrial & Trade Associations*, published by CBD Research, Beckenham, 6th edn, 1997

*Directory of European Professional & Learned Societies*, published by CBD Research, Beckenham, 5th edn, 1995

*Encyclopedia of Britain: The A–Z of Britain's Past and Present*, by Bamber Gascoigne, rev. edn, Macmillan, London, 1994

*English Historical Documents*, ed. D.C. Douglas, 12 vols, Eyre & Spottiswoode, London, 1953–75

*English Historical Review*, published quarterly since 1886; now by Addison Wesley Longman Ltd, Harlow, Essex

*English Short Title Catalogue 1473–1800*, on CD-ROM, British Library, London, 1998

*The Europa World Year Book*, 2 vols, published annually by Europa Publications, London

*European Historical Statistics 1750–1975*, ed. B.R. Mitchell, Macmillan, London, 2nd rev. edn, 1981

*European Political Facts 1900–1996*, eds Chris Cook and John Paxton, *Historical and Political Facts* series, Macmillan, London, 4th edn, 1998

*The Facts on File Weekly World News Digest*, published by Facts on File, New York

*The Guinness Book of Records*, published by Guinness Publishing, London; regularly updated

*Handbook of British Chronology*, Royal Historical Society, London, first published 1939; 3rd edn, eds. E.B. Fryde *et al*, 1986

*Handbook of Dates for Students of English History*, by C.R. Cheney, Royal Historical Society, London, first published 1945; latest reprint, with corrections, published by Cambridge University Press for the Society, 1996; new edition due February 2000

*The Historian*, quarterly magazine of the Historical Association, London

*Historical Facts* series, published by Macmillan, London: 6 vols covering the period 1485–1985 (first 2 vols entitled *English Historical Facts*, subsequent vols *British Historical Facts*), 1975–88

*Historical Research* (formerly the *Bulletin of the Institute of Historical Research*), since 1987 published three times a year by Blackwell, Oxford, for the IHR

*History*, published three times a year by the Historical Association, London

*A History of the English-Speaking Peoples*, by W.S. Churchill, 4 vols, Cassell, London, first published 1956–58; various reprints; one-volume abridgement, Cassell, London, 1998

*History of the Twentieth Century*, by Martin Gilbert, 4 vols, Harper-Collins, London, vols 1–3, 1997–99; vol. 4 forthcoming

*History Today*, published monthly since 1951, London

*Hollis Press & Public Relations Annual*, published by Hollis Directories, Teddington, Middx; also *Hollis Europe*, annually

*How to Find* series, British Library, London

*The Hutchinson Almanac 1999*, Helicon, Oxford, 1998; to be published annually

*The Hutchinson Factfinder*, Helicon, Oxford, 1999

*Illustrated London News*, weekly from May 1842; now 2–3 issues per year (summer and Christmas, plus occasional issues on special events), London

*International Historical Statistics: Africa, Asia, Oceania 1750–1993*, ed. Brian Mitchell, Macmillan, London, 3rd edn, 1998

*International Historical Statistics: Americas 1750–1993*, ed. Brian Mitchell, Macmillan, London, 4th edn, 1998

*International Historical Statistics Europe 1750–1993*, ed. Brian R. Mitchell, Macmillan, London, 4th edn, 1998

*IPO Directory*, published bi-annually by the Central Office of Information, London

*Keesing's Record of World Events* (formerly *Keesing's Contemporary Archives*), published since 1931; now 11 issues per year, published by Keesings Worldwide, Washington D.C. (UK office: 69A Lensfield Road, Cambridge CB2 1EN; tel. 01223 508050). Also available on CD-ROM back to 1960

*Key Resource* series, British Library, London

*Larousse Desk Reference Encyclopedia*, Larousse, London, 1998

*The Marcan Handbook of Arts Organisations*, Peter Marcan, London, 4th edn, 1995

*The Media Guide*, ed. Steve Peak and Paul Fisher, published annually by Fourth Estate, London, (a *Guardian Book*)

*Monthly Digest of Statistics*, Office for National Statistics, The Stationery Office (formerly HMSO), London

*The New Shell Book of Firsts*, ed. Patrick Robertson, Headline, London, 1995 (formerly entitled *Shell Book of Firsts*, 2nd rev. edn, Michael Joseph, London, 1984)

*The New York Public Library Science Desk Reference*, Macmillan, New York, 1996

*NUJ Freelance Directory*, National Union of Journalists, London, updated regularly

*Penguin Book of Firsts*, ed. Matthew Richardson, Penguin Books, London, 1997

*Punch*, published weekly 1841–1992, London; relaunched 1996, fortnightly since October 1997

*Royal Historical Society Transactions*, published annually, now by Cambridge University Press, Cambridge, for the RHS

*SCICAT*, catalogue of the former Science Reference and Information Service (SRIS) from 1968, now the Science, Business and Technology Service (STB), on microfiche; also on CD-ROM, updated quarterly, by annual subscription, British Library, London

*The Statesman's Year-Book*, published annually by Macmillan, London

*Statistics Europe*, published by CBD Research, Beckenham, 6th edn, 1997

*The Tatler*, first published in 1709, now monthly, London

*The Timetables of Technology*, by Bryan Bunch and Alexander Hellemans, Touchstone (Simon & Schuster), New York, 1993

*The Times*, London; microfilm edition from 1795, Primary Source Media (The Gale Group), Reading; current subscriptions updated every three weeks

*The Times Index*, 1785 to present day, currently by subscription, updated monthly, with annual cumulation; on microfilm from 1906 and on CD-ROM (as part of *British Newspaper Index*) from 1990. Also *Palmer's Index to The Times, 1790–1905* (print edition). All from Primary Source Media (The Gale Group), Reading

*Ulrich's International Periodicals Directory*, published annually in 5 vols by Bowker, New Providence, N.J., also on CD-ROM as *Ulrich's on Disc* (annual subscription with quarterly updates), and online

*Walford's Guide to Reference Material*, vol. 2, *Social and Historical Sciences, Philosophy and Religion*, Library Association, London, 7th edn, 1998

*Whitaker's Almanack*, published annually by The Stationery Office, London

*Writings on British History*, now *Annual Bibliography of British and Irish History*, *q.v.*

Note: From 1995 serial publications of the Royal Historical Society are published by Cambridge University Press. Back titles to 1990 are available from CUP; titles published before 1990 from Oxbow Books Ltd, Park End Place, Oxford OX1 lHN. Reprints of the first 15 volumes of *Writings on British History* are available from Dawson Book Service, Cannon House, Folkestone, Kent CT19 5EE: 12 volumes covering the period 1946–1974, published by the Institute of Historical Research, are available from the IHR. The *Annual Bibliography of British and Irish History*, covering the years since 1975, is published and distributed by Oxford University Press for the RHS.

# 5

# Research for Fiction Writers and Dramatists

The depth of research to be undertaken by the writer of fiction will depend upon his choice for the story's setting and his own knowledge of that setting, and upon his acquaintance with the kind of people he is writing about. Basically, the research will be concerned with the creation of an authentic background to the plot and with writing dialogue in the correct idiom. As the problems which face the writer of modern fiction and drama differ from those of the writer of historical fiction and drama, they are here examined separately. All that is said about the novel applies equally to the short story and to drama.

## The Modern Novel

### Background

There is no substitute for a personal visit to every place in which your story, or scene of a story, is to be set. Only through first-hand experience will you absorb the atmosphere of a place, find out exactly how long it will take your character to get from A to B and what buildings or other landmarks he will pass on the way; by using your eyes and ears and nose, by travelling on the local bus, and by spending a few evenings at the pub, you can learn pretty well everything you need to know about the way the locals live, behave and talk. Make a point of attending at least once each kind of event that is going to crop up in your story or play – whether it is a boxing match, a race meeting, a sale at Sotheby's, a ballet performance, a court hearing, or anything else.

Inevitably, sometimes, a personal visit is out of the question, and then you have no choice but to rely on secondary sources. If this is the case, equip yourself with a good, large-scale map or two – preferably a street map of each town in which the action of your story is to take place, as well as a map of the whole district. You can obtain much free information of this nature from town halls or tourist offices.

Travel brochures are always a helpful source, and there are any number of excellent general topographical guides to various regions of the United Kingdom. *The Blue Guides: England* and *London* (separate volumes) are detailed and up to date. Arthur Mee's *The King's England* series, originally published in the 1930s, is now available in a facsimile edition. Look also at the publications of the motoring organisations. (How to obtain information on places abroad is dealt with in chapter 9, 'Information from and about Foreign Countries', pages 162–79). The researcher wishing to find out more about the origin and meaning of place-names will find Adrian Room's *Placenames of the World* a useful source. Insofar as English place-names are concerned, both A.D. Mills' *A Dictionary of English Place-Names* and Kenneth Cameron's *English Place-Names* are recommended. For in-depth study consult the volumes (by county) published by the English Place-Name Society.

If you need to describe particular buildings you will find Nikolaus Pevsner's *Buildings of England* series, also one per county, enormously helpful; also the *Guide to Country Houses* series. In addition, all stately homes and castles open to the public produce their own guidebooks, some more comprehensive and informative than others. The annual publication, *Historic Houses, Castles and Gardens* and the AA's *Historic Houses in Britain*, both carry brief details of all such properties. The curators of these historic houses are well informed, but may be too busy to talk to you on days when the public is admitted; a telephone call or preliminary letter beforehand may lead to a special appointment and personally guided tour, with much additional information.

Other essential reference tools are railway and bus time-tables of the area you are describing and, if appropriate, an air time-table: these should save you from making an elementary mistake such as putting a character on a train or plane at the wrong rail or air terminus or misjudging the time taken for a particular journey. A writer setting his tale on board a cruise ship or private yacht will find the *World Cruising Handbook* a mine of information on harbour regulations, ports of call, and much else.

An excellent way to get the 'feel' of a place, when it is not possible for you to visit it, is to take out a subscription to the local newspaper and county magazine; you will find lists of these, under towns, in both *Benn's Media* and *Willing's Press Guide* (see chapter 3, 'Basic Sources of Information', page 54).

## People

Often the background to a story or play will concern a particular profession or industry, and here too the best method of research is to mix as much as possible with people in the field. The secretary of the relevant professional or trade association (check names and addresses either in the current *Directory of British Associations,* in the *Hollis Press & Public Relations Annual* or in *Whitaker's Almanack* – see chapter 4, page 83) will usually be very helpful if you do not have any personal contacts, and most large corporations or companies have a press and public relations department or member of staff who will assist you. You should not feel diffident about approaching such people; it is rare for a genuine request for information to be refused point blank, and very often the enquirer will be invited to visit a factory or training establishment or to attend as an observer one or two meetings of the relevant society – all this is grist to the mill. Nevertheless, it is unfair to impinge too much on someone else's time or expertise – even if this is being paid for by his company – and so a luncheon or dinner invitation is a nice gesture. An incredible amount can be learned from an hour's conversation face to face.

Much of what has been said about background research also applies to finding out about people, for there is nothing better than to spend time with whatever age, regional or occupational group the writer wishes to bring into his story. It is essential to observe at first hand how people behave, talk and dress. Every writer should try, therefore, to cultivate a wide circle of friends in all walks of life, and the fiction writer especially will do well to get to know a psychologist with whom he can discuss the actions and reactions of his characters, as well as a doctor with whom he can verify medical symptoms and treatments. The crime writer ought to be on friendly terms with at least one member of the police force, active or retired, who is willing to put him right on procedures and jargon. And so on.

Careers pamphlets and training manuals for the relevant trade or profession yield a good deal of information. The memoirs and diaries of eminent people in that trade or profession should be looked at, and also the relevant in-house or trade journals, for these will all provide up-to-date material and jargon, and sometimes also historical detail.

So far as the behaviour of your characters is concerned, personal observation may be supplemented by a simple textbook on psychology or behavioural study. Recommended titles are Desmond Morris's *Bodytalk: A World Guide to Gestures,* Peter Collett's *Foreign Bodies: A Guide to European Mannerisms* and Roger Axtell's *Gestures: The Dos and Taboos of Body Language Around the World.* A more academic study is the *Dictionary of Worldwide Gestures.*

Useful sources of information on nicknames (both modern and historical) are the *Handbook of Pseudonyms and Personal Nicknames* compiled by H. Sharp, and *A Dictionary of Pseudonyms and Their Origins, with Stories of Name Changes,* by Adrian Room.

On names in general, the best up-to-date source is Adrian Room's *Brewer's Dictionary of Names*, which has 8,000 entries and a guide to nearly 100 languages; it covers not only the origins of personal and place names, but brand names, literary characters, rock groups, and almost every other category. For recommendations on literary pseudonyms and names of characters in published fiction, see the penultimate paragraph of this chapter, page 106. More academic genealogical studies are mentioned in chapter 7, 'Family and Local History', pages 137–56.

# Language

It is highly dangerous for the writer who is unfamiliar with a foreign language, local dialect or occupational slang to dabble in these fields, but if he must do so he should always try to get what he has written verified by an expert. So far as English is concerned, your first step should be to consult The British Library National Sound Archive (96 Euston Road, London NW1 2DB; tel. 020 7412 7440; fax 020 7412 7441); an appointment will be arranged for you to listen to relevant recordings. (This can be in London or Yorkshire, see page 207) Among printed works Peter Trudgill's *The Dialects of England* is first class. Most reference libraries will also have the four-volume *Survey of English Dialects* by H. Orton and E. Dieth, and the *English Dialect Dictionary* by J. Wright.

There are a number of so-called 'slang dictionaries', and these have their uses. However, since it is necessary first to know the word or expression whose meaning you wish to look up in them, their value is somewhat limited. Happily there is now *The Thesaurus of Slang*, a splendid compilation containing an alphabetical list of 12,000 standard English words for which you can look up some 150,000 slang terms, common idioms and colloquialisms. The late Eric Partridge's *Slang Today and Yesterday*, with its separate sections dealing with slang spoken in chronological periods and in various occupational groups, is still valid historically. Eric Partridge also compiled *A Dictionary of the Underworld, British and American*, which will serve the crime writer well (although this too is arranged as a dictionary), and also a fascinating *A Dictionary of Catch Phrases* (British and American) from the 16th century to the present day.

A major new work by the lexicographer Jonathon Green, *The Cassell Dictionary of Slang*, is set to become the standard work. Among Dr Green's earlier compilations, *Newspeak: A Dictionary of Jargon*, *Slang Down the Ages* and *The Slang Thesaurus* each still has a different use to the researcher. Other recommended titles include Tony Thorne's *Dictionary of Contemporary Slang* and *The Macmillan*

*Dictionary of American Slang* by R.L. Chapman. The classic Anglo-Indian dictionary, *Hobson-Jobson*, an invaluable source first published in 1886, has recently been reprinted.

Quite often a writer is at a loss to know how one of his characters would address another, perhaps someone in an elevated position. Here either *Debrett's Correct Form*, *Debrett's New Guide to Etiquette and Modern Manners* or *Titles and Forms of Address* will provide the answer, supplying as a bonus a guide to practically every situation likely to arise, socially and professionally, including American usage. These books will also be invaluable for the researcher wishing to know how to write or talk to titled or official persons whom he needs to contact for information.

# The Historical Novel

The writer of an historical novel must be thoroughly familiar with the period in which his story is set, and especially knowledgeable about the manners, customs and daily life of the people concerned. He must also be accurate about major events and prominent people. This will not present any great difficulty so long as he keeps at his elbow as he works a general bibliography and authoritative history of the period, as well as a good biographical dictionary (suggested titles are mentioned in chapter 4, 'Factual and Historical Research' (pages 79–91) and chapter 6, 'Biography and Autobiography' (pages 116–36)). A trap that inexperienced writers sometimes fall into is one of anachronisms: that is, the mention of, say, ice cream or zip fasteners at a period before these came on the scene. You can avoid such errors by checking in an encyclopedic dictionary or *The New Shell Book of Firsts*.

In recent years a number of gifted historians, notably the French writers Fernand Braudel, Georges Duby and Roy Ladurie (all now translated into English) have added a new dimension to social history, for which we humble researchers, seeking ever more detail on the private lives of people through the ages, must be enormously grateful. For reasons of space I have had to be ruthlessly selective in considering which titles to recommend here in order to introduce some newer studies that are European in scope and written with the benefit of contemporary research. Readers who have read and absorbed my chapters 3 and 4 should be more than adequately equipped to ferret out other titles on more specific subjects.

It is of the utmost importance to use contemporary sources wherever possible, and you should make good use of the *English Historical Documents* series. Also recommended are the *They Saw It*

*Happen* and the *Human Documents* series; some of these are now out of print, but they will be found in most reference libraries. G.M. Trevelyan's *English Social History* remains one of the best general accounts of life in this country through the ages, while a more recent study is Asa Briggs' *A Social History of England*. Two admirable multi-volume works are Fernand Braudel's *Civilization and Capitalism 1400–1800* and *A History of Private Life*, edited by P. Aries and G. Duby. The lifestyle of the upper classes is admirably portrayed in Mark Girouard's *Life in the English Country House*. R. Graves and A. Hodge's *The Long Week-End* is very evocative of the years between the two world wars. Among numerous social histories relating to particular periods, I mention a few, to give readers an idea of what to look out for: E.N. Williams' *Life in Georgian England*, Dorothy Marshall's *English People in the Eighteenth Century*, J.H. Plumb's *Georgian Delights*, Venetia Murray's recent social history of the Regency period, 1788–1820, *An Impolite Society*, John Fisher's *The World of the Forsytes*, David Evans' *Victorians Early and Late*, in the *How We Used to Live* series from A & C Black (early Victorian times to the present) and Norman Longmate's *How We Lived Then: A History of Everyday Life during the Second World War*. G.D.H. Cole and R. Postgate's *The Common People 1746–1938* has become a standard work; see also *The Common People: A History from the Norman Conquest to the Present*, by J.F.C. Harrison, two studies by E.P. Thompson, *Customs in Common* and *The Making of the English Working Class*, and *The Labourer 1760–1832* by J.L. and Barbara Hammond. J.M. Brereton's *The British Soldier: A Social History* provides a reliable background to army life from the 17th century. *British Trials 1660–1900* contains first-hand accounts of thousands of trials. In lighter vein, but very informative, are C.L. Graves' *Mr Punch's History of Modern England*, covering the years from 1841 to 1914, and Leslie Baily's *BBC Scrapbooks 1896–1939*. Rona Randall's *The Model Wife* is a well-illustrated mine of information about marriage and the role of a wife in the 19th-century household. Phyllida Barstow's *The English Country House Party* is an excellent source for late Victorian and Edwardian high society. For the present century it is worth looking at the *Portrait of a Decade* series and at *Yesterday's Britain: The Illustrated Story of How We Lived, Worked and Played*.

Autobiographies and diaries are extremely useful as source material for the historical novelist in that they provide absolutely authentic accounts of day-to-day life and thought of the period, written in the contemporary idiom. *British Autobiographies*, compiled by William Matthews, is an annotated bibliography of material printed or published before 1951. John Burnett has made two useful studies of working-class material, the three volume *Autobiography of the Working Class*, covering the period 1790–1945, and a paperback, *Useful Toil: Autobiographies of Working People from the 1820s to the 1970s*.

William Matthews' *British Diaries 1442–1942* and John Stuart Batts' *British Manuscript Diaries of the 19th Century* are standard works, both listing the diaries under the year in which they commence, which enables the researcher to ascertain what material exists for a particular period. Matthews also compiled an annotated bibliography of *American Diaries* written prior to 1861 and *American Diaries in Manuscript 1580–1954*. His work has been updated, expanded and continued by another American bibliographer, Patricia Pate Havlice, in an invaluable volume, *And So To Bed: A Bibliography of Diaries published in English*; this contains an index to Matthews' listings and also a general index of authors, editors, titles and subjects. Also worth consulting are *English Family Life 1576–1716: An Anthology of Diaries*, edited by Ralph Houlbrooke, and *Women's Diaries, Journals and Letters: An Annotated Bibliography*, compiled by Cheryl Cline.

Most public libraries maintain a local collection, and you should always ask if there is a book dealing with a particular region, town, industry or local family, in the period about which you are writing. (For further suggestions, see chapter 7, 'Family and Local History' pages 137–56).

One good method of keeping the story of an historical novel or play in line with world or national events is to refer constantly to a published chronology. I highly recommend the new edition of *Chronology of World History*, in four volumes (you can buy it as a set or only the one you need). *The People's Chronology* contains much information on human events, inventions, etc. not listed elsewhere, from prehistory to modern times. The Dorling Kindersley *Chronicle of the 20th Century*, with its month by month listings, amply illustrated with news photographs, and a good index, is indispensable if you are setting a story in the last hundred years. A more detailed set of chronologies is the *Day By Day* series, the 1960s, 1970s and 1980s, two volumes per decade.

There is a wide choice of dictionaries of dates from various publishers. In these volumes the major events of each year are listed month by month, while also included are annual listings of the developments in the arts, sciences, politics, etc., together with the births and deaths of famous people.

Problems likely to be encountered by the writer of historical fiction and some suggestions as to how they may be solved are discussed below.

# Places

Many of the places and buildings you may want to mention in your novel or play still exist today, but have changed out of all recognition in the last few hundred years, and it is not easy to find out exactly how they looked at a particular date. You should always ask at the local library or record office if they have maps of approximately the right date, and where these exist you will find it valuable to keep a photocopy of the map in front of you as you write. There is an historical series of the Ordnance Survey, which may be useful, and you can buy reprints of the first (one inch) edition. A good historical atlas such as *The Times Atlas of World History* or the *Penguin Atlas of World History* is essential. Penguin also publish an excellent and relatively inexpensive series of historical atlases, with separate volumes for *Ancient, Medieval, Modern* or *Recent History*, and also for regions and individual countries. There is a new series of *Continental History Atlases* published by Macmillan in the USA.

Like the writer of modern fiction, the historical novelist should try to visit every place or building that comes into his story. If this is quite impossible, the best course is to enquire at your local library or county record office for a reliable parish history and for any books about life in the district during the period in which you are interested. If your story is set in the 18th century or later, you will be able to study the local newspaper. Where buildings have to be described, Nikolaus Pevsner's *Buildings of England* series, already mentioned, will be most useful. For buildings in London, there is the very detailed *Survey of London*. Other useful sources include the *Britain in Old Photographs* series, as well as current guidebooks to the historic castles and stately homes open to the public.

# Dates

The problems that arise over dating have been discussed in the previous chapter (see pages 86–7). In historical fiction work the writer will most often need to find out on what day of the week a certain anniversary or religious festival fell. This can be done very easily by first looking up the date of Easter in the chronological table at the back of the *Handbook of Dates for Students of English History* and then by turning to the appropriate calendar section, in which there is a double-page spread for all the years from AD 500 to 2000 in which Easter fell (or is going to fall) on that particular day. In the same *Handbook* you will find a list of saints' days and religious festivals, but if you need more detail on festivals you should consult the *British Calendar Customs* series published by the Folklore Society. *Whitaker's Almanack* contains an 'Any Year' calendar from 1770 to 2030.

## Weather

What the weather was like on a certain day, or if a particular winter was severe, or when there was a heatwave and how long it lasted, can be vital to an historical novel. *Whitaker's Almanack* (from 1868) is a good source, and so are local and regional newspapers. *The Times* has employed a regular weather correspondent since the early 1870s, but earlier reports – from 1731 – appeared in *Gentleman's Magazine*, where you will find not only monthly tables giving temperatures and rainfall, but a calendar with brief descriptions against each day, such as 'cloudy morning, but bright later'; 'windy and wet all day'; 'heavy rain in the south, snow in the north'.

Two excellent works which are rare books and to be found nowadays only at the major libraries are T.H. Baker's *Records of the Seasons, etc.... observed in the British Isles* and E.J. Lowe's *Natural Phenomena and Chronology of the Seasons* (of which Part I only was ever published, containing records from AD 220 to 1753). Among other useful reference books are Ingrid Holford's *The Guinness Book of Weather Facts and Feats*; D. Bowen's *Britain's Weather*, which has an appendix listing notable gales, blizzards, floods and frosts; J.H. Brazell's *London Weather*, with its useful chronology from AD 4 to 1964; and W. Andrews' *Famous Frosts and Frost Fairs in Great Britain*.

The best printed source of information about the weather in different regions of the globe is *The World Weather Guide*. The *World Climate Disc*, on CD-ROM, contains data from 1854 to 1990. For quick reference there is a splendid little book by Maria Harding, *Weather to Travel: The Traveller's Guide to the World's Weather*, which as a bonus suggests appropriate seasonal clothing under each country.

In England, the Meteorological Office has published records since the 1860s. Its Library at Bracknell, Berkshire, houses a collection of meteorological literature dating from the 16th century which is the most comprehensive in the world. Members of the public may use the Library and also the Archive, which is in the Scott Building nearby; the records stored here comprise a vast collection of meteorological data and charts from England, Wales and British overseas bases, including many ships' weather logs, and the archives of the Royal Meteorological Society. (Records from Scotland are stored in Edinburgh, and those from Northern Ireland in Belfast.)

Intending visitors should give prior notice to the Library or Archive Manager. Postal enquiries should be addressed to the National Meteorological Library and Archive, Meteorological Office, London Road, Bracknell, Berks RG12 2SZ (tel. 01344 854841; fax 01344

854840). The Librarian will usually recommend titles or may pass a specific query on to the relevant department; a search fee will be payable if extensive research has to be undertaken by staff. Many of the Library's books may be borrowed (proof of identity required); such loans are best arranged through your local library, but may also be requested by post, in which case there may be a search fee and handling surcharge. N.B. Much of the material in the Archive is classed as public records and may not be loaned.

## Language

Getting the idiom right in historical fiction is often a big worry to the writer. The best advice that can be given is that he should read extensively the best novels and plays of the relevant age; by so doing, he will gradually acquire the 'feel' of the spoken English of the time. Eric Partridge's *Slang Today and Yesterday*, as mentioned earlier in this chapter, has useful sections on the slang spoken at different periods (16th to mid-20th century). *Slang Down the Ages* is arranged by subject, with a word index. If you are setting your story in the last war, you should look at *The Language of World War II*, which covers not only spoken expressions but also the slogans and abbreviations then current, as well as the popular songs of the time.

## Cost of living, currencies and wages

How much people earned and what they paid for their food and clothing are queries that frequently crop up in historical writing. J. Burnett's *A History of the Cost of Living* will answer most needs: it has chapters dating from the Middle Ages to the present day, and also a good bibliography. Unfortunately it has been allowed to go out of print, but most libraries will have it; should you ever see it on offer secondhand, be sure to snap it up! A more recent paperback, written primarily for family and local historians, is Lionel Munby's *How Much is that Worth?* Another exceptionally informative source is the *What It Cost the Day Before Yesterday Book* by Harold Priestley, which is divided into three periods: 1851–1914, 1915–70 and (to take account of inflation) 1971–78. *Prices and Wages in England from the 12th to the 19th Century* by Lord Beveridge and others is a standard work, and Peter Wilsher's *The Pound in your Pocket 1870–1970* is a very readable and well-researched study of the pound and its purchasing power throughout that period. Newspapers and women's magazines are valuable sources from the early 19th century onwards – Alison Adburgham's *Shops and Shopping* covers the period 1800–1914, whereas a new publication,

Bill Lancaster's *The Department Store: A Social History*, deals with the subject from the mid-19th century to the present day, on both sides of the Atlantic.

*Currency Conversion Tables: A Hundred Years of Change* by R.L. Bidwell is a most useful guide to the fluctuations in rates of exchange of most countries of the world 1870–1970; it also has a table of London gold prices. For money values in earlier times I recommend John McCusker's *Money and Exchange in Europe and America 1600–1775*, Peter Spufford's *Handbook of Medieval Exchange* and Pierre Vilar's *A History of Gold and Money 1450–1920*. For more historical or monetary information, write or telephone to the Bank of England Library and Information Services, Threadneedle Street, London EC2R 8AH (tel. 020 7601 4715; fax 020 7601 4356).

## Fashion, etiquette and food

The best source for the history of costume is The Fashion Research Centre at 4 Circus, Bath, Somerset BA1 2EW (tel. 01225 477752; fax 01225 444793). The Centre houses an extensive library (books on the history of dress from the medieval period to the present day) as well as a study collection (dress, accessories and textiles) which, by appointment, you can study at close quarters. At the Museum of Costume nearby you will find some 200 dressed figures illustrating styles from the late 16th century to modern times. Bibliographies are available free of charge from the Centre (state period and type of costume, i.e. men's dress, underclothes, etc.).

Researchers seriously interested in fashion should consider joining The Costume Society. The Society's annual journal, *Costume*, now in its thirty-fourth edition (1999) is a valuable research tool, containing articles and book reviews on many aspects of the subject; it is available to non-members on subscription. Members also receive a newletter twice a year. Past issues and reprints are available. A new edition of the Society's *Costume: A General Bibliography* has recently been issued. (Note that the bibliography covers articles in the journal rather than general titles.) Members of the Society have the opportunity to attend lectures and other events throughout the year. Details from the Membership Secretary, 56 Wareham Road, Lytchett Matravers, Poole, Dorset BH16 6DS.

The classic work on English costume is the series by C.W. and P.E. Cunnington, which consists of *Handbooks* covering the medieval period and the 16th, 17th, 18th, 19th and 20th centuries in separate volumes. For quick reference there is J. Laver's *A Concise History of Costume*. Also useful is the revised edition of A. Racinet's *The Historical Encyclopedia of Costumes*. Alison Lurie's study *The Language of Clothes* is both a thoroughly researched and witty comment on dress and manners that will help both the modern and the historical novelist. The *Fashions of a Decade* series, published by Batsford, is useful for the 20th century. On hairdressing there is R. Corson's *Fashions in Hair: The First 5000 Years*, R. Turner Wilcox's *Modes in Hats and Headdress* (from ancient Egyptian to the present day) and G. de Courtais' *Women's Headdress and Hairstyles in England from AD 600 to the Present Day*.

The best guides to English manners and etiquette are J. Wildeblood and P. Brinson's *The Polite World* (covering the 13th to the 19th centuries) and *A Punch History of Manners 1841–1940*, by A. Adburgham. On eating habits and diet there are Arnold Palmer's *Movable Feasts*, J.C. Drummond and A. Wilbraham's *The Englishman's Food: A History of Five Centuries of English Diet*, J. Burnett's *Plenty and Want: A Social History of Diet in England from 1815 to the Present Day*, Reay Tannahill's *Food in History* and Margaret Visser's *The Rituals of Dinner*.

## Transport and travel

Finding out exactly how long a particular journey would have taken at a particular date is not easy. So far as train journeys are concerned, try to find an early *Bradshaw* (first published in 1839) – you may have to settle for the one nearest in date to your story. Stage-coach time-tables will be found in the early London directories. OAG Worldwide (formerly ABC International), now part of the Reed Travel Group, have a collection of old rail and air time-tables; telephone them on 01582 695242. Alternatively, contact the National Railway Museum Library and Archive, Leeman Road, York YO26 4XJ (tel. 01904 621261; fax 01904 611112); the Caird Library of the National Maritime Museum, Greenwich, London SE10 9NF (tel. 020 8312 6607; fax 020 8312 6632); or the Civil Aviation Authority Library and Information Centre, Aviation House, South Area, Gatwick Airport South, West Sussex RH6 0YR (tel. 01293 573725; fax 01293 573181).

There is an important Transport History Collection at Leicester University Library, University Road, Leicester LE1 9QD (tel. 0116 252 2042; fax 0116 252 2066).

One of the best general studies is E.A. Pratt's *History of Inland Transport and Communications*. The publishers who specialise in transport history are Sutton Publishing of Thrupp, near Stroud, Gloucestershire (tel. 01453 731114; fax 01453 731117). Researchers requiring information should send both for the firm's general catalogue and for their separate catalogues of 'Road and rail titles' and 'Inland waterway and maritime books'.

# Children's Fiction

Research done by the children's writer is not much different from that carried out by the writer of stories for adults. Children of all ages being highly critical and quick to spot mistakes, it is very important that background and language are absolutely right.

The correct idiom is vital. It is a good idea, if you are embarking on a modern story, to study a selection of juvenile magazines for a time. You will also want to keep up to date with, and read, published children's books. Ask at your local children's library enquiries desk for the *Children's Fiction Index* and *Sequels, Volume II: Children's Books*.

Young Book Trust, which is part of Book Trust (Book House, 45 East Hill, London SW18 2QZ; tel. 020 8516 2977; fax 020 8516 2978), maintains an excellent library and information service; it holds a copy of every children's book published in the past two years. After two years, these books are passed on to the Bethnal Green Museum of Childhood, Cambridge Heath Road, London E2 9PA. The Museum of Childhood also houses the Renier Collection of Historic and Contemporary Children's Books, spanning five centuries, and other smaller collections. Access is by appointment: contact the Curator of Children's Books for information (tel. 020 8983 5217; fax 020 8983 5225). Leaflets are available on how to use the collections, as well as lists featuring different aspects of the Renier Collection (send A4 size stamped addressed envelope). Computer cataloguing is in progress, with records being entered into the National Art Library database at the Victoria & Albert Museum in London. The National Art Library also has a collection of around 6,500 children's books.

On sources generally, highly recommended are the *Children's Fiction Sourcebook*, and two works by Tessa Rose Chester, *Children's Books Research: A Practical Guide to Techniques and Sources* and *Sources of Information about Children's Books*. For general reference, in addition to the standard work, *The Oxford Companion to Children's Literature*, you will find Arthur Mortimore's *Index to Characters in Children's Literature* very useful. If you write for young children, you may want to have works such as *The Classic Fairy Tales*, *The Fairies in Tradition and Literature* or the *Oxford Dictionary of Nursery Rhymes* on your reference bookshelf.

So far as school stories are concerned, you cannot do better than delve into Peter Opie's *The Lore and Language of School Children*. Isabel Quigly's *The Heirs of Tom Brown*, with its excellent bibliography, will help with a public school setting. Another very useful book is *Children's Games in Street and Playground*, by Iona and Peter Opie.

Various slang dictionaries have been mentioned on pages 95–6. However, it cannot be stressed too strongly that language is changing all the time – and especially the language of the young – so that there can be no substitute for the writer mixing with, and talking and listening to, the younger generation, in order to get the idiom exactly right.

Background too must be up to date: remember single-parent families and the mixed nationalities encountered by children today in playgroup and school!

# Crime Fiction

The best research tool I have come across recently in this field is Douglas Wynn's *The Crime Writer's Handbook*. This slim and inexpensive reference publication is a goldmine of information on methods of murder (including weapons and poisons), methods of detection and forensic science, police procedures and much else. The bibliography will lead you to pretty well every other source you need.

# Science Fiction

The best source in this country is the Science Fiction Foundation Research Library, at Liverpool University Library, PO Box 123, Liverpool L69 3DA (tel 0151-794 2733/2696; fax 0151-794 2681). This collection, which includes the library of the British Science Fiction Association, is the largest in this field outside the United States. Intending researchers should telephone in advance for an appointment. A useful reference to published works is *The Ultimate Guide to Science Fiction: An A–Z of Science Fiction Books by Title* by D. Pringle.

# Finding out about Published Fiction

In addition to the specific research problems connected with his own work, the fiction writer or playwright frequently wants to know what other novels or plays or short stories have been published with similar themes or backgrounds. He may also wish to check on whether any other writer has used the title which he has in mind. (There is no copyright in titles, but for the exact legal position, see the Society of Authors' *Quick Guide* on the 'Protection of Titles'.)

Most public libraries possess copies of the *Fiction Index*, the *Play Index* and the *Short Story Index*; you should ask for them at the readers' enquiry desk. There are cumulated volumes of the *Fiction Index* for 1945–60 and 1960–69; since 1970 every five years. Titles are listed under some 3,000 subject headings. Another useful tool is the *Reference Guide to Short Fiction*, which covers the 19th and 20th centuries and includes foreign language writers and translations. There is also the British Library *Fiction on Fiche*, listing adult and teenage fiction published since 1950. New as I go to press is *The Modern Library: The 200 best novels in English since 1950*, by Carmen Callil and Colm Tóibín.

If you want to check up on sequels to published fiction, ask at the library enquiry desk for *Sequels* (*Volume I: Adult Books*; *Volume II: Children's Books*).

The researcher wishing to find out about published historical fiction should consult Daniel S. Burt's *What Historical Novel Do I Read Next?* This fairly recent 2-volume American compilation not only covers over 7,000 novels, it contains a number of indexes which enable the user to track down historical fiction under author, subject, fictional and historical characters, location and period. It also evaluates the novels for historical accuracy. Persuade your local library to acquire it if they haven't already done so.

Literary pseudonyms may be traced in Frank Atkinson's *Dictionary of Literary Pseudonyms*. There are three useful sources for finding out about characters in published fiction: the *Dictionary of British Literary Characters*, the *Dictionary of Fictional Characters* and the *Dictionary of Real People and Places in Fiction*.

A new and vast reference source for English and American literature, *Literature Online*, is available on the World Wide Web, by subscription, from Chadwyck-Healey of Cambridge. There are flexible rates for access (to all, or any single or combination of databases), and it is worth asking whether your library subscribes.

Finally, but by no means least, for the advice of a successful novelist (as opposed to that of myself, a humble researcher, albeit one who has worked for many novelists), read Jean Saunders' *How to Research your Novel*.

*American Diaries: An Annotated Bibliography of American Diaries written prior to Year 1861*, by William Matthews, University of California Press, Berkeley and Los Angeles, 1945, 1959

*American Diaries in Manuscript, 1580–1954*, by William Matthews, University of Georgia Press, Athens, 1974

*And So To Bed: A Bibliography of Diaries published in English*, by Patricia Pate Havlice, Scarecrow, Metuchen, 1987

*Autobiography of the Working Class*, by John Burnett, 3 vols, Harvester, Hemel Hempstead, 1984–89

*BBC Scrapbooks*, by Leslie Baily, 2 vols: 1, *1896–1914*; 2, *1918–1939*, Allen & Unwin, London, 1966–68

*Benn's Media*, 3 vols, published annually by Miller Freeman PLC, Tonbridge (formerly Benn Business Information Services)

*Bodytalk: A World Guide to Gestures*, by Desmond Morris, Jonathan Cape, London, 1994

*Bradshaw's Monthly Railway Guide*, 1839–1961

*Brewer's Dictionary of Names*, compiled by Adrian Room, Helicon, Oxford, 1995

*Britain in Old Photographs* series, published by Sutton Publishing, Thrupp, Stroud

*Britain's Weather*, by David Bowen, David & Charles, Newton Abbot, 1969

*British Autobiographies: An Annotated Bibliography of British Autobiographies published or written before 1951*, by William Matthews, University of California Press, Berkeley and Los Angeles, 1955

*British Calendar Customs: England*, 3 vols; *Scotland*, 3 vols; *Orkneys and Shetland*, 1 vol, published by The Folklore Society, London, 1936–46

*British Diaries 1442–1942: An Annotated Bibliography of British Diaries written between 1442 and 1942*, by William Matthews, University of California Press, Berkeley and Los Angeles, 1950

*British Manuscript Diaries of the 19th Century: An Annotated Listing*, by John Stuart Batts, Centaur Press, Fontwell and London, 1976

*The British Soldier: A Social History*, by J.M. Brereton, Bodley Head, London, 1986

*British Trials 1660–1900*, microfiche series, Chadwyck-Healey, Cambridge

*Buildings of England* series, originally ed. by Nikolaus Pevsner, 46 vols, 1951 onwards, Penguin Books, Harmondsworth; revised editions, by Bridget Cherry and others, in progress

*The Cassell Dictionary of Slang*, by Jonathon Green, Cassell, London, 1998

*Children's Books Research: A Practical Guide to Techniques and Sources*, by Tessa Rose Chester, Thimble Press/Westminster College, Oxford, 1989

*Children's Fiction Index*, published by the Career Development Group of the Library Association, London, 7th edn, eds Margaret Hobson and Jennifer Madden, 1995

*Children's Fiction Sourcebook*, compiled by J. Madden and M. Hobson, Scolar Press, London, 1995

*Children's Games in Street and Playground,* by Iona and Peter Opie, Oxford University Press, Oxford, 1969; paperback edn, 1984

*Chronicle of the 20th Century,* first published by Dorling Kindersley, London, 1988; rev. edn, 1995

*Chronology of World History,* 4 vols: 1, *Prehistory–1491AD*; 2, *1492–1775*; 3, *1776–1900*; 4, *1901–present day,* Helicon, Oxford, 1999

*Civilization and Capitalism 1400–1800,* by Fernand Braudel, 3 vols: 1, *The Structures of Everyday Life*; 2, *The Wheels of Commerce*; 3, *The Perspective of the World,* Collins, London, 1981–85

*The Classic Fairy Tales,* by Iona and Peter Opie, Oxford University Press, Oxford, 1974; reprinted 1992

*The Common People 1746–1938,* by G.D.H. Cole and R. Postgate, Methuen, London, 1938; reprinted 1965

*The Common People: A History from the Norman Conquest to the Present,* by J.F.C. Harrison, Fontana, London, 1984

*A Concise History of Costume,* by J. Laver, Thames & Hudson, 1969

*Continental History Atlases*: vols for *Asia, Europe, North America, South America,* Macmillan, New York,1998

*Costume,* illustrated journal of The Costume Society, published annually (available on subscription from W.S. Maney Ltd, Hudson Road, Leeds LS9 7DL)

*Costume: A General Bibliography,* by P. Anthony and J. Arnold, published by The Costume Society, London, new edn, 1999 (available from W.S. Maney Ltd, Hudson Road, Leeds LS9 7DL)

*The Crime Writer's Handbook,* by Douglas Wynn, Allison & Busby, 1997

*Currency Conversion Tables: A Hundred Years of Change,* by R.L. Bidwell, Rex Collings, London, 1970 (out of print)

*Customs in Common,* by E.P. Thompson, Merlin, London, 1991

*Day by Day* series: *The Sixties, The Seventies, The Eighties,* published by Facts On File, New York, 2 vols per decade, 1983, 1988, 1994

*Debrett's Correct Form,* Headline, London, new edn, 1999

*Debrett's New Guide to Etiquette and Modern Manners,* by John Morgan, Headline, London, 1996

*The Department Store: A Social History,* by Bill Lancaster, Leicester University Press (Cassell), London, 1995

*The Dialects of England,* by Peter Trudgill, Blackwell, Oxford, 1990

*Dictionary of British Literary Characters, 18th, 19th and 20th Century Novels,* by John R. Greenfield, Facts On File, New York, 3 vols, 1993, 1994

*A Dictionary of Catch Phrases British and American, from the Sixteenth Century to the Present Day,* by Eric Partridge, ed. Paul Beale, 2nd edn, Routledge, London 1986; paperback edn, 1990

*Dictionary of Contemporary Slang,* by Tony Thorne, Bloomsbury Reference, London, 1997

*A Dictionary of English Place-Names,* by A.D. Mills, Oxford University Press, 1991; 2nd edn (paperback), 1998

*Dictionary of Fictional Characters,* by William Freeman, Everyman Reference series, Dent, London, 3rd edn revised, 1973

*Dictionary of Literary Pseudonyms,* compiled by Frank Atkinson, Library Association, London, 4th edn, 1987

*A Dictionary of Pseudonyms and Their Origins, with Stories of Name Changes,* by Adrian Room, McFarland, Jefferson, North Carolina, 3rd edn, 1998

*Dictionary of Real People and Places in Fiction,* compiled by M.C. Rintoul, Routledge, London, 1991

*A Dictionary of the Underworld, British and American,* compiled by Eric Partridge, Routledge, London, 3rd edn revised, 1968

*Dictionary of Worldwide Gestures,* by Betty J. Bäuml and Franz H. Bäuml, Scarecrow Press, Lanham, Maryland, 2nd edn, 1997

*Directory of British Associations 1998/99,* published by CBD Research, Beckenham, 14th edn, 1998; also on CD-ROM

*England: Blue Guide,* by Ian Ousby, A & C Black, London, 11th edn, 1995

*The English Country House Party,* by Phyllida Barstow, Sutton Publishing, Thrupp, Glos., 1998

*English Dialect Dictionary,* compiled by J. Wright, 6 vols, Frowde, London, 1896–1905; new edn, Oxford University Press, Oxford, 1981

*English Family Life 1576–1716: An Anthology of Diaries,* ed. R. Houlbrooke, Blackwell, Oxford, 1989

*English Historical Documents,* ed. D.C. Douglas, 12 vols, Eyre & Spottiswoode, London, 1953–75

*English People in the Eighteenth Century,* by Dorothy Marshall, Longman, London, 1956

English Place-Name Society, volumes by county, in progress since 1923, published by the Society, c/o University of Nottingham

*English Place-Names,* by Kenneth Cameron, Batsford, London, 1996

*English Social History,* by G.M. Trevelyan, Longman, London, new edn, 1978; paperback edn, Penguin Books, Harmondsworth, 1986

*The Englishman's Food: A History of Five Centuries of English Diet,* by J.C. Drummond and A. Wilbraham, Cape, London, 1958; reprinted, Pimlico, London, 1991

*The Fairies in Tradition and Literature,* by K.M. Briggs, Routledge, London, 1977; reprinted Bellew, London, 1989

*Famous Frosts and Frost Fairs in Great Britain,* by W. Andrews, Redway, London, 1887

*Fashions in Hair: The First 5000 Years*, by R. Corson, Peter Owen, London, 1965

*Fashions of a Decade* series (1920s–1990s), published by Batsford, London, 8 vols, 1991–92

*Fiction Index*, published annually by the Association of Assistant Librarians (now the Career Development Group of the Library Association), London, since 1970; cumulated vols covering the period 1945–1989, now every 5 years. Latest editions, compiled by Marilyn E. Hicken: *Fiction Index 1995* and *Cumulated Fiction 1990–1994*, both published 1997

*Fiction on Fiche*, microfiche, published quarterly on annual subscription by the British Library National Bibliographic Service, Wetherby

*Food in History*, by Reay Tannahill, Eyre Methuen, London, 1973; paperback edn, Penguin Books, 1989

*Foreign Bodies: A Guide to European Mannerisms*, by Peter Collett, Simon & Schuster, London, 1993

*Gentleman's Magazine*, 1731–1922; weather reports

*Georgian Delights*, by J.H. Plumb, Weidenfeld & Nicolson, London, 1980

*Gestures: The Dos and Taboos of Body Language Around the World*, by Roger E. Axtell, John Wiley, London, 1991

*Guide to Country Houses* series, Burkes' Peerage/Savill, London, in progress

*The Guinness Book of Weather Facts and Feats*, by Ingrid Holford, Guinness Superlatives, Enfield, 1977

*Handbook of Dates for Students of English History*, ed. C.R. Cheney, Royal Historical Society, London, first published 1945; latest reprint 1995 published by Cambridge University Press; new edn due February 2000

*Handbook of English Costume* series, by C.W. and P.E. Cunnington, Faber, London, 1952–73

*Handbook of Medieval Exchange*, by Peter Spufford, Royal Historical Society, London, 1986

*Handbook of Pseudonyms and Personal Nicknames*, compiled by Harold S. Sharp, 2 vols, Scarecrow Press (formerly of Metuchen, N.J., now Lanham, Maryland, USA), 1972; supplements, 1975, 1982

*The Heirs of Tom Brown*, by Isabel Quigly, Chatto & Windus, London, 1982; paperback edn, Oxford University Press, Oxford, 1984

*Historic Houses, Castles and Gardens*, published annually by Johansens, London

*Historic Houses in Britain*, AA Publishing, Basingstoke, 1994; reprinted 1999

*The Historical Encyclopedia of Costumes*, originally compiled by A. Racinet, rev. edn, Studio Editions, London, 1988

*A History of the Cost of Living*, by John Burnett, Penguin Books, Harmondsworth, 1969

*A History of Gold and Money 1450–1920*, by Pierre Vilar, Verso, USA, 1991 (distributed in UK by Marston Book Services, Oxford)

*History of Inland Transport and Communication*, by E.A. Pratt, 1912; reprinted, David & Charles, Newton Abbot, 1970

*A History of Private Life*, eds P. Aries and G. Duby, translated from French, 5 vols, Belknap, Harvard University Press, Cambridge, Mass. and London, 1987–91

*Hobson-Jobson: The Anglo-Indian Dictionary*, by Henry Yule and A.C. Burnell, 1886; paperback edn, Wordsworth Reference, Ware, Herts, 1996

*Hollis Press & Public Relations Annual*, published by Hollis Directories, Teddington, Middx

*How Much is that Worth?*, by Lionel Munby, Phillimore, Chichester, 2nd edn, 1996

*How to Research your Novel*, by Jean Saunders, Allison & Busby, London, 1993

*How We Lived Then: A History of Everyday Life during the Second World War*, by Norman Longmate, Hutchinson, London, 1971; paperback edn, Arrow, London, 1977

*How We Used to Live: Victorians Early and Late*, by David Evans, A & C Black, London, 1990

*Human Documents* series, ed. R.E. Pike, Allen & Unwin, London (out of print)

*An Impolite Society: A Social History of the Regency Period 1788–1820*, by Venetia Murray, Penguin Books, London,1998

*Index to Characters in Children's Literature*, compiled and published by Arthur D. Mortimore, Bristol, 1977

*The King's England* series, by Arthur Mee, introductory vol. and 40 vols (county by county), facsimile edition, The King's England Press, Rotherham, South Yorkshire, 1998

*The Labourer 1760–1832*, by J.L. and Barbara Hammond, 1-vol. paperback edn, Sutton Publishing, Thrupp, Stroud, 1995

*The Language of Clothes*, by Alison Lurie, Heinemann, London, 1981; paperback edn, Hamlyn, London, 1983

*The Language of World War II*, compiled by A.M. Taylor, H.W. Wilson, New York, 1948

*Life in the English Country House*, by Mark Girouard, Yale University Press, New York and London, 1978; paperback edn, Penguin Books, Harmondsworth, 1980

*Life in Georgian England*, by E.N. Williams, Batsford, London, 1962

*Literature Online*, World Wide Web database, by subscription, Chadwyck-Healey, Cambridge

*London: Blue Guide*, by Ylva French, A & C Black, London, 16th edn, 1998

*London Weather*, by J.H. Brazell, HMSO, London, 1968

*The Long Week-End: A Social History of Great Britain 1918–1939*, by Robert Graves and Alan Hodge, Hutchinson, London, 1985

*The Lore and Language of School Children*, by Iona and Peter Opie, Oxford University Press, Oxford, 1959; reprinted 1987

*The Macmillan Dictionary of American Slang*, compiled by R.L. Chapman, Macmillan, 1995

*The Making of the English Working Class*, by E.P. Thompson, Gollancz, London, 1980

*Mr Punch's History of Modern England*, by C.L. Graves, 4 vols, Cassell, London, 1921–22

*The Model Wife*, by Rona Randall, Herbert Press, London, 1989

*The Modern Library: The best 200 novels in English since 1950*, by Carmen Callil and Colm Tóibín, Picador, London, 1999

*Modes in Hats and Headdress*, by R. Turner Wilcox, Scribner's, New York, rev. edn, 1959

*Money and Exchange in Europe and America 1600–1775*, by John McCusker, Macmillan, London, 1978

*Movable Feasts: Changes in English Eating-Habits*, by Arnold Palmer, Oxford University Press, Oxford, 1984

*Natural Phenomena and Chronology of the Seasons*, by E.J. Lowe, Part I only, London, 1870

*The New Shell Book of Firsts*, ed. Patrick Robertson, Headline, London, 1995; previously entitled *The Shell Book of Firsts*

*Newspeak: A Dictionary of Jargon*, by Jonathon Green, Routledge, London, 1984; paperback edn, 1985

*Ordnance Survey*: first edition, ed. J.B. Harley, reprinted by David & Charles, Newton Abbot; modern editions, Ordnance Survey, Southampton

*The Oxford Companion to Children's Literature*, by H. Carpenter and M. Prichard, Oxford University Press, Oxford, 1984; paperback edn, 1998

*Oxford Dictionary of Nursery Rhymes*, eds Iona and Peter Opie, Oxford University Press, Oxford, first published 1951; new edn 1997

*Penguin Atlas* series, various compilers and dates: *Ancient, Medieval, Modern* and *Recent History*; also *Historical Atlases* of individual countries, peoples and regions of the world, Penguin Books, Harmondsworth

*Penguin Atlas of World History*, 2 vols, Penguin Books, Harmondsworth, 1974; reprinted 1984

*The People's Chronology*, compiled by James Trager, Heinemann, London, 1980; 3rd rev. edn, Henry Holt, New York, 1992 (distributed in UK by Littlehampton Book Services, Worthing)

*Placenames of the World: Origins and Meanings of the Names for Over 5000 Natural Features, Countries, Capitals, Territories, Cities and Historic Sites*, by Adrian Room, McFarland, Jefferson, North Carolina, 1997

*Play Index*, published by H.W. Wilson, New York, since 1949 (9 vols to date, covering 1949–1997)

*Plenty and Want: A Social History of Diet in England from 1815 to the Present Day*, by John Burnett, Routledge, London, 3rd edn, 1989

*The Polite World: A Guide to English Manners and Deportment from the 13th to the 19th Century*, rev. edn by J. Wildeblood and P. Brinson, Oxford University Press, Oxford, 1974

*Portrait of a Decade* series, published by Batsford, London, 9 vols covering the period 1900–1980s

*The Pound in Your Pocket 1870–1970*, by Peter Wilsher, Cassell, London, 1970

*Prices and Wages in England from the 12th to the 19th Century*, by Lord Beveridge and others, Frank Cass, London, 1965

'Protection of Titles', Society of Authors *Quick Guide* (free to members or available from the Publications Department of the Society of Authors, 84 Drayton Gardens, London SW10 9SD, £2.00 post free)

*A Punch History of Manners 1841–1940*, by Alison Adburgham, Hutchinson, London, 1961

*Records of the Seasons and Prices of Agricultural Produce & Phenomena observed in the British Isles*, by T.H. Baker, Simpkin Marshall, London, 1883

*Reference Guide to Short Fiction*, ed. Noelle Watson, St James Press, Detroit, 2nd edn, 1998

*The Rituals of Dinner*, by Margaret Visser, Penguin Books, Harmondsworth, 1991

*Sequels: Volume I: Adult Books*, compiled by Marilyn E. Hicken, 12th edn, 1998; *Volume II: Children's Books*, compiled by Margaret Woodcock, 9th edn, 1999, Career Development Group of The Library Association, London

*Shops and Shopping*, by Alison Adburgham, Allen & Unwin, London, 2nd edn, 1981

*Short Story Index*, published annually with 5-year cumulations by H.W. Wilson, New York; 10 permanent retrospective volumes covering 1900–93; a single volume *Collections Indexed 1900–1978*

*Slang Down the Ages*, by Jonathon Green, Kyle Cathie, London, 1993

*The Slang Thesaurus*, by Jonathon Green, Penguin Books, Harmondsworth, 1988; revised edn due 1999

*Slang Today and Yesterday*, by Eric Partridge, Routledge, London, 4th edn, 1970

*A Social History of England*, by Asa Briggs, Weidenfeld & Nicolson, London, 1983; paperback, 3rd rev. edn, Penguin Press, Harmondsworth, 1999

*Sources of Information about Children's Books*, by Tessa Rose Chester, Thimble Press, Oxford, 1989

*Survey of English Dialects*, by H. Orton and E. Dieth, introductory vol. and 4 regional vols, E.J. Arnold, Leeds, 1962–70

*Survey of London*, 41 vols to date, originally published by the LCC, subsequently by Athlone Press, London, 1900–

*The Thesaurus of Slang*, compiled by Esther and Albert E. Lewin, Facts on File, New York, rev 2nd edn, 1997

*They Saw It Happen* series, published by Blackwell, Oxford; 4 vols covering 55BC–1940 (out of print)

*The Times*, London; weather reports, from c. 1870

*The Times Atlas of World History*, 4th edn, 1993; *Concise Times Atlas of World History*, 5th edn, 1994; HarperCollins, London, updated regularly

*Titles and Forms of Address: A Guide to Correct Use*, A & C Black, London, 20th edn, 1997

*The Ultimate Guide to Science Fiction: An A–Z of Science Fiction Books by Title*, by D. Pringle, Scolar Press, London, 1995

*Useful Toil: Autobiographies of Working People from the 1820s to the 1970s*, by John Burnett, Penguin Books, Harmondsworth, 1984

*Weather to Travel: The Traveller's Guide to the World's Weather*, by Maria Harding, Tomorrow's Guides Ltd, London, Millennium Edition, 1998

*What Historical Novel Do I Read Next?*, compiled by Daniel S. Burt, The Gale Group, Detroit, USA, 2 vols, 1997

*What It Cost the Day Before Yesterday Book*, by H. Priestley, Kenneth Mason, Emsworth, 1979

*Whitaker's Almanack*, now published annually by The Stationery Office, London

*Willing's Press Guide*, 2 vols, now published annually by Hollis Directories, Teddington, Middx

*Women's Diaries, Journals and Letters: An Annotated Bibliography*, compiled by Cheryl Cline, Garland, New York and London, 1989

*Women's Headdress and Hairstyles in England from AD 600 to the Present Day*, by G. de Courtais, Batsford, London, rev. edn, 1986

*World Climate Disc*, CD-ROM, Chadwyck-Healey, Cambridge, 1995

*World Cruising Handbook*, by Jimmy Cornell, A & C Black, London, 2nd edn, 1991

*The World of the Forsytes*, by John Fisher, Secker & Warburg, London, 1976

*The World Weather Guide*, by E.A. Pearce and C.G. Smith, Helicon, Oxford, new edn, 1998

*Yesterday's Britain: The Illustrated Story of How We Lived, Worked and Played*, Reader's Digest Association, London, 1998

*Note:* Scarecrow Press and McFarland titles are available in the UK through Shelwing Ltd, 127 Sandgate Road, Folkestone, Kent CT20 2BL (tel. 01303 850501; fax 01303 850162). Facts On File titles are distributed in the UK by Michael O'Mara Books Limited, London (order from Biblios PDS, Star Road, Partridge Green, West Sussex RH13 8LD; tel. 01403 710851; fax 01403 711143).

# 6

# Biography and Autobiography

Biographical writing may consist of a short article on a celebrity, past or present, to be published perhaps in commemoration of a centenary or an eightieth birthday, or it may be a full-length study. It sometimes happens that a book grows out of the research undertaken for a newspaper or magazine article. Occasionally biographies are written of people who during their lifetime were neither renowned nor eminent, but whose papers (usually diaries or letters) make a unique contribution to the social history of their time. Autobiographies, whether of celebrities or of lesser mortals, are also of value, provided that they are well researched and well written and not mere exercises in self-promotion or name-dropping.

There is a growing trend for biographies to be written while their subjects are still alive, or very soon after their death; this may have something to do with the fear of the modern biographer that once the biographee and his contemporaries have gone, there may be little material to work on, seeing that letter-writing is a dying art and telephoning an increasing convenience. The academic view of such work, however, is that it constitutes a 'study' or 'profile' of the person concerned rather than a true biography, and that while the study or profile as such may prove to be of inestimable value to a future biographer, it is essential for a certain number of years to have elapsed before any life can be properly evaluated and seen in perspective to its time.

The autobiography of a well-known personality is often published at the peak of that person's career rather than towards the end of his or her life; subsequent volumes may follow. There is much to be said for starting to write your memoirs early on or at least assembling the material – while the people you need to mention are alive and events fresh in your mind. You may not know at that stage whether you will achieve the status that merits a published autobiography, but if in the event you do not, then at least you will have written a piece of family history that can be handed down to the grandchildren. And if you deposit a copy with your local record office or at the Society of Genealogists in London, you will have made a worthwhile contribution towards the social history of the period for which future researchers and historians will be immensely grateful. Such documentation may be rather thin on the ground for researchers of the 21st century!

The author who embarks on a biographical project normally has some good reason for wanting to write it – kinship to the subject, or an intimate working relationship with him or her, and/or the possession of – and access to – original papers. Or, if a number of 'lives' have already been published on the person concerned, the writer may simply have a burning desire to write from a fresh angle, to 'set the record straight' or to throw new light on some controversial aspects as a result of recent research. It is generally accepted that the famous characters of history will stand new biographies every ten years.

Whatever the motive, it is advisable to try to get the work commissioned and – especially where a full-length book is envisaged – to secure a cash advance, for there will be a considerable amount of research to be undertaken and expenses to be met. In calculating the likely total costs, you should not forget to take into account your own working time. Out-of-pocket expenditure will include travel, meals away from home, postal and telephone charges, photocopying, photographs and stationery, at the very least; there may well be 'extras' such as library search fees, fees payable to a genealogist or research assistant, the cost of professional typing and indexing, reproduction fees for illustrations, and so on.

Before a publisher signs a contract, or parts with any money to a writer who is unknown to him, he will normally ask to see a synopsis, or maybe even a chapter or two, of the proposed work. The research that has to be done for the purposes of writing this synopsis is roughly the same as that required for a short biographical article: both must include the salient points of the life and mention the existence of any hitherto unpublished material and/or recent research that provide a new angle. It must be done in sufficient depth so as to convince the potential publisher that the book will be a good investment.

The writer who has reached this stage is bound to be familiar with the outline life of his subject. However, it may not be out of place to record here, as an *aide-mémoire,* the main sources open to biographers and to researchers seeking biographical information for use in other work.

The importance of researching 'in the round' has been stressed in an earlier chapter. In biographical research this is particularly important. It is essential to uncover the whole person, 'warts and all', so that at the research stage nothing should be avoided or glossed over or left unexplored. Motives for a person's actions may be discussed in the final work, and whether the biographer writes from a more or a less sympathetic angle is a matter of interpretation rather than one of research: this is a decision each individual writer must make once he has satisfied himself as to the true facts.

## Private Papers

One good reason for allowing a certain amount of time to elapse before writing a biography is that there may not be access to private papers for a given number of years after a person's death; although the writer may have possession of his subject's own papers and the blessing of the family concerned to make use of them, it is very probable that some relevant material will be contained in the papers of others and that this may be subject to restrictions. Papers deposited in record offices and other archives are normally subject to the thirty-year closure rule or, in special cases, to an even longer period. Permission may be needed from the family or the estate before the documents may be seen. Although the copyright of correspondence belongs to the writer, the actual letters belong to the recipient or to his heirs or executors, or to anyone else who has acquired them; in practice, unless there is some good reason to the contrary, permission is usually forthcoming – but it may be stipulated that the text of the biography must be submitted before going to press. It is important always to make due acknowledgment to the source of such material and to comply with any request for prior submission of the text.

It is true that modern biographies *are* often written without the permission of the subject's family and thus without access to the private papers, but a writer who decides to embark on such a work should be fully aware beforehand of the difficulties that can arise. Quite apart from missing out on material and close family recollections and anecdotes, it may be less easy to obtain other people's help (there is no doubt that when seeking interviews or writing for information, magic phrases such as 'the official biography', 'sanctioned by the family', and so on, do carry weight and often swing the balance in the biographer's favour where someone is hesitant about supplying information). More serious can be the reaction of relatives to an 'unauthorised' biography, with the possibility that if they are seriously displeased they may seek an injunction through the courts.

The location of unpublished source material in general has been discussed in an earlier chapter (see pages 61–7). The biographer needing to find out whether any private papers exist and, if so, their whereabouts, should make his first point of call the National Register of Archives (NRA), maintained by the Royal Commission on Historical Manuscripts at Quality House, Quality Court, Chancery

Lane, London WC2A 1HP. Enquiries should preferably be made in person (a reader's ticket is not required). Limited or specific queries only will be answered by post (or fax, 020 7831 3550) but not by telephone. The Commission's Website is http://www.hmc.gov.uk.

The NRA was set up in 1945 to collect and disseminate information about manuscript sources for British records outside the public records domain. It now consists of more than 40,000 unpublished lists and catalogues of major manuscript collections, including those of private individuals. The database is available on the Internet (direct Telnet access at public.hmc.gov.uk).There are several computerised indexes to the NRA, the most useful for biographical purposes being the Personal Index, which enables the researcher to find details of the nature and location of an individual's own papers as well as that person's correspondence housed in other collections.

The Commission's publications include an ongoing series of *Guide to Sources for British History*, based on private papers and other unpublished information held in the National Register of Archives; the ten volumes published to date include guides to the papers of cabinet ministers, churchmen, colonial governors, diplomats, politicians and scientists (full list on page 72). Another valuable research tool is *Surveys of historical manuscripts in the United Kingdom: a select bibliography*, available in hard copy from the Commission direct, and also on the Internet.

The Department of Manuscripts in the British Library and the Public Record Office are both major sources. Many universities have important holdings. The National Maritime Museum at Greenwich has a comparatively recent manuscript collection of interest to the naval biographer. The Churchill Archives Centre at Churchill College, Cambridge is collecting papers of 20th-century politicians, scientists and both military and naval commanders. To check on other holdings use the 'General Index to Collections' at the back of *British Archives: A Guide to Archive Resources in the United Kingdom*.

The papers of lesser-known persons are more difficult to track down. If you are not in touch with the family or cannot trace any relatives, and the local record office has no deposited papers, you may be able to trace executors or other persons likely to be in possession of a deceased person's papers through a will at First Avenue House (see chapter 7, 'Family and Local History', pages 146-7). If you are writing a biography of someone who lived in the last fifty years, even if you do have access to family and private papers, an advertisement in the national or local press is recommended: many unexpected and valuable 'fish' are netted in this way, in the shape of replies from friends, teachers, colleagues, employees and others who have known or met the subject at some period of his life, and may well produce fascinating and very usable factual or anecdotal material of which you would otherwise remain unaware.

It is important to remember that the papers of even the most eminent public personages contain a certain amount of correspondence from people in lesser walks of life, and if you have reason to believe that the subject of your biography had dealings with someone whose papers have been catalogued and/or deposited, do not overlook this source. When researching for biographical information on professional people, it is always worth contacting the librarian or archivist of the relevant society or institution; some of these bodies hold collections of important private papers and most have biographical information that you may not find easily elsewhere, going back to the date of their foundation.

'Private papers' in this context are not limited to correspondence, but may consist of almost any kind of documentary material, such as account books, scrapbooks and photograph albums, visitors' books, personal diaries, and so on.

# Printed and Other Sources

## Biographical dictionaries

The major source of biographical information on nationals of this country is the *Dictionary of National Biography*, known to scholars, librarians and researchers as 'the *DNB*'. There are 22 main volumes containing entries in alphabetical sequence for persons who died up to 1900, and 10 supplementary volumes up to 1990. A *Missing Persons* volume containing entries for all those worthy persons 'omitted' from the main *DNB* from its beginning up to 1985 was published in 1993. Also very useful is the *Chronological and Occupational Index to the DNB*. Few individuals can afford the money or the shelf space for the complete set, but the *Concise DNB*, in three volumes, should be in every writer's study: it contains entries for every person in the main *DNB*, with finding references to the relevant volume and page number, which you can then look up at the library. A CD-ROM of the complete *DNB* is available. Many foreign countries publish their own equivalent to the *DNB*: these are listed under 'Biography' in *Walford's Guide to Reference Material,* vol. 2, under each country.

Probably the most important biographical reference tool currently in progress is the massive World Biographical Information System launched by K.G. Saur Verlag of Munich in 1982. This consists of a series of *Biographical Archives* on microfiche (23 to date), each supplemented by printed index volumes, and also the *World*

*Biographical Index*, a cumulated index of the *Biographical Archives*, available on CD-ROM and on the Internet. Eventually this mammoth undertaking, which has a wide international, regional and occupational coverage and spans many centuries, will cover the entire world. For some countries there is so much source material that there will be more than one series. The German Biographical Archive was the first to be published, in 1982; like the *British Biographical Archive (BBA)*, which appeared in 1986, it is already in its second series. There are now *Archives* for Africa, America, Australia, China, most European countries and Latin America; also a *Jewish Biographical Archive*. Others in progress and planned include Canada, India, Japan, Korea, Russia, Turkey, a *Biographical Archive of the Classical World* and an *Arab-Islamic Biographical Archive*. A detailed brochure is available from K.G. Saur Verlag, PO Box 701620, 81316 Munich, Germany.

*The Encyclopedia of World Biography*, originally published by McGraw Hill and now by The Gale Group of Detroit, USA, is another major source, comprehensively indexed and cross-referenced. It is currently available in a 17-volume hardback edition, also on CD-ROM. Annual supplements are published, and there is a new 6-volume abridged edition.

The *Biography Index*, published by H.W. Wilson of New York, claims to be international, but has a definite American bias. More useful is the regularly updated *Biography and Genealogy Master Index*, produced by The Gale Group of Detroit, USA, which, in its microfiche cumulative version, is available at most major libraries in the United Kingdom and is known as the 'Bio-Base'. In the current edition some 1,350,000 biographical sketches are indexed, the information being extracted from more than 260 English-language biographical dictionaries and who's who. Birth and death dates are stated, together with the source (in abbreviated form), which may be verified in an accompanying booklet.

With such massive modern tools at the researcher's disposal (see also the subheading 'Bibliographies' below), it seems unnecessary to list the many biographical dictionaries on offer. However, every writer needs at least one for quick reference. Outstanding among such compilations are *Chambers' Biographical Dictionary*, *The Cambridge Biographical Encyclopaedia* and the *St James Guide to Biography*. The best quick reference for contemporary biography is *Who's Who*. There are also eight *Who Was Who* volumes containing entries for those who died during the years 1897–1990, and a *Cumulated Index* volume (1897–1990). *Debrett's People of Today* carries entries for a number of people who have not qualified for inclusion in *Who's Who*.

International reference works of contemporary biography include the *International Who's Who*, the *Dictionary of International Biography* and *Who's Who in International Affairs*. Many foreign countries publish their own *Who's Who* volumes; a selection of these are listed under individual countries in chapter 9 (see pages 162–79). The *Almanach de Gotha*, the definitive who's who of European royalty, has recently reappeared after an absence of more than half a century.

There are now biographical dictionaries and *Who's Who* volumes relating to almost every trade or profession from acting to zoology, some of which are published annually and others at irregular intervals. Readers will find some recommended titles listed by subject in Appendix I (see pages 191–221). These should be easily located in the reference library, or ask at the enquiry desk for them. The *Oxford Companion* series is another useful source of biographical information.

Encyclopedias are invaluable for quick reference, both for contemporary and historical lives; the articles are often followed by a brief bibliography which will lead the researcher on to other sources. The *Who's Who in British History* series covers the British Isles from Roman to Victorian times.

## Bibliographies

If you want to find out whether a biography has been published about a particular individual, your best sources are the *British National Bibliography* (*BNB*) (look under 'Biographies') and the *International Bibliography of Biography 1970–1987*. Try also your own library's subject catalogue.

In Germany a massive international research tool, the *Index Bio-Bibliographicus Notorum Hominum*, is in progress and likely to take many more years. Of the 200 volumes planned, 98 have been published to date and will be found in most major reference libraries; these have recently become available on CD-ROM.

Most scholarly non-fiction works contain up-to-date bibliographies, and if you find there is a recently published study of your subject or of any of his close friends or contemporaries, it will probably be a good investment to buy rather than borrow such a book, so that you can keep it at your elbow and make notes and underlinings in it of special sources, people and places. If you cannot buy the book, then be sure to photocopy the bibliography – it will make an excellent starting point for your research. With luck, it will include references to newspaper and periodical articles. If it does not, you should make a search in the *British Humanities Index* or, if appropriate, one of the earlier subject indexes to periodicals mentioned in chapter 3 (see pages 57–8).

## Obituaries

Obituaries are an excellent source and often the starting point for biographical research, since the more recent notices usually provide both an outline of a person's life and an evaluation of his career.

To find notices of people who died earlier than the mid-19th century, the six-volume *Musgrave's Obituary* is the first place to look; you should also use the *Indexes to the Biographical and Obituary Notices* in the *Gentleman's Magazine* (the two volumes cover the years 1731–1819) and, if you know the approximate year of death, *The Annual Register.* For obituaries of prominent persons who have died since the early 1800s, *The Times* is the best source; in recent years as many as 600 obituary notices have been printed annually in that paper. Provided you have an approximate date of death, a search in *The Times Index* should not take long. There are three published volumes, *Obituaries from The Times*, for the years 1951–60, 1961–70 and 1971–75.

Not everyone you may expect to find in *The Times* has achieved an obituary there (much depends on how many other eminent people died the same day), and so the *Daily Telegraph*, the *Guardian* and the relevant local newspapers should be checked. The local paper of the area in which a person was resident often prints a notice that did not 'make' the nationals or one that goes into greater detail. Professional and trade journals, where appropriate, are especially useful for the evaluation of a person's career.

International notices, but with an American bias, are best checked in the *New York Times Obituaries Index*, from 1858, or in the *New York Times Personal Name Index*, from 1851. For notices relating to persons of other countries, look also at the relevant national paper.

## Diaries, letters and memoirs

A great deal of information will be obtained about a person from the published diaries, letters or memoirs of his friends and contemporaries. As research progresses, therefore, it is an excellent plan to keep an ongoing list of all names that crop up and systematically to check these out at the library. Use the indexes to these books to locate the relevant passages. If you think there may be unpublished journals or correspondence, consult the National Register of Archives, as explained earlier in this chapter under the heading 'Private Papers' (pages 118–20).

## School and university records

School and university records provide excellent source-material, not only for details of a person's scholastic and academic achievement, but also for information concerning his extra-curricular activities (sports, drama, public-speaking, etc.) and – especially important – the names of his contemporaries and friends, school masters and tutors. Should any of these people still be alive, they may have useful contributions to make and can usually be traced through the school or university, or – if they themselves have achieved eminence – in the current *Who's Who*.

The registers of many universities, schools and colleges in the United Kingdom have been printed. If the particular one you seek is not listed in the library catalogue, get in touch with the college or school secretary. Research of this nature may involve you in a visit to the educational establishment concerned, or you may be put in touch with the secretary of the relevant 'Old Boys' or 'Old Girls' association. Don't overlook the college or school magazines, as these will yield important information on your subject's contemporaries as well as (possibly) on his or her own classroom or sporting achievements. Addresses, with names of current headmasters and headmistresses, will be found in the *Independent Schools Yearbook* and the *Education Authorities Directory and Annual*. Universities and colleges are listed in *The World of Learning*. The registers of Oxford and Cambridge, *Alumni Oxonienses* and *Alumni Cantabrigienses*, and A.B. Emden's *Biographical Registers* of both these universities to 1500 are of special value to the historian, while the *Historical Registers* series for Oxford and Cambridge brings the records up to the present day.

## Service records

You should encounter no great problem in obtaining details of a person's Service career. Records more than one hundred years old are held at the Public Record Office, where there are also complete runs of the *Army*, *Navy* and *Air Force Lists*; current volumes of these are usually available in all reference libraries. Guides to the records at the Public Record Office include *Army Records for Family Historians*; *Records of the Militia and Volunteer Forces 1757–1945*; *Army Service Records of the First World War*; *Naval Records for Genealogists*; *Records of the Royal Marines*; *Records of Merchant Shipping and Seamen*; and *RAF Records in the PRO*.

Regimental histories are another good source and may be traced in the Society for Army Historical Research's *Bibliography of Regimental Histories*. J.M. Brereton's *Guide to the Regiments and*

*Corps of the British Army* includes, along with other information, addresses of regimental headquarters to whom to write for further details. Another highly recommended book, now out of print but available in libraries, is G. Hamilton Edwards' *In Search of Army Ancestry.*

So far as naval records are concerned, apart from those mentioned above, the National Maritime Museum has published a useful list, *The Commissioned Sea Officers of the Royal Navy 1660–1815.* Another informative source-book is the *Dictionary of British Ships and Seamen.*

The first port of call for research into Air Force records should be the Royal Air Force Museum (Department of Aviation Records, Grahame Park Way, Hendon, London NW9 5LL; tel. 020 8205 2266; fax 020 8200 1751).

The whereabouts of the records of all three Services can be ascertained from R. Higham's admirable *Guide to the Sources of British Military History.*

## Business records

Details of a person's business career can sometimes be obtained from the organisation or company by whom he was employed. Naturally there are often restrictions on the amount of information that will be divulged to an outsider, but in special circumstances the researcher may be allowed access to the relevant files. Check first in the *Dictionary of Business Biography*, which contains entries for business people active in Britain in the period 1860–1980.

There may be a company history, either published or printed for private circulation, which will provide extremely useful background material. You can check this in the *International Directory of Company Histories* or the *International Bibliography of Business History*. Annual returns and other statutory documents, including lists of all directors and company secretaries, of public, private limited and guarantee companies may be inspected (on microfiche) at Companies House (Department of Trade and Industry), 21 Bloomsbury Street, London WC1B 3XD or the original files at the Companies Registration Office, Crown Way, Maindy, Cardiff CF4 3UZ (for all enquiries tel. 029 2038 0801); a modest search fee is payable per file, and there are full photocopying facilities. The Business Archives Council, 3rd/4th floors, 101 Whitechapel High Street, London E1 7RE (tel. 020 7247 0024; fax 020 7422 0026), maintains a library and will advise researchers about records available; its Scottish counterpart, the Business Archives Council of Scotland, is at Glasgow University Archives and Business Records Centre, 13 Thurso Street, Glasgow

GL11 6PE (tel. 0141-330 4543; fax 0141-330 4158). Researchers may also make use of the British Library Business Information Service in the Science 3 reading room at the British Library, 96 Euston Road, London NW1 2DB (tel. 020 7412 7457; fax 020 7412 7453).

## Members of Parliament and government officials

*Dod's Parliamentary Companion*, first published in 1832, is the indispensable British biographical source-book for the modern period. Earlier information will be found in the Institute of Historical Research series (12 volumes published to date), *Office Holders in Modern Britain*. There is one volume per ministry, some of the lists beginning in 1660 and covering the entire period up to 1870; recent additions to the series are volumes on officials of Royal Commissions of Inquiry 1870–1939 and on officers of the Royal Household. Another good source is the 4-volume *Members of Parliament*, in which you will find the names of all MPs in England from 1213 and in Scotland and Ireland from 1357 and 1559 respectively; the lists continue up to 1874, for the United Kingdom, and there is an index volume. For further information, or if you fail to find what you are seeking in printed sources, write to the Clerk of the Records at the House of Lords Record Office, House of Lords, London SW1A 0PW. For the location of private papers of Members of Parliament and selected public servants, consult the Royal Commission on Historic Manuscripts' *Guides to Sources for British History*, volumes 1 (*Papers of British cabinet ministers 1782–1900*) and 7 (*Papers of British politicians 1782–1900*), and the *Guide to the Papers of British Cabinet Ministers 1900–1951*, published by the Royal Historical Society. The papers of a number of 19th-century British prime ministers, statesmen and politicians are marketed on microfilm by Primary Source Media (The Gale Group) of Reading.

## Public speeches and broadcasts

Speeches of significance are usually reported in the national press and may be traced in *The Times Index* either under the speaker's name or under the name of the society or conference addressed. The texts of Members' speeches in Parliament are printed in *Hansard: Parliamentary Debates* (separate series for the House of Commons and the House of Lords). Lectures or papers read before learned or professional bodies will normally be found in the transactions or proceedings of such institutions at a later date.

To check on broadcast or televised speeches and interviews, your best plan is first to contact the British Library National Sound Archive,

96 Euston Road, London NW1 2DB (tel. 020 7412 7440; fax 020 7412 7441); an appointment will be made for you to listen to or view the relevant transmission, provided it is in their collections. (Note that the NSA includes a collection of Parliamentary sound recordings.) Once you have ascertained the date, it may be possible to obtain a transcript from the BBC Written Archives Centre at Peppard Road, Caversham Park, Reading RG4 8TZ (tel. 0118 946 9280/1/2; fax 0118 946 1145) or the independent radio or television company. (The availability of transcripts is subject to certain copyright restrictions.)

## Travel

Obtaining information about a person's travel may be unexpectedly complicated, where no diary or travelogue was kept. Hotel registers and shipping company records are not always retained for more than a few years, although it is always worth asking. (For example, the P & O Group's archives were deposited at the National Maritime Museum in Greenwich in the autumn of 1977.)

British Transport historical records are now at the Public Record Office in Kew, and so are the records of the former Board of Trade (now the Department of Trade and Industry) from c. 1890; the latter contain lists of all arrivals in, and departures from, the United Kingdom, but only a sample (roughly one-tenth) of passengers' lists and ships' logs, so that it is very much a matter of luck whether the information you seek will be obtainable. For more recent information you should contact the Library and Information Service of the Department of the Environment, Transport and the Regions, Ashdown House Information Centre, 123 Victoria Street, London SW1E 6DE (tel. 020 7890 3039; fax 020 7890 6098); you may be directed to one of several site libraries in London. Factual details such as dates of departure, ports of call, tonnage and which company owns a particular vessel may be quite easily verified in *Lloyd's Shipping Index* or *Lloyd's Voyage Record*.

# Further Research

Having cast your net, and hauled in your initial catch of material, your next task will be to sort the documentation into periods, or other natural chapters, of the life and, as you proceed, to make a note of any supplementary research to be undertaken. For a short biographical feature or the synopsis of a book, you can fairly safely rely on the standard or most recent work, plus your own special knowledge; but if you are embarking on a full-length biography you must go through and evaluate for yourself all the published material. It is a good idea to make index cards or slips for each book or article read, and to keep these in alphabetical sequence; this will take only a few minutes at the time and will be of immense value both for quick reference as you write and at the end of the day, when it comes to compiling the bibliography (see chapter 10, 'Preparation for the Press', page 182).

Some professional help may be required for your chapter on family ancestry (see chapter 8, 'Specialist Research', pages 141–5) and if so, this should be arranged at the earliest possible moment, as good genealogists are frequently booked up for several months ahead. At the same time the question of employing outside researchers should also be carefully considered: where the source material is located at some distance from your home, or if it is essential to go through several years of a particular paper that is available only at the British Library Newspaper Library at Colindale, for instance, it may pay you to off-load part of the routine research and leave yourself free to tackle the more complicated aspects of the work.

Inevitably some travelling will be involved, and it makes sense to plan this so that several sources and/or interviews can be combined on each trip. A visit to the family home, if it still exists, is essential, and on such a visit time must be allowed for conversations with local inhabitants and – particularly important – with anyone close to the family who is still alive, such as a gardener, nanny or cook, where appropriate, or perhaps the vicar or local schoolmaster or publican. It goes without saying that this applies only when you are researching for biographies of people who are either still alive or recently deceased; in the case of subjects who were born, say, earlier than 1900, you have no choice but to rely on documentary sources such as the local newspaper or church magazine, or the records of any local societies with which the family is known to have been connected. The local librarian or secretary of the local historical society will usually be helpful in this respect, and you could strike lucky in that the descendants of an old family retainer may have cherished stories handed down verbally from one generation to the next, along with old photographs or other mementoes, so that any opportunity of visiting such people should always be taken up.

Corroboration of family births, marriages and deaths since 1837 may be obtained at the Family Records Centre, and of divorces, wills and administrations (since 1858) from the Principal Registry of the Family Division now at First Avenue House (for details and how to trace earlier records, see chapter 7, 'Family and Local History', pages 137–56). To verify the date of an engagement you may need to search the appropriate pages of *The Times, Daily Telegraph* or local paper; these papers will also carry reports of christenings, weddings, funerals and memorial services in the case of prominent members of society.

If the subject of your biography was involved in any major legal proceedings, you will be able to check this in the *All England Law Reports*, which begin in 1558 and are indexed; or use *The Times Index* and look up the law report in that paper (these have been published since January 1788). Once you have the date of the court proceedings you can, if you require a more popular account or a 'sensational' headline to quote, then go to other newspapers of the same date. Those who do not have access to law libraries (normally open only to members of the profession) may like to know that there is a complete set of the *All England Law Reports* on the open shelves at Holborn Public Library, 32–38 Theobalds Road, London WC1X 8PA (tel. 020 7413 6345).

# Special Problems

The problems most likely to crop up during research for an auto-biography or a biography are the following:

## Names

In private correspondence and diaries people are often mentioned by nickname or given name only, and their identity may not be clear to you at the outset of research. It is an excellent idea to keep an alphabetical list or card index of everyone who crops up in the course of your work on a biography; apart from its value to you personally as a private 'who's who' of identification, it will come in very useful should any editorial note be required and also later on for the index. Among pitfalls to avoid are the danger of confusing titles (always check on which duke or earl you are referring to at any one time) and the various names by which a woman may be known during her life, due to a series of marriages and/or divorces and the possibility that she may have reverted to her maiden name for professional or other reasons. To add to the confusion, titled persons are sometimes referred to by title and sometimes by surname, which may not be the same.

## Dating letters

Letters all too frequently present the biographer with unforeseen problems. Far too many people had (and still have) the habit of dating their correspondence 'Thursday', 'Sunday, 12th' or 'Amsterdam,

Monday', or – which is worse from the researcher's point of view – of not dating them at all. You should also be aware that some individuals are prone to stuff free hotel or club stationery into their briefcases and to use it weeks or even months later, so that although such correspondence may be dated, you cannot be absolutely certain that the writer was actually resident at the hotel or club at the time: if there is any doubt at all in your mind on this score, try to verify the date and/or place in another source.

Some expert detective work will sometimes be needed before you can establish the correct chronological sequence of a bundle of correspondence. The most obvious clues are: the address from which the letter is, or is alleged to be, written; the person to whom it is written; the subject-matter. Look also at the handwriting; the ink; the paper: should there be a watermark, this will not give you the precise date of the letter, but it will provide firm evidence that the document cannot have been written earlier than the date of the watermark.

If, on first reading, a letter does not appear to offer any clue of this kind, do not despair. Re-examine it closely for mention of any family, national or world event – perhaps the death of a well known person, an exhibition or play seen, a new novel read, and so on, the dates of which can then be checked out in the national press, *Whitaker's Almanack* and other sources. Letters that you cannot even guess at dating should be kept apart from the rest; sooner or later, as work progresses, you are more than likely to stumble on some information (nearly always when you are not looking for it) that will enable you to slot such letters into their right sequence. The use of the *Handbook of Dates for Students of English History* for checking the day of the week of given dates has been explained on page 99.

Handwriting is a great revealer of character, and in recent years many biographers have sought the help of trained graphologists (a trend which has spread from France). However, you should not be tempted to try to do it yourself with the aid of any one of a number of books on the subject, entertaining as many of them are (on doodles, for example), as you could go very wrong. It takes years to qualify as a professional graphologist; there are approximately only 100 in the United Kingdom with an internationally recognised diploma. Costs depend on the depth of the analysis required. At the Graphology Bureau Ltd, The Studio, 1B Limpsfield Avenue, London SW19 6DL (tel/fax 020 8780 9530) there is a minimum charge of £100. If you decide to ask for an analysis, you will need to send a selection of original, not photocopied or faxed, letters or other documents, preferably of varying dates. Before embarking on this course, you may like to read an article, 'Graphology and the Biographer', by the graphologist Mary Nicholson in the winter 1994 issue of *The Author*.

# Verbal information

It is beyond the scope of this chapter to examine in detail all the possibilities open to the biographical researcher, but if the basic principle is followed of taking each natural phase of the life in turn, verifying dates and events in printed and other records and supplementing the documentary material with the recollections of contemporaries wherever obtainable, you will not go far wrong. A word of warning about the use of verbal information, however: human nature being what it is, people do frequently tend to try to enhance their own status (either in the researcher's eyes or their own or with a view to their name appearing in print) by exaggerating their intimacy or acquaintance with a well-known person, and memories in general are, sadly, far from infallible. Similarly with autobiography. How many of us can rely on being able to recall with 100 per cent accuracy the exact sequence of events in a particular week or how passionately we felt about something or someone, say, twenty or more years ago? We *think* we remember. But *do we – truthfully?* Imagining how it was is a poor substitute for the comment recorded at the time. The human memory plays strange tricks. Always therefore make a point of double-checking any story that is told to you or any event you think you remember. If you cannot verify it from a reliable printed source, try to get corroboration from a second person. Confidences must, of course, be respected at all times, and care must be taken to avoid giving offence to relatives or other persons who are still alive. Where private individuals have been especially helpful or informative, it is good manners to let them see the draft text before going to press, and to acknowledge their assistance in the book.

Happily for the responsible writer of biography and autobiography in Britain, the 'infringement of privacy' legislation under discussion a few years ago, and mentioned in my previous edition, appears to have been put on hold for the time being, if not scrapped altogether. The traditional liberty to portray one's subject 'warts and all' is sacrosanct.

*Air Force List*, published annually since 1949, formerly by HMSO, now by The Stationery Office, London

*All England Law Reports*: reprint 1558–1935, 36 vols + index, published 1966–68; since 1936 weekly, with 4 bound vols and cumulative index annually, Butterworth Publishers, London

*Almanach de Gotha*, 1998; updated 1999 (available from Boydell & Brewer Ltd, PO Box 9, Woodbridge, Suffolk IP12 3DF)

*Alumni Cantabrigienses: A Biographical List of all known Students,*

*Graduates and Holders of Office to 1900*, by J. and J.A. Venn, 10 vols, Cambridge University Press, 1940–54; Kraus reprint, 1974

*Alumni Oxonienses: The Members of the University of Oxford 1500–1886*, by J. Foster, 8 vols, Parker, Oxford, 1888–92; Kraus reprint, 1968

*The Annual Register of World Events*, published since 1758; now by Keesings Worldwide, Washington D.C. (UK office: 69A Lensfield Road, Cambridge CB2 1EN)

*Army List*, first published 1814, now annually by The Stationery Office (formerly HMSO), London (an earlier series from 1754 may be seen at the PRO, Kew)

*Army Records for Family Historians*, by Simon Fowler and William Spencer, PRO Publications, London, rev. edn, 1998

*Army Service Records of the First World War*, by Simon Fowler, William Spencer and Stuart Tamblin, PRO Publications, London, rev. edn, 1998

*Bibliography of Regimental Histories*, compiled by A.S. White, Society for Army Historical Research with The Army Museums Ogilby Trust, London, 1965. (Now out of print, but the library of the National Army Museum, Royal Hospital Road, London SW3 4HT (tel. 020 7730 0717) maintains a regularly updated interleaved version)

*Biographical Archive*, ongoing international series published on microfiche by Saur, Munich, in progress since 1982; printed index volumes and cumulative *World Biographical Index*, on CD-ROM and on the Internet

*Biographical Register of the University of Cambridge to 1500*, by A.B. Emden, Cambridge University Press, Cambridge, 1963

*Biographical Register of the University of Oxford to 1500*, by A.B. Emden, 3 vols, Oxford University Press, Oxford, 1957–59; reissued 1989. *Supplement 1501–1540*, 1974

*Biography and Genealogy Master Index*, published by Gale Research International (now The Gale Group), Detroit, USA, 2nd edn, 1980–81, plus 14 updated vols, 1982–95; 1999 edn, published 1998; 2000 edn, published 1999; abridged 2nd edn, 3 vols, 1995. On microfiche as *Bio-Base 1996–99* and *Bio-Base 1995 Master Cumulation*

*Biography Index*, published by H.W. Wilson, New York, since 1946; now updated quarterly on CD-ROM, magnetic tape and in print; monthly online

*British Archives: A Guide to Archive Resources in the United Kingdom*, by Janet Foster and Julia Sheppard, Macmillan, London, 4th edn, 1998

*British Biographical Archive (BBA)*, on microfiche, with 4 vols printed index, Saur, Munich, 1984–88; Series II, 1991–94

*British Humanities Index (BHI)*, first published 1915; quarterly 1963–89, with annual cumulations, by the Library Association, London, and from January 1990 quarterly by Bowker-Saur, East Grinstead; available on CD-ROM as *BHI Plus*, annually since 1985, with quarterly updates

*British National Bibliography (BNB)*, weekly since 1950, with cumulative monthly, annual and some 5-yearly volumes; now published by British Library National Bibliographic Service, Wetherby, on various subscription options (printed, microfiche and CD-ROM); there is a complete set from 1950 on two CD-ROMs, also two cumulations on microfiche, 1950–1984 and 1981–1992. There is a complete *BNB* file on BLAISE

*The Cambridge Biographical Encyclopedia*, ed. David Crystal, Cambridge University Press, Cambridge, 2nd edn, 1998

*Chambers' Biographical Dictionary*, first published 1897; centenary edn, Chambers Harrap, Edinburgh, 1997

*The Commissioned Sea Officers of the Royal Navy 1660–1815*, National Maritime Museum, London, 1954

*Debrett's People of Today*, published by Debrett's Peerage, London, annually since 1990; available on CD-ROM from 1997

*Dictionary of British Ships and Seamen*, by G. Uden and R. Cooper, Allen Lane, Harmondsworth, 1980

*Dictionary of Business Biography*, ed. David J. Jeremy, 5 vols, Butterworth, London, 1984–86

*Dictionary of International Biography*, published since 1963; 26th edn, Melrose Press, Cambridge, 1998

*Dictionary of National Biography (DNB)*: to 1900, 22 vols, Oxford University Press, London, 1885–1900; 10 later vols, for the period 1901–1990, published 1912–96. *The Concise DNB*, to 1985, 3 vols, 1992. *A Chronological and Occupational Index to the DNB*, 1985. *Missing Persons*, 1993. CD-ROM edition of complete *DNB*, 1995

*Dod's Parliamentary Companion*, published annually since 1832 by Dod's Parliamentary Companion Ltd, London

*Education Authorities Directory and Annual*, published by the School Government Publishing Company, Redhill

*Encyclopedia of World Biography*, 2nd edn, 17 vols, The Gale Group, Detroit, 1998; also on CD-ROM. *1998 Supplement* (vol 18), 1998; abridged edn, 3 vols, 1999

*Gentleman's Magazine: Index to the Biographical and Obituary Notices*, 2 vols: *1731–1780*, British Record Society, London, 1891; *1781–1819*, by B. Nangle, Garland Publishing, New York and London, 1980

'Graphology and the Biographer', by Mary Nicholson, *The Author*, Society of Authors, winter 1994

*Guide to the Papers of British Cabinet Ministers 1900–1951*, compiled by C. Hazelhurst and C. Woodland, Royal Historical Society, London, 1974; new edn published by Cambridge University Press for the Society, 1996

*Guide to the Regiments and Corps of the British Army*, by J.M. Brereton, Bodley Head, London, 1985

*Guide to Sources for British History*, Royal Commission on Historical Manuscripts, London, in progress since 1982, 11 vols to date (see list on page 72)

*Guide to the Sources of British Military History*, ed. R. Higham, Routledge, London, 1972; supplement, ed. G. Jordan, Garland, New York and London, 1988

*Handbook of Dates for Students of English History*, ed. C.R. Cheney, Royal Historical Society, London, first published 1945; latest reprint, with corrections, published by Cambridge University Press for the Society, 1996; new edn due February 2000

*Hansard: Parliamentary Debates (House of Commons and House of Lords)*, 1803 onwards; now published daily during sessions by The Stationery Office (formerly HMSO), London. Chadwyck-Healey, Cambridge, publishes various series of Reports and Parliamentary Papers from 1715 on microfilm, microfiche and CD-ROM

*Historical Register* series (Universities of Cambridge and Oxford): Cambridge University Press and Oxford University Press respectively

*In Search of Army Ancestry*, by G. Hamilton-Edwards, Phillimore, Chichester, 1977

*Independent Schools Yearbook (Boys' Schools, Girls' Schools, Co-educational Schools and Preparatory Schools)*, published annually by A & C Black, London

*Index Bio-Bibliographicus Notorum Hominum*, Biblio Verlag, Osnabruck, in progress, 1972– (98 vols to date); also on CD-ROM

*International Bibliography of Biography 1970–1987*, published by Bowker, New Providence, N.J., 12 vols, 1988

*International Bibliography of Business History*, compiled by S. Goodhall, Routledge, London, 1996

*International Directory of Company Histories*, St James Press, now part of The Gale Group, Detroit, USA, in progress, 1988– (29 vols to date)

*International Who's Who*, published annually by Europa Publications, London

*Jewish Biographical Archive*, on microfiche, Saur, Munich, 1994–96

*Lloyd's Shipping Index*, first published as *Lloyds Weekly Index* in 1882, now weekly by Lloyd's of London Press, Colchester, Essex

*Lloyd's Voyage Record*, published weekly since 1946 by Lloyd's of London Press, Colchester, Essex

*Members of Parliament*, 4 vols: I–II, *England 1213–1702*; III, *Great Britain 1705–1796, United Kingdom 1801–1874, Scotland 1357–1707, Ireland 1559–1800*; IV, *Index*, HMSO, London, 1878–91

*Musgrave's Obituary prior to 1800*, ed. Sir G.J. Armytage, 6 vols, Harleian Society, London, 1899–1901

*Naval Records for Genealogists*, by N.A.M. Rodger, PRO Publications, London, 1998

*Navy List*, published annually since 1814, now by The Stationery Office, London (formerly HMSO); earlier listings at PRO, Kew

*New York Times Obituaries Index*, from 1858; cumulative volumes 1858–1968 and 1969–79, Glen Rock, N.J., now annually by Mecklen Corporation, N.Y.

*New York Times Personal Name Index 1851–1974*; supplement *1975–1984*, compiled by B.A. and V.R. Falk, Roxbury Data, Succasunna, N.J.

*Obituaries from The Times*, 3 vols covering the period 1951–75, Research Publications International (now Primary Source Media), Reading, 1975–79; no later vols

*Office Holders in Modern Britain*, Institute of Historical Research, London, 12 vols, 1972–98; recent additions to series: vol 10, *Officials of Royal Commissions of Inquiry 1870–1939*, compiled by E. Harrison, 1995; vols 11 and 12, *Officers of the Royal Household 1660–1870: Part 1, Department of the Lord Chamberlain and Associated Offices*; *Part 2, Departments of the Lord Steward and the Master of the Horse*, compiled by J.C. Sainty and R.O. Bucholz, 1997, 1998. Further vols in preparation

*Oxford Companion* series (over 40 titles), Oxford University Press, Oxford, regularly revised; some paperback editions

*Papers of British cabinet ministers 1782–1900*, Royal Commission on Historical Manuscripts Commission, *Guide to Sources for British History No. 1*, London, 1982

*Papers of British politicians 1782–1900*, Royal Commission on Historical Manuscripts Commission, *Guide to Sources for British History No. 7*, London, 1989

*RAF Records in the PRO*, by Simon Fowler, Peter Elliott, Roy Conyers Nesbit and Christina Goulter, PRO Publications, London, 1994

*Records of the Militia and Volunteer Forces 1757–1945*, by William Spencer, PRO Publications, London, 1997

*Records of Merchant Shipping and Seamen*, by Kelvin Smith, Christopher T. Watts and Michael J. Watts, PRO Publications, London, 1998

*Records of the Royal Marines*, by Garth Thomas, PRO Publications, London, 1994

*St James Guide to Biography*, St James Press, Detroit, 1991

*Surveys of historical manuscripts in the United Kingdom: a select bibliography*, 3rd edn, 1997, available only from the Royal Commission of Historical Manuscripts, Quality House, Quality Court, Chancery Lane, London WC2A 1HP; also on the Internet

*The Times Index*, first published 1790; now monthly with annual cumulations, Primary Source Media, Reading; *Palmer's Index to The Times, 1790–1905*, on CD-ROM, Chadwyck-Healey, Cambridge

*Walford's Guide to Reference Material*, vol. 2, *Social and Historical Sciences, Philosophy and Religion*, eds Alan Day and Michael Walsh, Library Association, London, 7th edn, 1997

*Whitaker's Almanack*, published annually by The Stationery Office, London

*Who Was Who*, published by A & C Black, London, 9 vols to date, covering the period 1897–1995; *Cumulated Index 1897–1990*; also available on CD-ROM as *Who's Who 1897–1996*, published jointly by A & C Black and Oxford University Press

*Who's Who*, published annually by A & C Black, London

*Who's Who in British History*, Shepheard Walwyn, London, 8 vols, hardback and paperback editions

*Who's Who in International Affairs*, Europa Publications, London, 2nd edn, 1998

*World Biographical Index*, Saur, Munich, 6th CD-ROM edn, 1999; also online

*The World of Learning*, published annually by Europa Publications, London

*Note:* Space does not permit a full listing of the *Who's Who* volumes for the various professions and foreign countries, of which there are now over 70 titles published by different firms; the researcher should have no difficulty in tracing these in the major library cataloguing systems. Selected titles are listed in chapter 9 under country and by subject in Appendix I.

# 7

# Family and Local History

In recent years people have become increasingly interested in tracing their own family ancestry. Largely as a result of teaching in schools and evening classes, many students embark on a local or family history project which they later wish to develop into a full-length study. Biographers and authors of historical novels also need to do some research in this field, and some of the problems they are likely to encounter have been outlined in chapters 4 and 6, 'Factual and Historical Research' and 'Biography and Autobiography'.

The first thing to be aware of is that research for family or local history can be exceedingly complex and costly, both in terms of research time and search fees. For those who look on it as a hobby and for whom time is no object, it will be a lengthy and often frustrating, but always in the end rewarding, task. Writers with publishers' press deadlines to meet, and who need only certain facts to fill out their work – for example, ancestral research for the first chapter of a biography, or the tracing of a particular will, or the detail of some event in a certain parish needed for an historical novel – should consider using the services of a professional genealogist or record agent (see 'Specialist Research', pages 157–61). Those who wish to undertake their own research in this field should be prepared to do a considerable amount of preliminary study so as to familiarise themselves with the classes of records available and the kind of information to be derived from them.

Space does not permit to do more here than suggest the major sources of information, as well as some of the standard textbooks on genealogy and local archives. Most adult education centres run courses on local history and genealogy, but very few on palaeography (the study of old handwriting). For details of a comprehensive course, leading to a diploma, that may be followed on a full- or part-time basis, or as a correspondence course, write to the Registrar, Institute of Heraldic and Genealogical Studies, 79–82 Northgate, Canterbury, Kent CT1 1BA (tel. 01227 768664; fax 01227 765617).

The Society of Genealogists, 14 Charterhouse Buildings, Goswell Road, London EC1M 7BA (tel. 020 7251 8799; fax 020 7250 1800) periodically organises day-conferences and lectures for beginners (members only). Members of the Society have free use of the library, with its unique collection of printed, manuscript, microfiche and microfilmed material (including the largest collection of parish register copies in the country), free attendance at lectures and the benefit of a reduced rate for research carried out by members of the staff; they also receive a quarterly journal, *Genealogists' Magazine*. The Society's other quarterly periodical, *Computers in Genealogy*, is offered to members at a reduced subscription. A leaflet, 'Using the Library of the Society of Genealogists', is available. The writer who intends to do any extensive genealogical research, and who lives in or with good access to London, will find membership very worthwhile. Non-members may use the library on payment of a small fee, currently £3.00 for one hour, £8.00 for four hours, £12.00 for a day, or a day and evening, and may subscribe to both publications.

There are family history societies and local history groups in most counties of the United Kingdom. Subscriptions are modest, and members benefit from advice on their researches as well as the exchange of information with fellow genealogists and historians. An up-to-date list of these societies, giving the secretaries' names and addresses, is available on receipt of a first-class stamped addressed envelope or two international reply coupons from the Administrator, Federation of Family History Societies (FFHS), c/o Benson Room, Birmingham & Midland Institute, Margaret Street, Birmingham B3 3BS.

A subscription to the Guild of One-Name Studies, which is closely associated with the Society of Genealogists and the FFHS, would be worthwhile in the long term, but probably not if you are engaged on a 'one-off' search for the ancestry chapter of one book. Members receive a quarterly journal, *One-Name Studies*, and also a Register listing the names that are currently being researched worldwide, with the name and address of a 'registered member' to contact for information on each name. Members may register a name for a small fee, provided it has not already been registered; but when you do this, you give an undertaking to deal with all reply-paid enquiries about that name – so consider carefully before you commit yourself (it could be a drain on your writing time!). The Hon. Secretary of the Guild may be contacted at Box G, 14 Charterhouse Buildings, Goswell Road, London EC1M 7BA.

The leading publishers of family and local history in this country are Phillimore & Co. Ltd, Shopwyke Manor Barn, Chichester, West Sussex PO20 6BG (tel. 01243 787636; fax 01243 787639) and Sutton Publishing, Phoenix Mill, Thrupp, Stroud, Gloucestershire GL5 2BU (tel. 01453 731114; fax 01453 731117). The Phillimore bookshop, at Shopwyke Manor Barn (see above), also stocks titles from other publishers and will supply books by post. Ask to be put on their catalogue mailing list. There is also a bookshop at the Society of Genealogists. Both the Society of Genealogists, FFHS and *Family Tree Magazine* publish handbooks and leaflets to assist the amateur family and local historian; these are updated regularly.

Among a number of journals of interest are *Family History News and Digest*, published twice a year (April and September) by the FFHS; *Family Tree Magazine*; *The Local Historian* (formerly *The Amateur Historian*); and *Practical Family History*. A subscription to the annual *Genealogical Research Directory* entitles you to register up to fifteen names in which you are interested; the book is circulated throughout the world and may eventually bring you the bonus of an exchange of information with other subscribers.

# Using County Record Offices, Archaeological Societies and Other Collections

Your first port of call, when embarking on a family or local history, should be your local record office, where the archivist or an assistant archivist will usually be glad to discuss the project and to explain what records are available. Some county record offices publish useful pamphlets for students on how to trace the history of a parish or of a family, and most have a printed or microfiche guide to their collections, as well as regularly updated lists of parish registers and other documents that have been deposited.

A short list of record offices will be found in Appendix I, but more detailed information is contained in the booklet *Record Repositories in Great Britain*. An excellent guide is J.S.W. Gibson and P. Peskett's *Record Offices: How to Find Them*. Jane Cox's *New to Kew?* will help those unfamiliar with the PRO to find their way through the labyrinth of sources available there.

The principal public libraries have local history collections, and those of local archaeological societies are usually open to *bona fide* researchers (non-members may be asked to pay a modest search fee). Where information is needed from outside your own district, it is always worth sending a preliminary letter (with self-addressed stamped envelope) to the local archivist or chief reference librarian. Most county archivists are happy to answer simple enquiries, such as the verification of not more than one or two entries in a parish register (a baptism, marriage or burial), but especially nowadays, owing to the severe cutback in local government expenditure, staff cannot undertake extensive searches. However, advice will always be given on the records available for consultation, as well as practical help over any problems encountered in the search room; and most county record offices will, on request, also supply the names and addresses of local record agents. Occasionally a record office or public library will offer to do research for you, on a fee-paying basis; however, it has to be said that you will almost certainly obtain results faster by employing a freelance record agent direct. You should nevertheless always enquire on your first visit whether there is any member of staff who happens to have a special knowledge of, or interest in, your subject. Photocopies and photographs of most documents are usually obtainable.

A list of local archaeological societies, with names and addresses of secretaries, will be found in *Whitaker's Almanack*.

# Family History

A family history may have as its starting point a rough tree drawn up by a relative or ancestor, or – if you are lucky – a more professional pedigree and possibly also a collection of papers handed down from one generation to another or recently discovered in an attic of the ancestral home. The first thing to do is to make reasonably sure that a history has not already been written or a tree drawn up. This can be checked in one of several ways: in the catalogue or subject index of one of the copyright libraries; at the library of the Society of Genealogists; at the College of Arms; at the local record office nearest to the family home. Remember that many family histories are privately printed or may have been deposited at the record office, or donated to the local library, in typescript.

If the family is likely to have been recorded in any of Burke's publications, the place to look is *Burke's Family Index*. This useful volume has references to some twenty thousand different family histories.

The next step is to verify, one by one, the dates of all births, marriages and deaths, and – other people's memories being what they are – also to check the names, allowing for variations in spelling. The usual procedure is to work methodically backwards in time, either from yourself or from the person you are writing about, first to the parents, then the grandparents, and so on, generation by generation. If you are fortunate enough to own a personal computer, you could invest in some specially designed software to help you store and sort the fruits of your research. Alternatively, set up a card index system, with a separate card for each individual, on which you enter each piece of information as it is verified; or there are specially printed genealogical record cards or 'research work-books' on the market (available from the Society of Genealogists, among others).

You can draw up your own draft family tree as you proceed; but if the tree is to be published, it is best to have it professionally drawn.

Terrick Fitzhugh's *How to Write a Family History*, although out of print, is highly recommended reading for the beginner.

## Verifying births, marriages and deaths

Since 1 July 1837 all births, marriages and deaths in England and Wales, together with some overseas (consular) and service returns, births and deaths at sea, etc., have been centrally recorded at the General Register Office (GRO) in London. Formerly at St Catherine's House, these records are now kept at the Family Records Centre (FRC), 1 Myddleton Street, London EC1R 1UW. In Scotland registration began in 1855, the records being housed at the office of the Registrar General, New Register House, Edinburgh EH1 3YT. In Ireland, the records from 1864 to 1921 are at the office of the Registrar General, Joyce House, 8–11 Lombard Street East, Dublin 2, for the whole of the country and for the Republic since 1922; Northern Ireland records dating from partition are in the care of the Registrar General, Oxford House, 49–55 Chichester Street, Belfast BT1 4HL.

In London searches may be made in person at the Family Records Centre, where there is a computerised link to the indexes at the GRO in Scotland. It should be remembered that access is to the indexes only, not to the actual registers. The index volumes are arranged according to the quarter of the year in which the event (birth, marriage or death) was registered, and alphabetically under surnames. Unless you have an approximate date to go on, you must be prepared for a long haul – and an exhausting one, as pulling out one heavy volume after another is exceedingly tiring. The information printed in the indexes is minimal, so that sometimes you may not be certain that you have found the correct entry; but if you request a copy of the relevant certificate and the parentage and/or spouse does not match with the information you have to give on the application form, a refund will be made. As full certificates now cost £6.50 apiece, this is an important consideration. (There is a shorter form of certificate – available for births only – but this is insufficient for genealogical research purposes as it contains only the name, sex, date and place, but *not* the parentage.)

There is an Adopted Children's Register from 1927 at the FRC, and adopted persons over the age of 18 may apply there for their original birth certificate.

It is always worth getting copies of birth, marriage and death certificates, as the detail given on them, such as the occupation of a child's father, the witnesses to a marriage, the cause of death and the address at which it occurred, will be invaluable and may lead you on to other channels of enquiry. For those who live a long way from London (or Edinburgh, Dublin or Belfast), copies of certificates may be obtained by post, in which case a higher fee is charged (currently £9.00 if you supply the GRO Index reference or £12.00 without a reference; this includes a search carried out by staff over a five-year period). Certificates ordered in person at the FRC are available for collection after four working days, or will be posted first class on the fourth day. Postal applications, with cheque or postal order payable to 'ONS' should be sent to the General Register Office, PO Box 2, Southport, Merseyside PR8 2JD; if the GRO Index reference is quoted, certificates will be posted within ten days, without a reference within twenty-eight days. A priority service is available by post, telephone or fax, with payment by credit or debit card; certificates will be posted on the day following receipt of application (tel. 0151-471 4816; fax 01704 550013).

The best starting point for family history research is the Family Records Centre. This joint facility provided by the Office for National Statistics (ONS) and the Public Record Office was officially opened in July 1997. At 1 Myddleton Street, London EC1R 1UW, the FRC is within walking distance of several other major sources such as the London Metropolitan Archives, the Society of Genealogists, and the Probate Search Rooms at First Avenue House, High Holborn. A useful photocopy map of the area is available from the Centre, showing public transport; there are also instructions on how to get from the FRC to the PRO at Kew. The staff are friendly and helpful; a series of leaflets on how to use the various facilities may be picked up from the New Customers Desk on the first floor, where there is also a Research Enquiries Desk. There is also a printed handbook: *Never Been Here Before? A Genealogist's Guide to the Family Records Centre*, by Jane Cox and Stella Colwell.

As well as the indexes to births, marriages and deaths mentioned above, other records kept at the FRC include miscellaneous foreign returns of births, marriages and deaths; census returns and PCC Wills (see below under relevant headings); death duty and non-conformist registers; a microfiche copy of the 1992 International Genealogical Index (IGI); and ten sets of *Family Search*, a series of databases on CD-ROM compiled by and for the Mormons. This last important source for family historians has proved so popular that in busy periods its use is limited to one hour.

The mammoth International Genealogical Index of some 187 million names, mostly birth and baptismal (but also some marriage) entries dating from the early 1500s, compiled and computerised by the Genealogical Department of the Church of Jesus Christ of Latter-

Day Saints (known more familiarly as the Mormon Church) at Salt Lake City, Utah, USA, is a major research tool for all genealogists. It is updated approximately every four or five years. Entries in the IGI are alphabetical by surname within each county. Users should however be aware that it is neither comprehensive nor, sadly, 100 per cent accurate: coverage and accuracy vary from county to county, and the information should always be double-checked in original sources. Nevertheless it is an essential starting point for anyone embarking on family history research.

By using the *Family Search* CD-ROM system of databases researchers are able to access both the IGI and the Ancestral File (family trees donated by researchers, containing some 35 million names) also maintained by the Mormons of Salt Lake City. Records may be copied either as printouts or onto floppy disks.

You will find the IGI and *Family Search* both at the Family Records Centre, and at the Society of Genealogists' Library. Many record offices and some public libraries hold sections of the IGI relating to their own localities. In London you can also use them at the Hyde Park Family History Center of the Church of Jesus Christ of Latter-Day Saints, at 64–68 Exhibition Road, London SW7 2PA (tel. 020 7589 8561). This is open to all, but you must make an appointment in advance to reserve a computer. You will then be able to use the Family History Library Catalog, searching under both locality and surname to ascertain which records in the library contain the information likely to help you. These include the Ancestral File and the IGI mentioned above. The complete world listing of the IGI has been updated to 1997; if you feed in a family name and a county, you can obtain a print-out for 5p per page, or for 50p download the information you want (up to 2,000 names) onto a floppy disk (this has to be the best value in London!).

The IGI, Ancestral File and the Family History Library Catalog have recently been made available on the Internet at www. familysearch.org.

Nonconformist registers were required by law to be surrendered to the Registrar General in 1840, and these are now at the Family Records Centre. (Some registers were exempt – where they were kept in the same books as other records, such as members' lists, minutes of meetings, etc. – and you may be lucky enough to find them at local record offices.) The Religious Society of Friends, before surrendering their records, prepared 'Digest Registers' which, together with other valuable Quaker material, may be seen at Friends' House, Euston Road, London NW1 2BJ (tel. 020 7387 3601). Records of Huguenots in England since the mid-16th century have been published by the Huguenot Society, University College, Gower Street, London WC1E

6BT (tel. 020 7380 7094). The archives of the French Protestant Church of London, founded in 1550, may be inspected by appointment with the Honorary Archivist, on Tuesdays and Thursdays, at 8 & 9 Soho Square, London W1V 5DD (tel. 020 7437 5311). Access is to the archives listed in the Huguenot Society, Quarto series, volume L. For further information on the existence and whereabouts of Nonconformist registers, see *Sources for Nonconformist Genealogy and Family History* (volume II of the *National Index of Parish Registers*).

Researchers seeking material on Roman Catholic or Jewish families should look at volume III of the same series, *Sources for Roman Catholic and Jewish Genealogy and Family History*.

## Parish registers

Ministers in England were first ordered to keep records of all baptisms, marriages and burials in 1538; some registers therefore start in that year, but others were not commenced until a few years later or the earliest volumes have not survived. Not all parish registers have been deposited at the relevant local record office, but current legislation provides that clergy who do not have adequate facilities for preservation and storage must deposit them within a reasonable time.

The best way to find out whether or not a particular parish register has been deposited is to telephone to the local record office; with new registers being deposited all the time, the situation is constantly changing. If the record office does not have what you require – and often they will not have registers of recent date – they will give you the name and telephone number of the incumbent in whose possession the relevant registers are, or you can look this up in the current *Crockford's Clerical Directory*. To obtain access to these registers, you must write or telephone to make an appointment, as either the minister or his parish clerk must be present. A fee is payable to the incumbent for this service: based either on the time spent or on the number of years searched, this is no longer standard, but you can expect to be asked for up to £13 per hour. If you are making a long search, you will normally be able to negotiate a special rate. To avoid any difficulty, it is wise to establish the fee before you make the appointment. (N.B. If you cannot get to the vestry yourself and the incumbent agrees to do the search for you, he is entitled to charge a higher fee.)

It is as well to remember that directories such as *Crockford's* go to press months ahead of publication and cannot therefore be totally up to date. (The same, alas, applies to this book.) To avoid your letter of enquiry being forwarded on to another parish, should the incumbent listed have moved (which at best will cause delay and may mean that you never receive a reply), it is wise to address it impersonally, i.e. to 'The Incumbent', 'The Rector' or 'Vicar'.

It is important for the novice researcher to remember that parish registers do not give the exact dates of birth or death, but only those of baptism and burial. (Some of the more diligent parish priests also noted the dates of births and deaths, but not often.) In some parishes there are separate registers for baptisms, marriages and burials; in others, the baptisms and burials may be recorded in the same book, starting at different ends, and where the incumbent ran out of space the entries are sometimes continued a few pages later or, worse, may be merged – be careful not to overlook these.

Many registers have been transcribed and/or printed, and the Society of Genealogists issues a very useful booklet: *Parish Register Copies in the Library of the Society of Genealogists*. The *National Index of Parish Registers*, a vast project started over twenty years ago, is now periodically revising or reprinting some of its earlier volumes. The first three volumes of the *Index* constitute a guide to the pre-1837 registers of all denominations in England, Scotland and Wales; the final two volumes deal with sources for Scottish genealogy and family history and the parish registers of Wales respectively. Seven regional volumes have been published so far; others are in progress. *The Phillimore Atlas and Index of Parish Registers* is the best quick reference tool.

Other useful sources, especially when it is difficult to gain access to the registers, are Bishop's Transcripts (copies of parish registers made by each minister and sent annually to the Bishop of his diocese). Unfortunately these are not altogether reliable and indeed are sometimes different, as entries were often copied wrongly, or even omitted. It is essential to make a double-check in the original registers.

## Marriage indexes

*Boyd's Marriage Index*, compiled by Mr Percival Boyd from parish registers, Bishop's Transcripts and the marriage licences of England, covers most of the English counties in the period 1538–1837. It contains more than 3½ million names and is housed at the Society of Genealogists in London; a booklet published by the Society and entitled *List of Parishes in Boyd's Marriage Index* gives the dates for each parish included. This is an important source for the researcher who already knows the place or county of the marriage he wishes to trace. However, it is neither complete nor infallible (Mr Boyd died in 1955), and entries should always be verified in the relevant parish register. This is a golden rule in genealogical research when using any printed or transcribed registers or indexes.

Another important marriage index is *Pallot's*, containing some 4½ million marriages between 1780 and 1837; this is held at the Institute of Heraldic and Genealogical Studies in Canterbury. Enquiries may be sent by post, and searches will be made on a fee-paying basis, currently (1999) £15.00 for one entry, £25.00 for up to twenty entries.

There are also a number of local marriage indexes compiled both by family history groups and by individuals, and more are in progress. Ask at your local record office, or consult the FFHS booklet, *Marriage and Census Indexes for Family Historians*.

Marriage registers generally are separate from those of baptisms and burials; some are more informative than others. Supplementary information may be obtained from records of the intention to marry, such as banns, licences, marriage bonds and allegations. Advice on the availability of these will be given by staff on duty in the record office.

## Divorce records

Prior to the mid-19th century a full divorce could be effected only by a private Act of Parliament. Early records of Divorce Bills from 1669 will therefore be found at the House of Lords Record Office, House of Lords, London SW1A 0PW (tel. 020 7219 3074; fax 020 7219 2570). Since 1859 records have been kept by the Divorce Registry of the Family Division of the High Court, formerly at Somerset House, but now at First Avenue House, 42–49 High Holborn, London WC1V 6NP (tel. 020 7936 6000 ext. 6957). Copies of divorce decrees are available (£1.00 if you can quote the case number; or a 10-year search will be made by staff for £20.00). These records are useful to the researcher, as they give the date and place of the marriage.

## Wills and administrations

Probate records constitute one of the most useful sources of genealogical information. Since 11 January 1858 copies of all wills and administrations in England and Wales have been centralised at the Principal Registry of the Family Division, formerly at Somerset House but now at First Avenue House, 42–49 High Holborn, London WC1V 6NP; the telephone numbers for the Probate Search Rooms there (on the ground floor) are 020 7936 7000 or 020 7936 6948. Wills and administrations are calendared alphabetically under surnames in the year in which probate was granted (which may be the same as the year of death, but is sometimes later). The calendar volumes are on open shelves, and once you have traced the will or administration you need, the volume containing it will be produced on payment of a reading fee. Brief notes may be made (in pencil), or alternatively a photocopy ordered. At the time of writing (spring 1999) much concern was being expressed in genealogical circles over the greatly increased charges announced by First Avenue House. Due to pressure the charge for reading a will or administration has been reduced from the proposed £15.00 to £5.00 (compared to 25p in the days of Somerset House), but it will cost you £5.00, compared to the old £1.00, to have a photocopy of a will or administration posted to you. Researchers may like to know that there is a microfiche set of indexes to wills 1858–1943 at the Family Records Centre.

Prior to 1858 wills and administrations were proved by the courts which had general jurisdiction, of which the most important were the Prerogative Court of Canterbury (PCC) and the Prerogative Court of York (PCY). The PCC wills, formerly at the Public Record Office in Chancery Lane, London (which is now closed), have been transferred to the Family Records Centre (address above). PCY wills are at the Borthwick Institute, York (see page 203). Consult your local record office for details of other courts.

As a handbook for the first-time reader of these records I recommend Miriam Scott's *Prerogative Court of Canterbury Wills and Other Probate Records*. A standard work on PCC wills is *An Index to the Wills proved in the Prerogative County of Canterbury 1750–1800* edited by Anthony J. Camp, Director of Research of the Society of Genealogists. Eve McLaughlin's *Wills before 1858* is a useful introduction, and Audrey Collins' *About Wills after 1858 and First Avenue House* is an up-to-date and invaluable short guide.

## Census returns

The 19th-century census returns are a valuable source for the family historian and may be read on microfilm at the Family Records Centre. Returns exist from 1801, but individual names were not recorded until 1841. There is a surname index to the 1881 census on microfiche. The 1891 census is also on microfiche. As census records are subject to a 101-year rule, the most recent return available for public inspection is that of 1891. The 1901 census will become available in 2002.

Do not be misled by the CD-ROM on the market claiming to contain the 1991 census: it consists only of the statistics, *not* the names and addresses and occupations that are of such value to the family historian.

The great value of the census to the genealogist is that he will usually find the whole family (or at least those living under the same roof at the appropriate date) recorded together. The returns of 1851 onwards are the most informative, since they give exact ages and places of birth, and also each person's marital status and relationship to the household, whereas the 1841 census return states only their occupations, in what area of the country they were born and, for those over fifteen, ages to the lowest term of five.

It is of course essential to know, if not the exact address at which the family is believed to have been living at the date of the census, at least the parish. The relevant dates are:

> 6 June 1841
> 30 March 1851
> 7 April 1861
> 2 April 1871
> 3 April 1881
> 5 April 1891

Index books are on open shelves in the Census Room, in which you can look up the number of the book and the enumerator's district; this helps you to locate the precise place on the spool. Most towns are now street-indexed. There are pitfalls in that streets may appear half in one enumerator's district and half in another, and not all enumerators, especially in the earlier returns, were scrupulously accurate. It is a little complicated at first, but the FRC staff will assist anyone in difficulties over tracing the right entry or in deciphering the handwriting, which is often far from clear. As delving into census returns nearly always takes longer than one imagines it will, the wise researcher allows plenty of time for it. The best and most up-to-date guide is Susan Lumas' *Making Use of the Census*. Another excellent handbook is *Census Returns 1841–1891 on Microfilm: A Directory to Local Holdings* by Jeremy Gibson.

## Other records

The above-mentioned are but a few of the sources open to the genealogist/family historian. Searching these will enable you to draw up at least a skeleton family tree as a basis from which to work. The next stage will be to explore the various other classes of records likely to yield further information. Elucidation of the mysteries of Court rolls, Quarter Sessions records, poll books, service records, and so on, is best left to the expert.

In the last few years a number of excellent handbooks have been published which will help the researcher. Outstanding among these are Mark D. Herber's *Ancestral Trails: The Complete Guide to British Genealogy and Family History*; *The Oxford Companion to Local and Family History*, edited by David Hey; and Stella Colwell's *Family*

*History: A Guide and Troubleshooter.* The classic study remains Sir Anthony Wagner's *English Genealogy.* Other recommended handbooks include *Tracing Your Ancestors in the Public Record Office,* edited by Amanda Bevan; *Genealogy for Beginners* by A.J. Willis and K. Proudfoot; *The Family Historian's Enquire Within* by Pauline Saul and F.C. Markwell; and Terrick Fitzhugh's *The Dictionary of Genealogy.* The latter title has over a thousand entries: descriptions and locations of records by county, as well as explanations of obsolete terms and translations of those Latin phrases most likely to be encountered in ancestry research. An information sheet, *Beginning Family History,* is available from The Royal Commission on Historical Manuscripts.

Most of the above-mentioned books contain bibliographies which will lead you on to further reading. Write for the Society of Genealogists' Bookshop Catalogue, which is arranged under subject, and also the list of publications of the Federation of Family History Societies.

Use should also be made of the indexes to proceedings of local archaeological societies and to publications of local family history societies (see page 138). Most public libraries and county record offices possess complete sets of those relating to their districts. The standard works and guides mentioned above contain details of the records of special groups such as the Baptists, Huguenots, Methodists and Quakers.

The major printed biographical sources have been discussed under 'Biography and Autobiography' (pages 116–36), but special mention should be made here of the publications issued by Burke's Peerage Ltd. The long-awaited new (106th) edition of *Burke's Peerage and Baronetage* was published in 1998. *Burke's Family Index* has already been mentioned. Other titles include *Burke's Dormant and Extinct Peerages, Burke's Guide to the Royal Family, Burke's Irish Family Records, Burke's Landed Gentry* and, international in scope, *Ruvigny's Titled Nobility of Europe* (originally published in 1914, reprinted by Burke), *Burke's Presidential Families of the United States of America* and *Burke's Royal Families of the World.* The *Almanach de Gotha,* covering European royalty and their descendants, has recently been reissued after many years out of print.

*Debrett's Peerage and Baronetage* is revised at five-year intervals. The older, but more comprehensive, *Cockayne's Complete Peerage,* covering extant, extinct and dormant titles from 1265 was reprinted a few years ago; a final volume of addenda and corrigenda was added in 1998, bringing it fully up to date. *Cockayne's Complete Baronetage* is also available in a reprint. F.L. Leeson's *Directory of British Peerages,* which covers earliest times to the present day in one continuous alphabetical listing of titles and surnames, is an invaluable finding aid.

A good introduction to heraldic research, written for genealogists and local historians, is Stephen Friar's *Heraldry.* Also recommended

149

is *The Oxford Guide to Heraldry* by Thomas Woodcock and John Martin Robinson. The best place to look up an old coat of arms when you come across one and do not know to which family it belongs is Papworth's *Ordinary of British Armorials*.

# Local History

Local history writing may range from a short article in the local newspaper or county magazine to a full-length academic study. In all cases painstaking research and a good deal of detective work will be necessary; care must be taken to transcribe original documents accurately and to keep a note of all sources. References should normally be quoted in all but the shortest and most 'popular' articles.

There is a vast store of printed and manuscript material open to the local historian, much of it as yet untapped. Some of these sources have been discussed already under chapter 3, 'Basic Sources of Information and their Location' (pages 42–78). As with family history, before embarking on a project it is wise to check with the local record office whether the same ground has been covered by someone else; even if nothing has yet been published or deposited, archivists notoriously have their 'ears to the ground' and will usually be aware of any other writers, researchers or students working on parallel lines. A preliminary study of a work of a similar nature, even if it deals with a totally different district, can be of considerable help to a writer wondering how to tackle the particular subject he has in mind.

*The Oxford Companion to Local and Family History* has been recommended earlier in this chapter. Another useful tool is *A Guide to English County Histories*, edited by C.R.J. Currie and C.P. Lewis. The *Darwen County Histories* series begun in 1950 and published by Phillimore of Chichester are regularly revised. From the same publisher is Paul Hindle's *Maps for Historians* (an updated edition of the same author's *Maps for Local History*, published in 1988). Anyone writing about London or Greater London will find the *Greater London History and Heritage Handbook* (a borough by borough guide to local sources of information) invaluable.

If you are seeking the location of manorial records, go to the Royal Commission on Historical Manuscripts office (Quality House, Quality Court, Chancery Lane, London WC2A 1HP) to consult the *Manorial Documents Register*. Note that this is a location tool only; the Commission does not hold original manorial documents. Limited and specific enquiries will be answered by post, but it is best to visit the Commission in person. Telephone enquiries are not accepted. Ask at the Commission for their information sheet, *The Manorial*

*Documents Register and Manorial Lordships*. An excellent handbook is *Using Manorial Records* by Mary Ellis, published jointly by the Commission and the Public Record Office.

Difficulty may be encountered in reading early documents, and unless you have some knowledge of palaeography and Latin, you may need to use the services of an expert. If however you are serious about learning the necessary skills, help is at hand in the shape of the recent and very comprehensive *Palaeography for Historians*, by Elizabeth Danbury, and of *Latin for Local and Family Historians* by Denis Stuart. Eve McLaughlin's *Reading Old Handwriting* is a good guide for beginners. Those who have the time might consider attending a course on the subject, but these are not widely available. Madingley Hall, part of the University of Cambridge Board of Continuing Education, occasionally runs residential courses on palaeography, and also on various aspects of local history (write to the Courses Registrar, Madingley Hall, Madingley, Cambridge CB3 8AQ for the forthcoming programme).

The Latin of local records differs considerably from school Latin. C.T. Martin's *The Record Interpreter*, with its invaluable list of Latin abbreviations and glossary of Latin words used in English historical manuscripts and records, first published in 1892 and out of print for many years, became available again in a facsimile edition a few years ago. Another useful reference work is the *Revised Medieval Latin Word-List*, edited by R.E. Latham.

C.R. Cheney's *Handbook of Dates for Students of English History* and Fryde's *Handbook of British Chronology* are indispensable aids to dating: they contain not only lists of rulers (with regnal years), popes, archbishops and other officers of state, but also include saints' days and tables that enable you to work out the day of the week of any date from AD 500 to the year 2000. (A new edition of Cheney is scheduled for use after the year 2000.) Lionel Munby's *Dates and Time: A Handbook for Local Historians* is another invaluable tool.

As general introductions to the subject, David Dymond's *Writing Local History*, Robert Dunning's *Local History for Beginners* and John Richardson's *The Local Historian's Encyclopedia* are highly recommended. *The Oxford Companion to Local and Family History* has been mentioned earlier in this chapter. Among numerous other titles on the subject, there are the classics by W.G. Hoskins, *Local History in England* and *Fieldwork in Local History*, and W.E. Tate's *The Parish Chest*. The *Victoria County Histories* (a varying number of volumes per county) are immensely detailed architecturally and topographically. Of more general interest is the revised edition of W.B. Stephens' *Sources for English Local History*. The Historical Association's series, *Short Guides to Records* is always worthwhile.

The publications of many local record societies and the Index Library have been produced on microfiche by Chadwyck-Healey (a massive 5,136 microfiches) under the general title of *Publications of the English Record Societies, 1835–1972, and the Index Library*; relevant sections may be available in your local library.

# Depositing Papers

Every writer of family or local history, whether or not his work achieves publication, should consider depositing a copy of it, together with any original papers that may have come into his possession, and possibly also his research notes, at the appropriate local record office or, in the case of a family history, at the Society of Genealogists in London. By so doing he will be making a valuable contribution to the store of material on English social history and genealogy for the use of future generations of students and researchers.

*About Wills after 1858 and First Avenue House*, by Audrey Collins, FFHS 'Basic Facts' series, 1999

*Almanach de Gotha*, 1998; updated 1999 (available from Boydell & Brewer Ltd, PO Box 9, Woodbridge, Suffolk IP12 3DF)

*Ancestral Trails: The Complete Guide to British Genealogy and Family History*, by Mark D. Herber, Sutton Publishing, Thrupp, Stroud, Glos., in association with the Society of Genealogists, 1998

*Beginning Family History*, information sheet available from The Royal Commission on Historical Manuscripts, Quality House, Quality Court, Chancery Lane, London WC2A 1HP

*Burke's Dormant and Extinct Peerages*, Burke's Peerage, London, reprinted 1985

*Burke's Family Index*, Burke's Peerage, London, 1976

*Burke's Guide to the Royal Family*, Burke's Peerage, London, 1973

*Burke's Irish Family Records*, Burke's Peerage, London, 1976

*Burke's Landed Gentry*, 3 vols, Burke's Peerage, London, 1965–72

*Burke's Peerage and Baronetage*, Burke's Peerage, London, 106th edn, 1998

*Burke's Presidential Families of the United States of America*, Burke's Peerage, London, 1981

*Burke's Royal Families of the World*, 2 vols, Burke's Peerage, London, 1977, 1980

*Census Returns 1841–1891 on Microfilm: A Directory to Local Holdings*, compiled by Jeremy Gibson, FFHS, Birmingham, 6th edn, 1994; reprinted 1997

*[Cockayne's] The Complete Baronetage*, reprinted in 6 vols, Alan Sutton, Gloucester, 1982

*[Cockayne's] The Complete Peerage of England, Scotland, Ireland, Great Britain and the United Kingdom, Extant, Extinct or Dormant*, 13 vols, London, 1910–59; reprinted in 6 vols, Alan Sutton, Gloucester, 1982; vol. XIV: *Addenda and Corrigenda*, ed. Peter Hammond, Sutton Publishing, Thrupp, Stroud, Glos., 1998

*Computers in Genealogy*, quarterly periodical published by the Society of Genealogists, London, 1982–

*Crockford's Clerical Directory*, first issued in 1858, now biennial; latest edition (2000), by Church House Publishing, London, 1999

*Darwen County Histories* series, published by Phillimore, Chichester; regularly revised

*Dates and Time: A Handbook for Local Historians*, by Lionel Munby, published by Phillimore for the British Association for Local History (BALH), 1997

*Debrett's Peerage and Baronetage*, published by Debrett's Peerage Ltd and Macmillan, London, 1995; new edn scheduled for 2000

*The Dictionary of Genealogy*, by Terrick Fitzhugh, 5th edn, revised by Susan Lumas for the Society of Genealogists, A & C Black, 1998

*Directory of British Peerages from earliest times to the present day*, ed. F.L. Leeson, Society of Genealogists, London, 1984

*English Genealogy*, by Anthony Wagner, Phillimore, Chichester, 3rd edn, 1983, reprinted 1990

*The Family Historian's Enquire Within*, eds P. Saul and F.C. Markwell, FFHS, Birmingham, 5th edn, 1995, reprinted with amendments 1997; new edn scheduled for 2000

*Family History: A Guide and Troubleshooter*, by Stella Colwell, Sutton Publishing, Thrupp, Stroud, Glos., 1999

*Family History News and Digest*, published twice a year (April and September), by the Federation of Family History Societies (FFHS), Birmingham

*Family Tree Magazine*, monthly since 1984 by ABM Publishing, 61 Great Whyte, Ramsey, Huntingdon, Cambs PE17 1HL

*Fieldwork in Local History*, by W.G. Hoskins, Faber, London, 1982

*Genealogical Research Directory*, published in the USA annually since 1982; available from the UK agent, Mrs E. Simpson, 2 Stella Grove, Tollerton, Notts NG12 4EY

*Genealogists' Magazine*, published quarterly by the Society of Genealogists, London

*Genealogy for Beginners*, by A.J. Willis and K. Proudfoot, Phillimore, Chichester, 1996

*Greater London History and Heritage Handbook*, compiled and published by Peter Marcan, London, 1999

*A Guide to English County Histories,* ed. C.R.J. Currie and C.P. Lewis, Sutton Publishing, Thrupp, Stroud, Glos., 1994; paperback, 1997

*Handbook of British Chronology,* eds E.B. Fryde *et al.,* Royal Historical Society, London, 3rd edn, 1986

*Handbook of Dates for Students of English History,* by C.R. Cheney, Royal Historical Society, London, first published 1945; latest reprint, with corrections, by Cambridge University Press for the Society, 1996; new edn due February 2000

*Heraldry,* by Stephen Friar, Sutton Publishing, Thrupp, Stroud, Glos., 1992; paperback, 1996

*How to Write a Family History,* by Terrick Fitzhugh, A & C Black, London, 1988

*An Index to the Wills proved in the Prerogative Court of Canterbury 1750–1800,* ed. A.J. Camp, 6 vols, Society of Genealogists, London, 1976–93; some vols now out of print but on microfiche

*Latin for Local and Family Historians,* by Denis Stuart, Phillimore, Chichester, 1995

*List of Parishes in Boyd's Marriage Index,* Phillimore, Chichester, for the Society of Genealogists, London, 6th edn, 1987; reprinted 1994

*The Local Historian* (formerly *The Amateur Historian*), published quarterly by Phillimore, Chichester, for the British Association for Local History (BALH)

*The Local Historian's Encyclopedia,* by John Richardson, Phillimore, Chichester, 2nd edn, 1986; reprinted 1993

*Local History for Beginners,* by Robert Dunning, Phillimore, Chichester, 1980

*Local History in England,* by W.G. Hoskins, Longman, Harlow, 3rd edn, 1984; 4th impression 1990

*Making Use of the Census,* by Susan Lumas, PRO Publications, London, rev. edn, 1997

*The Manorial Documents Register and Manorial Lordships,* information sheet available from The Royal Commission on Historical Manuscripts, Quality House, Quality Court, Chancery Lane, London WC2A 1HP

*Maps for Historians,* by Paul Hindle, Phillimore, Chichester, 1998

*Marriage and Census Indexes for Family Historians,* by J. Gibson and E. Hampson, FFHS, Birmingham, 7th edn, retitled, 1998

*National Index of Parish Registers,* series ed. Cliff Webb, published by Phillimore, Chichester, for the Society of Genealogists, in progress (some vols revised/reprinted, some out of print, others in preparation): I, *Sources for Births, Marriages and Deaths before 1837,* 1968, reprinted 1976; II, *Sources for Nonconformist Genealogy and Family History,* 1973, reprinted 1981; III, *Sources for Roman Catholic and Jewish Genealogy and Family History,*

1974, reprinted 1986; IV, *South East England*, 1980: Part 1, *Surrey*, reprinted 1990; V, *South Midlands and Welsh Border*, 1966, 3rd edn revised, 1976; VI, *North Midlands*: Part 1, *Staffordshire*, 1982, 2nd edn, 1992; Part 2, *Nottinghamshire*, 1988, 2nd edn 1995; Part 3, *Leicestershire and Rutland*, 1995; Part 4, *Lincolnshire*, 1995; Part 5, *Derbyshire*, 1995; VII, *Cambridgeshire, Norfolk, Suffolk*, 1983; VIII, Part 1, *Berkshire*, 1989; Part 2, *Wiltshire*, 1992; Part 3, *Somerset*, 1997; Part 4, *Cornwall*, 1999; IX, Part 1, *Bedfordshire and Huntingdonshire*, 1991; Part 2, *Northamptonshire*, 1991; Part 3, *Buckinghamshire*, 1992; Part 4, *Essex*, 1993; Part 5, *London & Middlesex*, 1995; X, Part 1, *Cheshire*, 1995; Part 2, *Lancashire*, 1998; Part 3, *Cumberland & Westmorland*, 1999; XI, *North-East England*: Part 1, *Durham and Northumberland*, 2nd edn 1984, rev. edn 1992; Part 2, *Yorkshire: North and East Ridings and York*, 1997; Part 3, *Yorkshire: West Riding*, 1997; XII, *Sources for Scottish Genealogy and Family History*, 1970, reprinted 1980; XIII, *The Parish Registers of Wales*, 1986

*Never Been Here Before?: A Genealogist's Guide to the Family Records Centre*, by Jane Cox and Stella Colwell, Public Record Office Reader's Guide No. 17, PRO Publications, London, 1997, reprinted 1998

*New to Kew?*, by Jane Cox, PRO Publications, London, 1997

*One-Name Studies*, quarterly journal of the Guild of One-Name Studies, London

*Ordinary of British Armorials*, by A.W.W. Papworth, 1874; facsimile edn, Tabard Publications, London, 1961

*The Oxford Companion to Local and Family History*, ed. David Hey, Oxford University Press, Oxford, 1996

*The Oxford Guide to Heraldry*, by Thomas Woodcock and John Martin Robinson, Oxford University Press, Oxford, 1990

*Palaeography for Historians*, by Elizabeth Danbury, Phillimore, Chichester, 1999

*The Parish Chest*, by W.E. Tate, Phillimore, Chichester, 3rd rev. edn, 1983; reprinted 1985

*Parish Register Copies in the Library of the Society of Genealogists*, booklet published by Phillimore, Chichester, for the Society of Genealogists, London; updated at regular intervals

*The Phillimore Atlas and Index of Parish Registers*, ed. C.R. Humphery-Smith, Phillimore, Chichester, 2nd edn, 1995

*Practical Family History*, published monthly since summer 1997 by ABM Publishing, Huntingdon, Cambs

*Prerogative Court of Canterbury Wills and Other Probate Records*, by Miriam Scott, PRO Publications, London, 1997

*Publications of the English Record Societies, 1835–1972, and the Index Library*, on microfiche, Chadwyck-Healey, Cambridge

*Reading Old Handwriting*, by Eve McLaughlin, FFHS, Birmingham, 1987; reprinted 1991, now available from *Family Tree Magazine*

*The Record Interpreter*, by Charles Trice Martin, originally published 1892; facsimile of 2nd edn (1910), Kohler & Coombes, Dorking, 1976; reprinted 1982, 1994

*Record Offices: How to Find Them*, by J.S.W. Gibson and P. Peskett, FFHS, Birmingham, 8th edn, 1998

*Record Repositories in Great Britain*, Royal Commission on Historical Manuscripts, PRO Publications, London; updated regularly (latest, 11th edn, 1999)

*Revised Medieval Latin Word-List from British and Irish Sources*, ed. R.E. Latham, Oxford University Press, Oxford, 1965

*Ruvigny's Titled Nobility of Europe*, originally published 1914; reprinted by Burke's Peerage, London, 1980

*Short Guides to Records* series, Historical Association, London

*Sources for English Local History*, by W.B. Stephens, Phillimore, Chichester, rev. edn, 1994

*Tracing Your Ancestors in the Public Record Office*, ed. Amanda Bevan, PRO, London, 5th edn, 1998

*Using Manorial Records*, by Mary Ellis, PRO Publications, London, 1997

'Using the Library of the Society of Genealogists', leaflet published annually by the Society of Genealogists, London

*Victoria History of the Counties of England (VCH)*, over 200 vols published since 1901; Institute of Historical Research, London (distributed by Oxford University Press, Oxford)

*Whitaker's Almanack*, published annually by The Stationery Office, London

*Wills before 1858*, by Eve McLaughlin, FFHS, Birmingham, 4th edn, 1992; now available from *Family Tree Magazine, q.v.*

*Writing Local History*, by David Dymond, Phillimore, Chichester, for the British Association for Local History (BALH), 1988; revised edn 1996

*Note:* Publications of the Federation of Family History Societies are obtainable through local family history societies or from FFHS Publications, 2–4 Killer Street, Ramsbottom, Bury, Lancs BL0 9BZ. Send a stamped addressed envelope for a complete list of titles. For a list of publications obtainable from *Family Tree Magazine*, send a stamped addressed envelope to the magazine at 61 Great Whyte, Ramsey, Huntingdon, Cambs PE17 1HL.

# 8

# Specialist Research

While it is always more rewarding to undertake your own research, there are times when it pays to employ the expert. Books or records to be consulted may be accessible only at some distance; specialist knowledge of a subject may be required, or familiarity with local records which it would take the inexperienced researcher, or one from another district, months, if not years, to acquire – in these circumstances the employment of an expert will usually save time and money in the long term. If you have press deadlines looming, or other commitments, it may even pay you to off-load some of the more routine research as well.

The best advice I can give to anyone looking for a reliable professional researcher is to get a personal recommendation from another writer. Failing that, look in the *Writers' & Artists' Yearbook*, under 'Editorial, Literary and Production Services', in the Cassell and Publishers Association *Directory of Publishing*, under 'Trade and Allied Services: publishing consultancies and research services in Great Britain', and in *The Writer's Handbook*, under 'Editorial, Research and Other Services'. The British Library, the Public Record Office and some other libraries and local record offices maintain lists of researchers/record agents and will pass on names and addresses to enquirers (send a stamped addressed envelope); naturally, they do not accept any responsibility for the work undertaken by these people. Experts willing to do research may also sometimes be contacted through the secretaries or librarians of professional or trade societies or institutions; alternatively, an advertisement in a professional or trade journal may yield a suitable result. Some freelancers advertise their services in *The Times*, the *Times Literary Supplement*, *The Author* and similar papers. Teachers and university students often seek research assignments during the long vacation. For details of how to obtain the services of a qualified indexer, see page 188.

Contacting a suitable researcher abroad is rather more difficult. You can write to the national library of the country concerned, or to the library or archives centre where you want the research to be done (always enclose a sufficient number of International Reply Coupons for airmail if writing overseas – one is never enough); or you can approach the cultural attaché of the relevant embassy, legation or high commission in London.

The most obvious occasions when a writer may need this kind of help are in the fields of genealogy, when a complicated ancestral search may be necessary for the first chapter of a biography; in local or family history, for which not only a knowledge of the classes of records available is required, but also some skill in reading Latin and in palaeography (transcribing old handwriting); in picture research; and in translation.

# Genealogy

Experience in palaeography and genealogy is acquired only after considerable study, and there are many traps into which the unwary novice can fall. A working knowledge of Latin is essential for the study of medieval or earlier texts, while later source material demands the ability to read and transcribe both the 'secretary hand' (the script in use in England from the mid-16th to the mid-17th centuries) and the later 'court hand', each with distinctive forms of capital letters and contractions. Unless you are embarking on your family or local history as a hobby, therefore, and can afford the time to qualify yourself in these subjects, some professional assistance will be desirable.

It is wise to employ someone who lives in the area in which the relevant search is to be made, for he will be familiar both with the local records and with local family names, and thus can save the client time and money. Most local record offices maintain lists of recommended searchers; alternatively, names and addresses of professional genealogists and record agents who are members of the Association of Genealogists and Record Agents (AGRA) may be obtained from the Joint Secretaries, 29 Badgers Close, Horsham, West Sussex RH12 5RU (enclose £2.50 to cover cost and postage or six International Reply Coupons for overseas). All AGRA members have satisfied their Council as to integrity, qualifications and experience, and they adhere to a strict professional code of practice. There are similar associations in Scotland and Ireland: The Association of Scottish Genealogists and Record Agents (ASGRA), 51/3 Morton Hall Road, Edinburgh EH9 2NH; and The Association of Professional Genealogists in Ireland (APGI), 2 Kildare Street, Dublin 2.

The College of Arms (Queen Victoria Street, London EC4V 4BT) is open to enquiries of a genealogical and heraldic nature from members of the public (arms and pedigrees of English, Northern Irish and

Commonwealth families). For personal visitors only a brief search will be made free of charge to ascertain whether or not a family tree has been drawn up; further research will be conducted on a fee-paying basis. Debrett Ancestry Research Ltd, PO Box 7, New Alresford, Hants SO24 9EN (tel. 01962 732676), which formerly catered only for royalty and the aristocracy, now offers a worldwide genealogical research service to the commoner. So does Burke's Ancestry Research Department, 209 St John's Hill, London SW11 1TH (tel. 020 7924 5132; fax 020 7924 3369); this firm, which has the reputation of being very competitive, will give free advice on a genealogical search or provide a detailed feasibility assessment for £48, the cost of which will be deducted if they are commissioned to do further research. Simple research queries (i.e. for specific information) are charged on an hourly basis. At current (1999) rates a full family search is likely to cost in the region of £350–£480. Other firms and individuals offering genealogical research services in various parts of the United Kingdom and abroad advertise in the *Genealogists' Magazine*, the quarterly journal of the Society of Genealogists. The Society itself will carry out research, on a fee-paying basis, for members and non-members. Enquiries, accompanied by a stamped addressed envelope, should be addressed to the Director of Research, The Society of Genealogists, 14 Charterhouse Buildings, London EC1M 7BA.

# Picture Research

Picture research is immensely complicated and therefore beyond the scope of this book. Sometimes a writer will be expected to provide all the illustrative material for his book or article; in other cases the publisher will employ a professional picture researcher, who may be a member of his staff or a freelance, to locate and select pictures, commission photographers, and clear the copyright and reproduction fees on a particular project. Whether the author or the publisher foots the bill for the picture researcher is a matter for negotiation. A wise author makes sure that it is stipulated in his contract that it will be the publisher who bears responsibility for print and reproduction fees, since these can be very costly.

Writers wishing to obtain the services of a qualified picture researcher are recommended to contact the Picture Research Association (formerly SPREd): telephone Emma Krikler on 020 7431 9886, or write to the PRA at The Studio, 5a Alvanley Gardens, London NW6 1JD.

If you are tempted to undertake your own picture research, you should first read the excellent introductory article on the subject in the *Writers' & Artists' Yearbook*, published annually by A & C Black. Both the *Writers' & Artist's Yearbook* and *The Writer's Handbook*, published annually by Macmillan, carry comprehensive lists of picture libraries and agencies in the UK.

Among a variety of practical manuals and useful source books are the following:

*Art Historians and Specialists*, published by Peter Marcan, PO Box 3158, London SE1 4RA, 1995

*BAPLA Directory*, published annually by the British Association of Picture Libraries and Agencies, 18 Vine Hill, London EC1R 5DX (tel. 020 7713 1780; fax 020 7713 1211)

*Dictionary of British Cartoonists and Caricaturists 1730–1980*, compiled by M. Bryant and S. Heneage, Scolar Press, London, 1994

*The Picture Researcher's Handbook*, by Hilary and Mary Evans, 6th edn, Blueprint, London, 1996 (new edition in preparation, to be published by Pira, Leatherhead)

*Picture Sources UK: A Guide to more than 1200 Public and Private Picture Collections*, compiled by R. Eakins, Macdonald, London, 1985 (out of print but available in libraries)

*Practical Picture Research: A Guide to Current Practice, Procedure, Techniques and Resources*, by Hilary Evans, Blueprint (Chapman and Hall), London, 1992

*Sources of Illustration 1500–1900*, Adams & Dart, London, 1971 (out of print, but still a valuable source, available in libraries)

# Translation

Translation is another field in which professional help may be required from time to time. For basic research purposes a rough translation or précis may be adequate to work on, but any passage to be quoted in print should be prepared by a qualified translator. The best way to find one is to contact the Institute of Translation and Interpreting (ITI), 377 City Road, London EC1V 1NA (tel. 020 7713 7600; fax 020 7713 7650). The languages and skills of qualified members of the Institute, together with those of some members of the Translators Association of the Society of Authors, will be found in the *ITI Directory*. Alternatively, translation agencies are listed in the yellow pages of most telephone directories, but these normally handle commercial rather than literary texts.

*The Translator's Handbook* by Rachel Owens (3rd edn, Aslib, London, 1996) is an excellent introduction and source-book for all members of the profession; it will also be of use to writers who need to commission a translator.

# Research Fees

Fees for professional freelance assistance are negotiable and depend on the nature and complexity of the task. Genealogists, record agents and researchers usually work on an hourly basis plus out-of-pocket expenses (travelling, search fees, photocopying, postages, telephone, etc.); short pieces of translation are charged per thousand words. Most freelance workers have a sliding scale of fees; the professional bodies to which the majority of them belong recommend minimum standard rates for the job; if you are asked to pay 'above the odds' it will be either because the assignment is very specialised or complicated, or is needed in a great rush (necessitating week-end and evening work), or because the person engaged has special qualifications. As a guideline the current recommended hourly rates range from £13.50 to £17.50 an hour.

It is normal practice for the client commissioning the work to pay a lump sum on account (up to 50 per cent of the total cost estimated) and the balance on completion, but in the case of long-term commissions accounts may be rendered monthly. Estimates will be given on request; but do not expect your researcher to give one with any accuracy – neither he nor you will know at the outset precisely how much time he will spend on the job.

Fees paid to researchers, genealogists, translators and other workers may be set against a writer's income tax.

# 9

# Information from and about Foreign Countries

The writer/researcher who needs to obtain information about foreign countries or to use published or unpublished material from abroad has few problems these days, thanks to the new technology. Twenty years ago you might have had to budget (or squeeze an advance out of your publisher) for an extended trip in order to look at some vital records lurking the other side of the world. Today you can search the catalogues of almost all the great national library and archive collections online, if not from the comfort of your study, then via the library computer terminal, and download what you need onto your own PC. An enormous amount of material is available on CD-ROM and in microform, which again you can study either in the library or wherever it is you work; and if you so wish you can obtain and/or exchange up-to-date research information with fellow writers worldwide by email without leaving home. What once took weeks, or sometimes months – and a great deal of money – is now more or less instantly accessible at a reasonable cost.

It is true that you may still have to travel to get at some of your material. But by doing your initial searching from the home base (which in the first instance normally involves extracting biblio-graphical information), you will soon discover precisely what exists and where, if necessary, you must go to examine it. Often you will find that copies of the books or journals you need are held by some library or archive centre in the UK, or that they are on CD-ROM or have been – or can be – microfilmed for you to use at home. In the case of private papers you will almost always have to go to the source in person, possibly to a university abroad or to visit the family.

When it is a question simply of finding some factual or background information on a foreign country, the best place to start is the reference library. National encyclopedias, bibliographies and current works of reference are usually to be found on the open shelves; many are now available on online, on CD-ROM and on microfiche. One of the best sources is the *World Bibliographical Series* published by Clio Press of Oxford. The use of bibliographies and how to trace books has been outlined in chapter 2.

All the copyright libraries and university libraries in the UK have substantial foreign language holdings, and you should experience little difficulty in obtaining most standard works. Use *Walford's Guide to Reference Material* (details in chapter 3) to find out, under the country; also the principal encyclopedias, national bibliographies and major works (listed under subject).

Foreign newspapers and weeklies going back for many years are held at the British Library Newspaper Library in Colindale; there are some gaps during the two world wars. Today they are nearly all purchased on microfilm. You can trace the whereabouts of all foreign periodicals held in British libraries in *Serials in the British Library*. Current publications are listed in *Benn's Media, Ulrich's International Periodicals Directory* and *Willing's Press Guide* (see chapter 3, pages 54–5).

If you are thinking of subscribing to a foreign periodical you should contact Dawson UK Ltd, Cannon House, Park Farm Road, Folkestone, Kent CT19 5EE (tel. 01303 850101; fax 01303 850440; online http.//www/dawsonco.uk). This firm offers a range of services including online access to a database of 150,000 journal titles and a huge stock of back issues; any enquiries that cannot be answered directly from the database are automatically passed on to the Dawson Bibliographic Research Service. The subscription division's *Guide to International Journals and Periodicals* lists publications alphabetically by title, with frequency of issue and prices in £ sterling; there is a detailed subject index. CD-ROMs are also available.

So far as obtaining books published abroad is concerned, the London booksellers Grant & Cutler, 55–57 Great Marlborough Street, London W1V 2AY (tel. 020 7734 2012; fax 020 7734 9272) hold a large stock of foreign language titles and will order on any subject. Bay Foreign Language Books, Unit 3B, Frith Business Centre, Frith Road, Aldington, Ashford, Kent TN25 7HJ (tel. 01233 720020; fax 01233 721272) also import new books; although they specialise in foreign language dictionaries and in natural history, they will obtain other titles.

The number of countries or regions for which there is a *Biographical Archive* (on microfiches, from Saur, Munich) is growing fast. Many also have a *Biographical Index*, and these are included on the huge Saur database, the *World Biographical Index* (see chapter 6, pages 120–1). In printed form, there are biographical dictionaries and/or *Who's Who* volumes for most countries. For quick factual reference look out for the single-volume encyclopedias such as *Le Petit Larousse* (French), *Der Brockhaus in einem Band* (German) and *Pequeño Larousse Ilustrado* (Spanish), as they contain information not always included in their English equivalents.

For up-to-date general information you should contact the relevant tourist information offices (listed in the London telephone directory) or the cultural departments or press offices of the particular embassy or high commission. Many embassies publish short factual booklets about their country which they will send you free of charge. A personal approach is often productive; you will find the addresses, and names of cultural attachés, in the current *London Diplomatic List* (published twice a year by The Stationery Office and usually available at the library enquiry desk). For addresses of embassies and other diplomatic bodies worldwide look at *The World Directory of Diplomatic Representation*, published by Europa Publications. The same firm also publishes an *International Relations Research Directory* which contains information on every major research institute concerned with international relations, as well as an alphabetical list of relevant periodicals and journals. You should remember, too, that public relations officers of the major international companies are often able to provide useful source material and/or contacts; you will find their names and addresses in the current *Hollis Press & Public Relations Annual* and *Hollis Europe*.

Finally, and by no means least, you will find much first-class information about foreign countries in some of the quality travel guides. The *Blue Guides* published by A & C Black are excellent in this respect; there are volumes for most European countries, some for individual towns and regions, and they are regularly revised. For countries farther afield, look at the *Handbooks* produced by Footprint (formerly Trade & Travel); these contain a wealth of information and are very reliable.

Foreign libraries in the United Kingdom are listed in the *Aslib Directory*. *The World of Learning* is international. For information on libraries and the book trade generally, look at the two Bowker annuals, *Literary Market Place*, covering the United States and Canada, and *International Literary Market Place*, for the rest of the world. Other useful tools not already mentioned include the US *Public Affairs Information Service Index* (PAIS), which is worldwide in coverage, the *Regional Surveys of the World* series published by Europa Publications and the *International Historical Statistics* series published by Macmillan. Do not forget old favourites such as the *Europa World Year Book*, the *International Who's Who* and the *Yearbook of International Organizations*. As with every other kind of research, you need only one book title, or one contact, to start you off.

Readers who live in or near London may be able to make use of the following:

Bibliothèque de l'Institut Français (French Institute), 17 Queensberry Place, London SW7 2DT (tel. 020 7838 2144; fax 020 7838 2145). The library is open to the public for reference and information; loans are restricted to members. Tue–Fri, 12–7; Sat, 12–6.

Commonwealth Resource Centre, Commonwealth Institute, Kensington High Street, London W8 6NQ (tel. 020 7603 4535; fax 020 7603 2807). Mon–Sat, 10–6.

German Historical Institute Library, 17 Bloomsbury Square, London WC1A 2LP (tel. 020 7309 2019/2022; fax 020 7404 5573). Open Mon, Thu 10–8, Tue, Wed, Fri, 10–5.

Goethe-Institut (German Cultural Centre) Library and Information Service, 50 Princes Gate, Exhibition Road, London SW7 2PH (tel. 020 7596 4040/4044; fax 020 7594 0230). Open to the public, free of charge, for reference and study. Loan service to members only (£20 per year; three- and six-monthly membership, and concessions available). Mon–Thu, 12–8; Sat, 11–5. (N.B. There are also Goethe-Instituts at 3 Park Circus, Glasgow G3 6AX (tel. 0141-332 2555; fax 0141-333 1630); at Churchgate House, 56 Oxford Street, Manchester M1 6EU (tel. 0161-237 1077; fax 0161-237 1079); and at 61 Micklegate, York YO1 1LJ (tel. 01904 611122; fax 01904 612736).

Institute of Commonwealth Studies Library, London University, 27–28 Russell Square, London WC1B 5DS (tel. 020 7580 5876; fax 020 7255 2160). Open (during term) Mon–Wed, 9.30–7; Thu, Fri, 9.30–6; (during vacations) Mon–Fri, 9.30–5.30. A fee may be payable.

Instituto Cervantes (Cervantes Institute, formerly called the Spanish Institute) Library, 102 Eaton Square, London SW1W 9AN (tel. 020 7235 0324; fax 020 7235 0329). Mon, 12.30–6.30; Tue–Thu, 9.30–6.30; Fri, 9.30–5; Sat, 9.30–1.30.

Italian Institute Library, 39 Belgrave Square, London SW1X 8NX (tel. 020 7235 1461; fax 020 7235 4618). Mon–Fri, 10–1, 2–5, for reference only.

Oriental and India Office Collections (formerly the India Office Library), now at the British Library, 96 Euston Road, London NW1 2DB (tel. 020 7412 7873; fax 020 7412 7641). Mon, Thu, 9.30–6; Tue, Wed, 9.30–8; Fri, Sat, 9.30–5. Reader's pass required.

Polish Library, 238–246 King Street, London W6 0RF (tel. 020 8741 0474; fax 020 8746 3798). Mon, Wed, 10–8; Fri, 10–5; Sat, 10–1; closed Tue and Thu. Reference only (loans to scholars).

School of Oriental and African Studies Library, London University, Thornhaugh Street, Russell Square, London WC1H 0XG (tel. 020 7323 6109; fax 020 7436 3844). Mon–Thu, 9–7; Fri, 9–5; summer vacation, Mon–Fri, 9–5; closed for one week in June. Reader's ticket required (letter of introduction).

Sir Robert Menzies Centre for Australian Studies, 28 Russell Square, London WC1B 5DS (tel. 020 7862 8854; fax 020 7580 9627). Mon–Thu, 10–5.30.

United States of America Information Service Reference Center, American Embassy, 55/56 Upper Brook Street, London W1A 2LH (tel. 020 7408 8060). N.B. This is not a library open to the public. Telephone enquiry service only, Mon–Fri, 10–12.

# Short List of Foreign Source-material (arranged alphabetically under area or country)*

## Africa

### Sources of information in the UK:

African Studies Centre Library, University of Cambridge, Free School Lane, Cambridge CB2 3RQ (tel. 01223 334398; fax 01223 334396)

The School of Oriental and African Studies, University of London, Thornhaugh Street, Russell Square, London WC1H 0XG (tel. 020 7323 6109; fax 020 7436 3844)

### Recommended books:

*Africa South of the Sahara*, published annually by Europa Publications, London

*African Biographical Archive*, Saur, Munich, 1994–7

*The African Book Publishing Record*, published quarterly since 1975 by Hans Zell, Munich, available from Bowker-Saur, East Grinstead

*African Books in Print*, Hans Zell, Munich, 5th edn, 2 vols, 1998

*African Studies Abstracts*, quarterly by Hans Zell, Munich, available from Bowker-Saur, East Grinstead

*The Black Handbook: The People, History and Politics of Africa and the African Diaspora*, by Evangeline Bute and Harry Harmer, Cassell Academic, London, 1997

*East Africa Handbook 1999*, Footprint Handbooks, Bath, 5th edn, 1998

*Guide to Documents and Manuscripts in the British Isles relating to Africa*, by J.D. Pearson, 2 vols, Mansell, London, 1993–4

*Guide to South African Reference Books*, by Reuben Musiker and Naomi Musiker, Cassell, London, 6th edn, 1997

*Excluding the general histories and guides already mentioned in the body of this chapter. *Biographical Archives*, where they exist for regions of the world, are included, but not those of individual countries.

*International African Bibliography*, published quarterly since 1971 by Hans Zell, Munich, available from Bowker-Saur, East Grinstead

*Reference Guide to Africa: A Bibliography of Sources*, ed. Alfred Kagan and Yvette Scheven, Scarecrow Press, Lanham, Maryland, 1999**

*South Africa Handbook*, Footprint Handbooks, Bath, 3rd edn, 1999

*South African Bibliography*, Mansell, London, 3rd edn, 1996

## Arab States and the Middle East

### Sources of information in the UK:

British Library Oriental and India Office Collections Reading Room, British Library, 96 Euston Road, London NW1 2DB (tel. 020 7412 7873; fax 020 7412 7641; email reader-services-enquiries@bl.uk; Website http://www.bl.uk/collections/oriental/

Centre for Arab Gulf Studies, Documentation Unit, University of Exeter Old Library, Prince of Wales Road, Exeter, Devon EX4 4J7, (tel. 01392 264041; fax 01392 264023)

Middle East Centre, St Anthony's College, 68 Woodstock Road, Oxford OX2 6JF (tel. 01865 284764; fax 01865 311475) (collections of papers of individuals involved in the Middle East from 1800 to the present day)

### Recommended books:

*Arab-Islamic Biographical Archive*, Saur, Munich, 1995–

*Dictionary of the Middle East*, by Dilip Hiro, Macmillan, London, 1996

*Egypt Handbook*, Footprint Handbooks, Bath, 2nd edn, 1998

*Index Islamicus 1906–1955*, with 5-year supplements to 1985, Mansell, London, 1958–91; published quarterly since 1977; now by Bowker-Saur, East Grinstead and available on CD-ROM

*The Middle East and North Africa*, published annually by Europa Publications, London

*Saudi Arabia: A Bibliography on Society, Politics and Economics from the 18th Century to the Present*, Saur, Munich, 1984

*Who's Who in the Arab World 1997–98*, Saur, Munich, 13th edn, 1996

### Asia (see also under The Far East)

### Sources of information in the UK:

Asian and Indian Studies Centre, St Anthony's College, Woodstock Road, Oxford OX2 6JF (tel/fax 01865 274559)

British Library Oriental and India Office Collections, British Library, 96 Euston Road, London NW1 2DB (tel. 020 7412 7873; fax 020 7412 7641; email reader-services-enquiries@bl.uk; Website http://www.bl.uk/collections/oriental/)

Centre of South Asian Studies, University of Cambridge, Laundress Lane, Cambridge CB2 1SD (tel. 01223 338094; fax 01223 316913)

School of Oriental and African Studies Library, University of London, Thornhaugh Street, Russell Square, London WC1H 0XG (tel. 020 7323 6109; fax 020 7436 3844)

University of Cambridge Faculty of Oriental Studies Library, Sidgwick Avenue, Cambridge CB3 9DA (tel. 01223 335112; fax 01223 335110)

Recommended books:

*Asia: A Selected and Annotated Guide to Reference Works*, Mansell, London, 1980

*Cumulative Bibliography of Asian Studies 1941–1965*, Association for Asian Studies Inc., Boston, Mass; now annually with cumulative volumes

*India Handbook 1999*, Footprint Handbooks, Bath, 1998

*South-East Asia Biographical Archive*, Saur, Munich, 1997–

## Australasia

Recommended books:

*Australasian Biographical Archive*, Saur, Munich, 1990–94

*The Far East and Australasia*, published annually by Europa Publications, London

*The Penguin Historical Atlas of the Pacific*, by Colin McEvedy, Penguin Press, Harmondsworth, 1998

*Who's Who in Australasia and the Pacific Nations*, Melrose Press, Cambridge, 3rd edn, 1997

## The Far East

### Sources of information in the UK:

British Library Oriental and India Office Collections, British Library, 96 Euston Road, London NW1 2DB (tel. 020 7412 7873; fax 020 7412 7870; email reader-services-enquiries@bl.uk; Website http://www.bl.uk/collections/oriental/)

Daiwa Anglo-Japanese Foundation Library, Japan House, 13–14 Cornwall Terrace, London NW1 4QP (tel. 020 7486 3054; fax 020 7486 2914)

Japan Information and Cultural Centre, 101–104 Piccadilly, London W1V 9FN (tel. 020 7465 6580; fax 020 7491 9347)
The School of Oriental and African Studies Library, University of London, Thornaugh Street, Russell Square, London WC1H 0XG (tel. 020 7323 6109; fax 020 7436 3844)
University of Cambridge Faculty of Oriental Studies Library, Sidgwick Avenue, Cambridge CB3 9DA (tel. 01223 335112; fax 01223 335110)

## Recommended books:

*The Cambridge Encyclopedia of China*, Cambridge University Press, 1991
*The Cambridge Encyclopedia of Japan*, Cambridge University Press, 1993
*Facts about China*, eds E. Knappman and Xiao-bin Ji, H.W. Wilson, New York, 1999
*The Far East and Australasia*, published annually by Europa Publications, London
*A Guide to Reference Books for Japanese Studies*, edited and published by the International House of Japan Library, Tokyo, rev. edn, 1997
*Korea Annual*, published annually by Yonhap News Agency, Seoul
*Republic of China Yearbook*, Taipei, 1997

## The Commonwealth

### Sources of information in the UK:

Commonwealth Resource Centre, Commonwealth Institute, Kensington High Street, London W8 6NQ (tel. 020 7603 4535; fax 020 7603 2807; email info@commonwealth.org; Website http://www.commonwealth.org.uk). Mon–Sat, 10–6
Commonwealth Secretariat Library, Marlborough House, Pall Mall, London SW1Y 5HX (tel. 020 7747 6164; fax 020 7747 6168)
Foreign & Commonwealth Office Library, King Charles Street, London SW1A 2AH (tel. 020 7270 3925; fax 020 7270 3270)
Institute of Commonwealth Studies, University of London, 28 Russell Square, London WC1B 5DS (tel. 020 7580 5876; fax 020 7255 2160)
Rhodes House Library, Oxford University Bodleian Library, South Parks Road, Oxford OX1 3RG (tel. 01865 270909; fax 01865 270912)
Sir Robert Menzies Centre for Australian Studies, 28 Russell Square, London WC1B 5DS (tel. 020 7862 8854; fax 020 7580 9627; email mcintyre@sas.ac.uk)

Researchers should also contact the various high commissions in London, i.e. Australia House, Canada House, India House, New Zealand House, etc. (addresses and telephone numbers in the *Writers' & Artists' Yearbook*, *Whitaker's Almanack* under 'The Commonwealth' or in *Hollis Press & Public Relations Annual* under 'International and Overseas Information Sources in the UK', and the London telephone directory).

Recommended books:

General:
*The Commonwealth Yearbook*, 1999 edition published by Hanson-Cooke, London; 2000 and future editions annually by The Stationery Office, London

*Australia*
*Australian Books in Print*, D.W. Thorpe, Melbourne
*Australian Dictionary of Biography*, Melbourne University Press, 14 vols to date plus index vol
*Australian National Bibliography*, National Library of Australia, Canberra (previously known as *Annual Catalogue of Australian Publications*, published 1936–60): since 1972 published weekly, with monthly and 4-monthly cumulations and annual volumes
*Contemporary Australians 1998*, D.W. Thorpe, Melbourne, 1997
*Monash Biographical Dictionary of 20th Century Australia*, D.W. Thorpe, Melbourne, 1994
*Official Year Book of the Commonwealth of Australia*, published annually by the Government Printing Office, Canberra
*Resources for Australian and New Zealand Studies: A Guide to Library Holdings in the United Kingdom*, British Library, London and Australian Studies Centre, University of London, 1986
*Who's Who in Australasia and the Pacific Nations*, Melrose Press, Cambridge, 3rd edn, 1997
*Who's Who in Australia*, published triennially since 1906, now by Information Australia, Melbourne; new edn due 2000

*Canada*
*Canada Yearbook*, published annually by Statistics Canada, Ottawa; also on CD-ROM
*Canadiana*, national bibliography published monthly since 1951, with annual cumulations, National Library of Canada, Ottawa; also on CD-ROM
*Canadian Encyclopedia*, ed. J.H. Marsh, published by Hurtig, Edmonton, Alberta, 2nd edn, 4 vols, 1988

*Dictionary of Canadian Biography*, University of Toronto Press, 1966– (in progress)

*Encyclopedia of Canada's People*, ed. Paul Robert Mogocsi, University of Toronto Press, Toronto, 1998

*The USA and Canada*, Europa Publications, London, 3rd edn, 1998

*Who's Who in Canada*, published annually since 1907, now by Global Press, Toronto

### India

*Index India*, published quarterly by Rajasthan University, Jaipur, since 1967

*India: A Reference Manual*, published annually since 1953 by the Ministry of Information and Broadcasting, New Delhi

*India Handbook 1999*, Footprint Handbooks, Bath, 1998

*India Who's Who*, published annually since 1969 by INFA Publications, New Delhi

*Indian National Bibliography*, published monthly, with annual cumulations, since 1957 by the Central Reference Library, Calcutta

### New Zealand

*Encyclopedia of New Zealand*, ed. A.H. McLintock, 3 vols, Owen, Wellington, 1966

*New Zealand Books in Print*, D.W. Thorpe, Melbourne

*New Zealand National Bibliography*, monthly since 1967, National Library of New Zealand, Wellington

*New Zealand Official Year Book*, published annually by the Department of Statistics, Wellington

*Resources for Australian and New Zealand Studies*, see page 170 under 'Australia'.

Regrettably, space does not permit the listing of other Commonwealth countries in this section.

## Europe

Given the vast amount of material published each year, readers will understand that it is impossible to do more in the space of this chapter than to list some of the countries of Europe, with the location of their national libraries/archives and a selection of reference works. There are, however, a number of general guides which should first be mentioned. These include:

*Biographical Archive of the Benelux Countries*, Saur, Munich, 1992–94

*Directory of European Industrial & Trade Associations* and *Directory of European Professional & Learned Societies*, both CBD Research, Beckenham; updated regularly
*The Documentation of the European Community*, by Ian Thomson, Mansell, London, 1989
*European Historical and Political Facts* series, published by Macmillan, London
*The European Union Encyclopedia and Directory*, Europa Publications, London, 3rd edn, 1999
*Hollis Europe*, published annually by Hollis Directories, Teddington, Middx
*Statistics Europe*, CBD Research, Beckenham; updated regularly
*Western Europe 2000*, Europa Publications, London, 3rd edn, 1999
*What's What and Who's Who in Europe*, by Harry Drost, Cassell, London, 1994

*Note:* For purposes of this chapter, 'Europe' refers to Western Europe. The countries of Eastern Europe are included under the heading 'The Russian Federation (formerly the Commonwealth of Independent States) and Eastern Europe'. Readers may like to know of the following *Biographical Archives* from Saur, Munich: the *Baltic Biographical Archive* (1995–98); the *South-East European Biographical Archive* (1998– ); and the *Turkish Biographical Archive* (1999–).

## Austria
The Österreichische Nationalbibliothek in Vienna is the national library, and there is also the Staatsarchiv (national archives) in the same city.

*Austria, Facts and Figures*
*Dokumentation und Information in Österreich*
*Österreich Lexikon*
*Österreichische Bibliographie*
*Österreichisches Biographisches Lexikon 1815–1950*
*Who's Who in Austria*

## Belgium
The Bibliothèque royale, Albert l^er/Koninklijke Bibliotheek Albert I and the Archives générales du Royaume, both in Brussels, are the major library and archive sources.

*Bibliographie de Belge/Belgische bibliografie*
*Documentation sur la Belgique: bibliographie selective et analytique*

*Inventaire des centres belges de recherche*
*Who's Who in Belgium and the Grand Duchy of Luxembourg*

**Denmark** – see under 'Scandinavia'.

### France

Until recently the the Bibliothèque Nationale de France (BNF) was situated in the rue Richelieu in central Paris. There is now a new and elegant building, opened by President Chirac and Madame Mitterand in December 1996, at Quai François Mauriac, between the Pont de Bercy and the Pont de Tolbiac, on the banks of the Seine, in the 13th arrondissement, which houses printed documents, serials, audio-visual and electronic documents. Some specialised collections (manuscripts, maps, drawings and photographs) remain at rue Richelieu. In contrast to its British counterpart, 'Tolbiac' as the new library has become popularly known, is architecturally pleasing both from the outside and inside. Another major difference is that, unlike in our British Library, the major collections of the BNF are accessible by the general public on the '*haut-de-jardin*' level; there is a special research library on the '*rez-de-jardin*' level reserved for researchers. Day or annual passes (20 or 200 francs respectively in the *haut-de-jardin*; 2-day, 12-day or annual passes in the *rez-de-jardin*) are available (readers seeking access to the *rez-de-jardin* may be subjected to a preliminary interview), and there is every facility you would expect from a purpose-built, up-to-date library. In all the reading rooms assistance is available from staff; there is also an 'Initiation Centre' offering group sessions to readers seeking information on the library and its collections. The full address of the new Bibliothèque Nationale de France is 11 Quai François Mauriac, 75706 Paris Cédex 13 (tel. for information (1) 53 79 59 59; or on the Internet at www.bnf.fr).

Among many other libraries in Paris open to the public is the Bibliothèque du Centre National d'Art et de Culture Georges Pompidou, at the Centre Beaubourg: 19 rue Beaubourg, 75191 Paris (tel. (1) 42 77 12 33). This library has been closed recently, but will reopen in January 2000. If you need to find other libraries in the city, ask at one of the tourist offices or libraries for a most useful free map, *Paris en Bibliothèques*, which lists over a hundred, by name and by subject.

The Archives Nationales are at 60 rue de Francs-Bourgeois, 75141 Paris (tel. (1) 40 27 61 31).

**Recommended books:**
*Annuaire Statistique de la France*, published annually by the I.N.S.E.E., Paris

*Le Bottin Administratif* (yearbook of government departments and public offices), Bottin, Paris, annually

*Dictionnaire de biographie française*, Letousey, Paris, in progress, 1929– (approximately one instalment per year)

*Electre* (*Livres Disponibles/French Books in Print*), published annually by Editions du Cercle de la Librairie, Paris; also on microfiche, CD-ROM and online (database Electre)

*Grand Larousse Encyclopédique*, Larousse, Paris, 10 vols, 1960–64; supplements, 1968, 1975

*Livres Hebdo: Bibliographie de la France*, published weekly with monthly and quarterly supplements by Editions Cercle de la Librairie, Paris

*Qui est Qui en France/Who's Who in France*, published biennially since 1953 by Editions Jacques Lafitte, Paris

The Press Division of the Ambassade de France in London issues from time to time a most informative compact publication, entitled *France: a journalist's guide*, which is invaluable to any writer needing to do research in or about France (latest edition 1999). Contact the Ambassade de France en Grande Bretagne, Service de Presse, 58 Knightsbridge, London SW1X 7JT (tel. 020 7201 1000; fax 020 7201 1053 or 1059).

## Germany

The three major libraries are the Deutsche Bibliothek, in Frankfurt and Leipzig; the Staatsbibliothek Preussischer Kulturbesitz, in Berlin; and the Bayerische Staatsbibliothek, in Munich.

*Allgemeine Deutsche Biographie*
*Brockhaus Enzyklopädie* (also on CD-ROM)
*Deutsche Biographische Enzyklopädie*
*Deutsche Nationalbibliographie* (since 1991 for the united Germany)
*Encarta 99 Enzyklopädie* (CD-ROM)
*Neue Deutsche Biographie*
*Wer ist Wer?* (also on CD-ROM; includes some Austrian and Swiss entries)
*Who's Who in Germany*

## Greece

The National Library is in Athens.

*Greek Bibliography*
*Guide to Greek Libraries and Cultural Organizations*
*Hellenika Vivla* (bibliography)

*Modern Greece: A Bibliography*
*Mega Hellenikon Biographikon Lexikon* (biographical dictionary),
   in progress

**Republic of Ireland (Eire)**
The National Library of Ireland is at Kildare Street, Dublin 2 (tel.
   (00-353-1) 6030200; fax (00-353-1) 6766690
The National Archives are at Bishop Street, Dublin 8 (tel. (00-353-1)
   4072300; fax (00-353-1) 4072333

*Oxford Companion to Irish History*

**Italy**
The major libraries are the Biblioteca Nazionale Centrale Vittorio
Emanuele II in Rome and the Biblioteca Nazionale Centrale in
Florence; there are also national libraries in Milan, Naples, Palermo,
Turin and Venice.

*Bibliografia Nazionale Italiana*
*Dizionario Biografico degli Italiani*
*Enciclopedia Italiana di Scienze, Lettre ed Arti*
*Guida delle Bibliothece Italiane*
*Historical Dictionary of Modern Italy* * *
*Italian Books in Print*
*Lui, Chi, E?*
*Who's Who in Italy*

**The Netherlands**
The major collection is at the Koninklijke Bibliotheek (Royal Library)
in The Hague.

*Brinkman's Cumulatieve Catalogus van Boeken* (bibliography)
*Digest of the Kingdom of the Netherlands* (Government Information
   Service publication)
*Grote Nederlandse Larousse Encyclopedie*
*Grote Winkler Prins Encyclopedie*
*Historical Dictionary of The Netherlands* * *
*Nieuw Nederlandsch Biografisch Woordenboek*
*Pythersen's Nederlandse Almanak*
*Who's Who in the Netherlands*
*Wie is Dat?*

**Norway** – see under 'Scandinavia'.

## Scandinavia

Two biographical dictionaries covering the region are the *Dictionary of Scandinavian Biography* and *Who's Who in Scandinavia*; the *Scandinavian Biographical Archive* (Saur, Munich, 1989–91) contains entries for 155,500 individuals from Denmark, Finland, Iceland, Norway and Sweden.

## Denmark

The Kongelige Bibliotek (Royal Library) in Copenhagen is the national library; the archive collection is at the Kobenhavns Stadsarkiv.

*Bibliography of Books on Denmark 1900–1965*
*Dansk Biografisk Leksikon*
*Dansk Bogfortegnelse* (national bibliography)
*Denmark: An Official Handbook*
*Denmark: A Select Bibliography*
*Historical Dictionary of Denmark* * *
*Who's Who in Denmark*

## Norway

The national library is the Universitetsbiblioteket i Oslo (Royal University Library), and the national archives are at the Riksarkivet, also in Oslo.

*Facts about Norway*
*Guide to Norwegian Statistics*
*Hvem or Hvem?* (Norwegian who's who)
*Norsk Biografisk Leksikon*
*Norsk Bokfortegnelse* (national bibliography)
*Norway Year Book*

## Sweden

The Kungliga Biblioteket (Royal Library), the Riksarkivet (National Record Office) and the Statistika Centralbyráns Biblioteket (Library of Statistics) are all in Stockholm.

*Facts about Sweden*
*Svenskt Biografiskt Lexikon*
*Svensk Bokforteckning* (national bibliography)
*Vem är Det?* (Swedish who's who)

## Spain

The Biblioteca Nacional is in Madrid, as are the Archivo General de la Administración Civil del Estado (the General Archives of the Civil

Administration of the State) and the Archivo Historico Nacional (the National Historical Archives). There is also the Real Biblioteca (Royal Library) at El Escorial, near Madrid. The Archivo de la Corona de Aragon (the Royal Archives of Aragon) are in Barcelona, where there is also the Biblioteca de Catalunya (the Library of Catalonia).

*Bibliografia Española*
*Enciclopedia Universal Ilustrada Europeo-Americana*
*Gran Enciclopedia Rialp*
*Indice Cultural Español* (Spanish cultural index)
*Quién es quién* (Spanish who's who)
*Who's Who in Spain*

See also the *Spanish, Portuguese* and *Latin American Biographical Archive* listed under 'Latin America'.

**Sweden** – see under 'Scandinavia'.

*Switzerland*
The national library is the Schweizerische Landesbibliothek/ Bibliothèque Nationale Suisse in Berne; the Archives Fédérales (national archives) are in the same city. In Geneva there are the United Nations Library and the International Labour Office Library.

*Das Schweizer Buch/Le Livre Suisse* (national bibliography)
*Who's Who in Switzerland*

# Latin America and the Caribbean

Space does not permit the listing here of major libraries in the various countries and states, but these are in the *World Guide to Libraries*, published by Saur, Munich, 13th edn, 1998 and in *The World of Learning*, published annually by Europa Publications, London.

*Cambridge Encyclopedia of Latin America and the Caribbean*, Cambridge University Press, 1992
*Caribbeana, 1900–1965: A Topical Bibliography*, by L. Comitas, University of Washington Press, Seattle and London, 1968
*CARICOM Bibliography*, Caricom Secretariat, Georgetown, Guyana, 1977
*Latin America Bibliography*, ed. Juan Manuel Pérez, Scarecrow Press, Lanham, Maryland, 1999**
*Mexico and Central American Handbook 1999*, Footprint Handbooks, Bath, 1998

*South America, Central America and the Caribbean 1999*, Europa
  Publications, London, 7th edn, 1998
*South American Handbook 1999*, Footprint Handbooks, Bath, 1998
*Spanish, Portuguese, and Latin American Biographical Archive*, 3
  series, Saur, Munich, 1986–98

## The Russian Federation (formerly the Commonwealth of Independent States/Union of Soviet Socialist Republics) and Eastern Europe

The Rossiiskaya Nacionalnaya Biblioteka (National Library of
Russia) is in St Petersburg, as are the Central State Historical Archives
of the USSR. The State Public Historical Library of Russia and the
Central Archives of the USSR are in Moscow.

*The Biographical Dictionary of the Former Soviet Union*, Saur,
  Munich, 2nd edn, 1992
*Eastern Europe and the Commonwealth of Independent States*,
  Europa Publications, London, 3rd edn, 1997
*The Great Soviet Encyclopedia* (translation of *Bol'shaya Sovetskaya
  Entsiklopediya*, 3rd edn), 31 vols + 3 index vols, Macmillan, New
  York/Macmillan, London, 1973–83
*Guide to Russian Reference Books*, Stanford University, California,
  in progress, 1962–
*Official Publications of the Soviet Union and Eastern Europe 1945–
  1980: A Select Bibliography*, ed. G. Walker, Mansell, London, 1985
*Reinterpreting Russia: An Annotated Bibliography of Books on
  Russia, the Soviet Union and the Russian Federation 1991–1996*,
  by Steve D. Bollard, Scarecrow Press, Lanham, Maryland, 1997**
*Russian Biographical Archive*, Saur, Munich, 1997–
*The Territories of the Russian Federation*, Europa, London, 1999
*Who Was Who in the Soviet Union*, 2 vols, Saur, Munich, 1992
*Who's Who in Russia Today*, Saur, Munich, 1993

## United States of America

The Library of Congress, Washington, D.C. 20540 (tel. (202) 707
5000) is the national library, but it is not the exact equivalent of the
British Library in that it does not automatically acquire a copy of
every book published in the United States; it does, however, collect
and catalogue books published in other countries. The printed
volumes of the *National Union Catalog*, which has replaced the old
*Library of Congress Catalog*, will be found on open access at the
British Library and in major libraries of the UK. The *Pre-1956*

*Imprints*, an impressive run of 755 volumes, are clear and easy to use; their great value to the researcher is that they provide in one alphabetical sequence, under authors, the holdings of the Library of Congress together with those of the principal libraries of North America. Another bonus is that the *NUC* gives dates of authors (otherwise sometimes difficult to obtain). The *NUC* from 1968 may be accessed through BLAISE-LINE (LC MARC). A useful Website for the NUC and other American catalogs is www.lib.ncsu.edu.

The National Archives and Records Administration is at the National Archives Building, 8th Street at Pennsylvania Avenue NW, Washington, D.C. 20408 (tel. (202) 501 5000 (visitor information)).

**Recommended books:**
*Books in Print, Books in Print Plus, Books in Print with Book Reviews Plus, Books Out of Print with Book Reviews Plus, Subject Guide to Books in Print*, Bowker, New Providence, N.J.; some printed vols, some microfiche, some CD-ROM, some online
*Cambridge Dictionary of American Biography*, ed. John S. Bowman, Cambridge University Press, Cambridge, 1995
*Information Please Almanac*, published annually since 1947, now by Houghton Mifflin, Boston, Mass.
*National Inventory of Documentary Sources in the United States* (*NIDS*), on microfiche in three parts: 1, *Federal Records*; 2, *Manuscript Division, Library of Congress*; 3, *State Archives, State Libraries, Historical Societies, Academic Libraries and Other Repositories*; by subscription, Chadwyck-Healey, Cambridge
*Oxford Companion to American History*, Oxford University Press, Oxford, 1966
*Statistical Abstract of the United States*, published annually since 1879 by the Government Printing Office, Washington, D.C.
*The USA and Canada*, Europa Publications, London, 3rd edn, 1998
*Who's Who in America, Who Was Who in America, Who Was Who in American History*, Marquis, Chicago, printed vols, fiches, CD-ROM and online. The same publisher issues regional volumes for the East, Midwest, South and Southwest, and West of the United States. There is a printed index vol. entitled *Index to Marquis Who's Who Publications*, and also *The Complete Marquis Who's Who* on two CD-ROMs, updated every six months.

**The publications of Scarecrow Press Inc., including their *Historical Dictionary* series, are available in the UK from Shelwing Ltd, 127 Sandgate Road, Folkestone, Kent CT20 2BL (tel. 01303 850501; fax 01303 850162).

# 10

# Preparation for the Press

The research is done, the text drafted and polished to the writer's satisfaction, on screen or in typescript, the length approximately right. (Most word processor owners have a built-in word count facility, but those less fortunate must do it the hard way, taking an average number of words per page and multiplying by the number of pages – remembering to allow for any short pages and inserts – and rounding up the total to the nearest hundred words.)

If the great work is an article, a short story, a novel or a play, all that remains to be done is to produce the fair copy. This you may either type, or have professionally typed, or, using a word processor and printer, the latter preferably of inkjet or laser quality, print out. In all cases it is advisable initially to make three copies, two for the publisher and one for yourself; additional copies when needed, say, for an American or paperback publisher, can be made later. It goes without saying that before despatch to literary agent or publisher you will make a final check for spelling mistakes and simple errors.

Nearly all typing agencies and most freelance typists today offer a word processing service, which means that as well as the specified number of typescript copies you will receive one or more floppy disks. An ever-increasing number of publishers now ask for submission on disk, in which case normally they will expect to get at least one copy of the typescript as well (this is known as the 'hard copy').

The non-fiction book requires some extra attention. The prelims must be written, the notes and references section and the bibliography (if any) compiled, some thought given to the provision of an index, although this will not actually be prepared until later. None of these chores, strictly speaking, comes within the province of 'research', but their importance in giving the finished manuscript a professional look merits their mention here.

The word 'manuscript', abbreviated as MS (MSS in plural), which originally meant a handwritten document, in 20th-century literary jargon has become synonymous with 'typescript', a text that is either typed or prepared on a word processor and printed out. An

180

'electronic typescript' is a text on disk. As mentioned above, a typed manuscript is now usually referred to as a 'hard copy'.

Writers submitting their work on disk should consult their publishers well in advance to ascertain requirements. They will probably be expected to produce their text to the ASCII format. There are other ways of transferring large quantities of material direct to publishers, i.e. on 'zip' disks, but this need not concern the reader of this handbook. Publishers producing small runs of specialised books sometimes require what is called 'camera-ready' copy, which is then photographed and reproduced lithographically. Take professional advice if this is a requirement.

There are some excellent works to help the writer with his final preparation. Godfrey Howard's *The Good English Guide* and the *Bloomsbury Good Word Guide* should resolve any problems as to the current usage of particular words or phrases. G.V. Carey's *Mind the Stop*, first published some years ago and now a Penguin Reference paperback, is one of two layman's bibles on punctuation; the other is Eric Partridge's *You Have a Point There*, reprinted in 1999. The *Writers' & Artists' Yearbook* carries a short article on 'Preparation of Typescripts', and Judith Butcher's *Copy-Editing*, recently reprinted, although directed more at publishers than writers, contains many valuable hints on the final preparation of text for the printer. *The MHRA Style Book* is the standard work, not only for academics and editors, but for all authors writing for publication. Finally, the relevant *British Standards* are listed at the end of this chapter.

# Prelims

These are the preliminary pages at the beginning of a book, known in the printing and publishing trade as 'prelims'. Normally they will consist of a title page, dedication, list of contents, list of illustrations, acknowledgments, abbreviations, preface or foreword. Not all of these will be required for every kind of book, and the publisher normally has some say in the matter. It is up to the author to indicate, at this stage, what he intends to provide – i.e. if he wishes to include an 'Author's Note' or not. It does not matter if he cannot write the text of these as yet – all you need to do is to put a blank sheet in the typescript at the appropriate place or places, stating, for example, 'Acknowledgments' and below this, 'copy to follow'. The important thing is for the production manager and book designer to know that they are coming, so that they can allow for them in their calculations.

# Notes and References

Consistency is the keyword here. If the book has been commissioned, the publisher may have sent the author a copy of the 'house style', or will have discusssed with him in advance his preference for the numbering and style of notes and references, such as whether they should appear at the foot of each page, after each chapter, or in a separate section at the end of the book. Failing such instruction, or if you do not yet have a publisher, it is advisable to study some published titles in a similar category of book and follow a similar style. Bear in mind for the future that source references may include Websites, possibly with the dates visited.

# Bibliography

Depending on whether the work is aimed at the popular or academic market, the bibliography may be as selective or as comprehensive as you wish. If the latter, it is usual to divide the entries into 'primary' and 'secondary' (or 'printed' and 'manuscript') sources, and to include not only books, but articles in periodicals and learned journals, as well as references to private papers consulted. Provided careful notes have been kept of all material used in the course of research, as suggested in chapter 2, the compilation of a bibliography should be quite straightforward. The normal arrangement of books and articles is in an alphabetical sequence, under the surname of the author. Care should be taken to list the particular editions used and to indicate any subsequent revised editions or reprints of each work, where relevant.

The British Standard *BS 1629: Recommendations for references to published materials*, details an internationally accepted set of rules for the guidance of those compiling bibliographies in books.

# Preparation of the Typescript

The cardinal rules for the presentation of material for publication stipulate that the text should be typed on one side of the paper only, in double spacing, with good margins (1½ inches; approximately 4 cm) is the norm, both on left and right, and at top and bottom. It is helpful to the publisher if the same number of lines are typed per page; but try not to carry over onto the next page the last few words of a paragraph. With a word processor you will find that the page breaks are automatic: when you do your final check-through you should be able to remedy these breaks where necessary: in order to avoid a short line at the top of a page it is best to carry over the last two lines, even though it means that the previous page may be one line short. A4 size paper is now standard. Headings should be consistent throughout, and quoted matter of more than a few lines should be indented, without the use of quotation marks. Indent five spaces at the beginning of each paragraph, unless the publisher's house style asks for anything different. Start each chapter on a new page.

Apart from the obvious use of italics or underlining as necessary, writers using word processors should resist the temptation to adorn their pages with different fonts and type sizes for headings and sub-headings etc. This is the publisher's prerogative, and the book designer would far rather have a straightforward typescript to work on.

First impressions matter. New authors should aim to submit a pristine MS, especially if the work is going to a publisher unsolicited. One of the joys of word processing is that corrections may be made right up to the last minute and the revised texts printed out, without the need for laborious re-typing. Established authors often find that their publishers adopt a more relaxed attitude and that they can get away with a modest number of handwritten additions, deletions or amendments. So long as these are absolutely legible and their place of insertion or deletion clear to the printer, it is unnecessary to go to the trouble of re-typing each amended page. Be very careful, however, about numbering pages: an insertion between pages 14 and 15, for example, should be numbered 14a, 14b and so on; but if page 15 is to be deleted altogether, the previous page should be numbered 14/15. (This does not apply to text prepared on a word processor, as pages are automatically re-numbered to take account of all amendments.) Where an insertion does not take up a full page, always rule a line obliquely from left to right through the remaining part of the page to indicate that the text is continuous. When amending typewritten texts, it is better to use white correcting fluid and to type the correction in rather than to risk an erasure and handwritten alteration that may be ambiguous to the copy editor or printer. In the case of 'camera-ready' copy, always typed electronically, with variable spacing and justified lines, each page must of course be perfect, although pure spelling mistakes and punctuation may be corrected – very carefully – again with the aid of correction fluid.)

Those who still use a typewriter should make just one clean copy of their final draft, then photocopy the required number of additional copies. Photocopying has become so inexpensive these days that there is little point in messing about with carbons and flimsy paper, except possibly for correspondence. If you do not have a photocopier at home, take your typescript to a copy shop where you can either have it done for you or, at a reduced cost, use a self-operated machine.

You may be able to negotiate a special price for several copies of a long book.

When packing up your typescript for agent or publisher, do remember that staples should never be used. Short texts such as poems, articles or short stories may be fastened with paper clips, but a full-length hard copy should always be delivered as loose sheets, preferably packed into a box. Most copy shops will supply light-weight boxes of A4 size, similar to those in which reams of bond typing paper used to be sold (alas, no longer!).

# The Copy-Editing Process

Once your book has been accepted by the publisher, and before it goes to the printer, the typescript will be handed over to a copy editor. This copy editor, who may be an 'in-house' member of your publisher's editorial team, but more likely nowadays a freelance, will go through your text with the eyes of a hawk, ironing out discrepancies, repetitions, and errors of grammar, punctuation and spelling. Be prepared, at this stage, to receive what may appear to be an exasperatingly long list of queries: part of the copy editor's job is to challenge everything that he considers to be less than clear, in need of amplification, or basically incorrect. This is why it is so vital that you should hang on to your research notes; otherwise you could find yourself having to re-do some of that early research.

Some copy editors are more ruthless than others, and authors in general do not take kindly to having their work 'tampered with'. Naturally you should not stand for anyone meddling with your individual style or with the opinions you express, but on most other matters it is wise to bear in mind that, far from 'nit-picking', the copy editor is genuinely trying to improve your book. He may not be knowledgeable about the subject-matter, however, and a good deal of patience, justifying and explanation may be required from you, the expert, as you wade through his queries. At the end of the day it may come as a surprise to you just how many inadvertent slips the copy editor has saved you from making.

That said, standards do vary, which is something that the Society of Freelance Editors and Proofreaders (SFEP), founded in 1988, is striving to improve through training and accredited membership. If you are unhappy and wish to check up on your copy editor's qualifications for the job, you could ask the publisher if he is a member of SFEP.

Writers should not lose sight of the fact that a first-class copy editor is worth his weight in gold.

# Proof-correction

As a book writer you will normally be sent one set of page proofs, which you are required to read and correct. At the same time the proofs will be read by the publisher's own proofreader, either in or out of 'house'. If the corrections are heavy, a set of revised proofs will be forthcoming.

It should be borne in mind that while printers' errors are not charged, any changes made by the author at proof stage which amount to more than 10–15 per cent of the cost of composition are payable by him (and will be deducted from royalties). The time to make major last-minute amendments is *before* the copy editor passes the work to the printer.

Sometimes, where the work is one of topical interest and some important event has taken place between the date of completion of the manuscript and delivery of proofs, the publisher will find the space to include a brief note to the effect that 'Since this book went to press [such and such] has occurred', but this cannot always be counted on.

A list of signs used in proof correction will be found in Judith Butcher's *Copy Editing*, in the *Writers' & Artists' Yearbook* and in the *British Standard BS 5261C: Marks for copy preparation and proof correction*. Other valuable guides for spelling, punctuation, division of words, and the use of capital and lower case, are *Hart's Rules for Compositors and Readers* and the *Oxford Writers' Dictionary*.

If for any reason you require the services of a qualified proof reader, you should contact the Administration Officer of the Society of Freelance Editors and Proofreaders at Mermaid House, 1 Mermaid Court, London SE1 1HR (tel. 020 7403 5141). Some proofreading services are listed in the *Writers' & Artists' Yearbook* under 'Editorial, literary and production services by specialisation' and in *The Writer's Handbook* under 'Editorial, research and other services'.

# The Index

Every non-fiction book merits a good index, and reviewers these days are paying more attention than ever before to the quality of indexing and commenting unfavourably, where appropriate, on the lack of indexes.

Most authors' contracts stipulate that the author shall provide the index. It is however sometimes possible – and when, if ever, most publishers have accepted the Minimum Terms Agreement negotiated by the Society of Authors and the Writers' Guild it should become normal practice – for the publisher to contribute 50 per cent of the cost, especially if a professional indexer is to be employed. Some publishers have their own team of freelance indexers on whom they can call; others seek recommendations from the Society of Indexers, which was founded in 1957 to safeguard and improve indexing standards and which maintains a register of indexers suitably qualified in different subjects and types of indexing. To assist those seeking an indexer for their work, the Society now issues annually a booklet entitled *Indexers Available*, which is distributed throughout the book trade and is on the Web at http://socind.demon.co.uk; it lists practising members' names, addresses, telephone numbers and their specialist subjects. At the time of writing (spring 1999) the Society's recommended minimum rate for indexing is £14 per hour for basic skills; specialist work commands more. Rates are revised annually.

There has long been controversy as to whether writers should or should not index their own books. Some people feel that an author is the ideal person, but others hold strongly to the view that he may be too close to his own work to be able to produce a truly objective index. Certainly, as a general rule, it will almost always take him longer than the trained professional. It is not generally realised that there is a great deal more to indexing than extracting the names of people and places and stringing them together in alphabetical order, so that when an author does decide to attempt it, he would be well advised to take the time and trouble to learn the basic rules.

Firstly, he must choose – and stick to – the form of alphabetical arrangement most suited to his book: either 'letter-by-letter' or 'word-by-word'. Then – and this is governed largely by space – he should give some thought to the layout and balance of the index and whether the sub-headings and sub-sub-headings (if any) will be indented or run on; both in layout and wording the sub-headings throughout must be consistent. There must be adequate cross-referencing of names and concepts, but not so much as to make the index unnecessarily long; care must be taken to avoid what is known as a 'wild goose chase', i.e. cross-references that never lead to the location of the subject-matter in the text, as in, for example, 'Indexers, Society of, *see* Society of Indexers' and 'Society of Indexers, *see* Indexers, Society of'. The main function of an index is to direct the user quickly to the place or places in the text where he will find precisely the information he seeks.

Indexing is normally undertaken at page proof stage and, for this reason, it nearly always has to be done at speed in order to meet the printers' deadline. Here the computer has really come into its own, and now that there is sophisticated software that has been specially designed to meet the professional indexer's needs (see details at end of this chapter), two of the most time-consuming stages of the job – the sorting of entries into the required order, and the printing out of the edited index copy – can be accomplished very quickly. Beware, however, of the so-called 'automatic indexing' programs on offer, as these are inadequate for book indexing. Although a growing number of indexers now use computers, much manual indexing still goes on, the usual method being to mark on the page proofs (either with highlighter pen or by underlining) each name or concept to be indexed, and to write these on separate cards or slips which are filed alphabetically in a box as work proceeds; a certain amount of tightening up and editing of entries has to take place when all entries are assembled. It is a good plan for the author who intends to prepare his own index to start building it as he writes, making slips for the main entries and possible sub-headings; these can be edited later and the page numbers added. In the course of his work the indexer may come across inconsistencies or inaccuracies that both the author and the copy editor have missed; these should be telephoned through to the editorial office immediately. The index should be typed in double-spacing, with a maximum of 32 characters per line. The publisher will usually say that his tight production deadline does not permit him to send the indexer a proof for correction, but this should be insisted on wherever possible. Even the best printer can make a nonsense out of an index by failing to indent a sub-heading or by omitting or misprinting the occasional page reference – something that may not be spotted if the index is checked in the editorial office – and an index that is inaccurate is worse than no index at all.

These are but a few of the problems that confront the indexer. Authors interested in acquiring some basic training in indexing may take the Training in Indexing course administered by the Society of Indexers, successful completion of which entitles members of the Society to the status of 'Accredited Indexer' and, ultimately, following assessment of their experience and competence in practical indexing, to that of 'Registered Indexer' (details from the Training Course Administrator, Society of Indexers, Globe Centre, Penistone Road, Sheffield S6 3AE; tel. 0114 281 3060; fax 0114 281 3061). The course consists of five units, which may be purchased separately; you are not committed to taking the formal tests. Also available is a Book Indexing Postal Tutorials (BIPT) course, based on the compilation of indexes to short texts (details from Ann Hall, The Lodge, Sidmount Avenue, Moffat, Dumfriesshire DG10 9BS; tel./fax 01683 220440).

The two most comprehensive and up-to-date manuals, recommended by and available from the Society, are Nancy C. Mulvany's *Indexing Books* and Hans Wellisch's *Indexing from A to Z*, both published in the United States. The *British Standard BS 1749* and *International Standard BS ISO 999* (details at the end of this chapter) are the authoritative guides to current practice. R.F. Hunissett's practical guide to indexing historical texts, *Indexing for Editors*, has recently been reprinted and is available from the British Records Association, c/o London Metropolitan Archives, 40 Northampton Road, London EC1R 0HB.

Names of suitably qualified indexers, general or specialist, may be obtained from the Registrar of the Society of Indexers, Mrs E. Wallis, 25 Leyborne Park, Kew Gardens, Surrey TW9 3HB (tel. 020 8940 4771). For a copy of *Indexers Available*, or other information about the Society, write to the Hon. Secretary, Liza Weinkove, Society of Indexers, Globe Centre, Penistone Road, Sheffield S6 3AE or contact the Administrator, Wendy Burrow, any weekday between 10 a.m. and 2 p.m. (tel. 0114 281 3060; fax 0114 281 3061; email admin@ socind.demon.co.uk; Website http://www.socind.demon. co.uk).

# A Last Word of Advice

Once the proofs have been corrected and returned to the publisher, you may safely return all borrowed books and documents to their respective libraries and/or owners. Parcel up and store your original notes and early drafts. *It is important not to throw these away.* When eventually your book is published, there is always the possibility that it may arouse unexpected interest and may even lead to other related commissions; almost certainly you will receive a number of readers' letters either asking you to justify certain statements or to give further information. Some of these enquiries may come from researchers working in the same field. Bearing in mind the enormous help you yourself have derived from the work of others, would it not be churlish and ungenerous to refuse or not to be in a position to pass on the fruits of your own research – especially any information gathered but not used – to other *bona fide* writers?

It should not be forgotten that all writers feed to a lesser or greater extent on the work of other writers. As the Californian playwright Wilson Mizner put it, 'When you steal from one author, it's plagiarism; if you steal from many, it's research'.

*British Standards* (available from the British Standards Institution, Sales Department, 389 Chiswick High Road, London W4 4AL (tel. 020 8996 7000; fax 020 8996 7001):

| | |
|---|---|
| BS 1629: 1989 | *Recommendations for references to published materials* |
| BS 1749: 1985 | *Recommendations for alphabetical arrangement and the filing order of numbers and symbols* |

| | |
|---|---|
| *BS 5261 Part 1: 1975 (1983)* | *Copy preparation and proof correction. Recommendations for preparation of typescript copy for printing* |
| *BS 5261 Part 2: 1976 (1995)* | *Specifications for typographical requirements, marks for copy preparation and proof correction, proofing procedure* |
| *BS 5261C: 1976* | *Marks for copy preparation and proof correction* (extract from *BS 5261 Part 2*) |
| *BS 5605: 1990* | *Recommendations for citing and referencing published material* |
| *BS ISO 999: 1996* | *Guidelines for the content, organisation and presentation of indexes* (This has replaced the earlier *BS 3700*) |

*Bloomsbury Good Word Guide*, ed. M.H. Manser, Bloomsbury, London, 2nd edn, 1990; paperback edn, 1991

*Copy-Editing*, by Judith Butcher, Cambridge University Press, Cambridge, 3rd edn, 1992; latest reprint, with corrections, 1999

*The Good English Guide: English Usage in the 1990s*, by Godfrey Howard, Macmillan, 1993; paperback edn, 1997

*Hart's Rules for Compositors and Readers at the University Press Oxford*, Oxford University Press, Oxford, 39th edn, 1983

*Indexers Available*, annual list of accredited and registered indexers, Society of Indexers, Sheffield

*Indexing Books*, by Nancy C. Mulvany, University of Chicago Press, Chicago, 1994*

*Indexing for Editors*, by R.F. Hunissett, first published in 1972; reprinted by British Records Association, London, 1997

*Indexing from A to Z*, by Hans Wellisch, H.W. Wilson, New York, 2nd edn, 1995*

*The MHRA Style Book*, eds A.S. Maney and R.L. Smallwood, Modern Humanities Research Association, London, 5th edn, 1998; obtainable from W.S. Maney & Son Ltd, Hudson Road, Leeds LS9 7DL (tel. 0113 249 7481)

*Mind the Stop: A Brief Guide to Punctuation*, by G.V. Carey, Penguin Books, Harmondsworth, 1971; reprinted 1993

*Oxford Writers' Dictionary*, Oxford University Press, Oxford, 1990

*Both these titles are available from the Sales Manager of the Society of Indexers, Dorothy Frame, 26 Draycot Road, London E11 2NX (tel. 020 8530 2727)

*Writers' & Artists' Yearbook*, published annually by A & C Black, London; articles on 'Preparation of Typescripts' and 'Research and the Internet'
*You Have a Point There*, by Eric Partridge, Routledge, London, 1978; reprinted 1999

The recommended indexing program is:
MACREX, compiled by Hilary and Drusilla Calvert and available from Macrex Indexing Services, Beech House, Burn Road, Blaydon-on-Tyne, NE21 6JR (tel. 0191 4142595; fax 0191 4141893)

# Appendix I

## Selective List of Major Sources in the United Kingdom

This list is limited by space and should be used as a guideline only, in conjunction with the *Aslib Directory of Information Sources in the UK*, the booklet *Record Repositories in Great Britain* and other reference source-guides mentioned in earlier sections of this book. Unless otherwise stated, the libraries and record offices are open to the public without formality. Addresses, telephone numbers and hours of opening are subject to change with alarming frequency; most libraries and record offices have fax numbers, but some have asked for them not to be listed. Websites and email addresses, where not given here, will be found in the above guides. While every effort has been made to bring information up to date at the time of going to press, it is advisable that researchers should check in advance before travelling any distance.

*Note:* This listing gives the new telephone codes and prefixes that are to apply from 22 April 2000 to London, some provincial cities and Northern Ireland. Prior to that date both the old and new numbers may be dialled. After 22 April 2000 it will not be necessary to include the area code 020 for London numbers when dialling locally. (See note on page xiii for further details.)

## The Copyright Libraries

The British Library, 96 Euston Road, London NW1 2DB (general enquiries: tel. 020 7412 7676; fax 020 7412 7609; emails: reader-services-enquiries@bl.uk and reader-admissions@bl.uk). Reading rooms: Humanities 1 and 2; Rare Books and Music; Oriental and India Office; Maps; Manuscripts; Science 1, 2 and 3. Admission to reading rooms by reader's pass (apply to Reader's Admissions Office, or tel. 020 7412 7677; fax 020 7412 7794). Mon, from 10; Tue-Sat, from 9.30; closing times vary. For general enquiries and advance reservations telephone 020 7412 7676 or fax 020

7412 7609. Information is available on Portico, the Library's World Wide Web server (http://www.bl.uk). Access to the British Library catalogue OPAC 97 (http://opac97.bl.uk).

Bodleian Library, University of Oxford, Broad Street, Oxford OX1 3BG (tel. (enquiries) 01865 277000; fax 01865 277182; email reader.services@bodley.ox.ac.uk). Admission by reader's ticket (fee may be payable). Mon–Fri, 9–10 (term), 9–7 (vacation); Sat, 9–1.

[Cambridge] University Library, University of Cambridge, West Road, Cambridge CB3 9DR (tel. 01223 333000; fax 01223 333160; email library@ula.com.ac.uk). Admission by reader's ticket (letter of introduction required). Mon–Fri, 9.30–7; Sat, 9.30–1; closed for one week in September.

National Library of Scotland, George IV Bridge, Edinburgh EH1 1EW (tel. 0131-226 4531; fax 0131-622 4803; email enquiries@nls.uk). Admission by reader's ticket. Mon–Fri, 9.30–8.30; Sat, 9.30–1.

National Library of Wales, Aberystwyth, Dyfed SY23 3BU (tel. 01970 632800; fax 01970 615709; email holi@llg.org.uk). Admission by reader's ticket. Mon–Fri, 9.30–6; Sat, 9.30–5.

N.B. Trinity College Library, College Street, Dublin 2, in the Republic of Ireland (tel. 00353 1 6772941; fax 00353 1 9003; email library@tcd.ie) is a copyright library. Mon–Fri, 10–5; Sat, 10–1. Letter of introduction required.

# Public Record Offices

Public Record Office, Ruskin Avenue, Kew, Richmond, Surrey TW9 4DU (tel. 020 8876 3444; fax 020 8878 8905; email enquiry@pro.gov.uk). Admission by reader's ticket. Mon, Wed, Fri, Sat, 9.30–5; Tue, 10–7; Thu, 9.30–7.Closed for stocktaking for two weeks usually in early December. Further information on Website http://www.pro.gov.uk N.B. The Public Record Office at Chancery Lane, London, is now closed.

Scottish Record Office, H.M. General Register House, Edinburgh EH1 3YY (tel. 0131-535 1314; fax 0131-557 9569; email research@nas.gov.uk). Admission by reader's ticket. Mon–Fri, 9–4.45.

Public Record Office of Northern Ireland, 66 Balmoral Avenue, Belfast BT9 6NY (tel. 028 9025 5905; fax 028 9025 5999; email proni@nics.gov.uk). Admission by reader's ticket. Mon–Wed, Fri, 9.15–4.45; Thu, 9.15–8.45. Closed for two weeks late November/ early December.

# General Register Offices

General Register Office (part of the Office for National Statistics): indexes to registers of births, marriages and deaths from 1837, and census returns 1841–1891, at the Family Records Centre, 1 Myddelton Street, London EC1R 1UW (tel. 020 8392 5300; fax 020 8392 5307; email: certificate.service@ons.gov.uk; Website http://www.open.gov.uk/pro/frc.htm). Admission without ticket. Mon, Wed, Fri, 9–5; Tue, 10–7; Thu, 9–7; Sat, 9.30–5. Address for postal applications for certificates: General Register Office, PO Box 2, Southport, Merseyside PR8 2JD; priority service tel. 0151-471 4816/fax 01704 550013.

Principal Registry of the Family Division, First Avenue House, 42–49 High Holborn, London WC1V 6NP. Probate Search Rooms, tel. 020 7936 7000. Divorce registry, tel. 020 7936 6000 ext. 6957. Mon–Fri, 10–4.30.

General Register Office for Scotland, New Register House, Edinburgh EH1 3YT (tel. 0131-334 0380; fax 0131-314 4400; email: nrh.gros@gtnet.gov.uk). Mon–Fri, 9.30–4.30.

General Register Office (Northern Ireland), Oxford House, 49–55 Chichester Street, Belfast BT1 4HL (tel. 028 9025 2021/22/23/24; fax 028 9025 2044). Mon–Fri, 9.30–4.

N.B. The records for the whole of Ireland from 1864 to 1921 are at the office of the Registrar General, Joyce House, 8–11 Lombard Street East, Dublin 2, which houses the records of the Republic only since 1922.

# Manuscript Collections/Registers of Archives

British Library, 96 Euston Road, London 2DB: Manuscripts Reading Room (tel. 020 7412 7513; fax 020 7412 7745; email mms@bl.uk) and Oriental and India Collections Reading Room (tel. 020 7412 7873; fax 020 7412 7641). Reader's pass required (apply to Reader Admissions Office, tel. 020 7412 7677; fax 020 7412 7794). *Note.* A higher-level pass is required for access to the Manuscripts Reading Room. All reading rooms are open Mon, from 10; Tue–Sat, from 9.30; telephone for details of closing times.

National Register of Archives (Scotland). This is maintained by the Scottish Record Office, see under 'Public Record Offices'.

Royal Commission on Historical Manuscripts/National Register of Archives, Quality House, Quality Court, Chancery Lane, London WC2A 1HP (tel. 020 7242 1198; fax 020 7831 3550; email nra@hmc.gov.uk; Website http://www.hmc.gov.uk). Mon–Fri, 9.30–5.

Many collections of manuscripts are also housed at the Public Record Offices (see page 192) and at the various County Record Offices and University Libraries (see pages 194–204).

# County Record Offices/Regional Archives Centres

In this list opening times are not given for the individual offices: some are open all day throughout the working week, others close for lunch (or do not produce material during the lunch period), some are open late one evening in the week (but material must be ordered beforehand), others are shut either on Mondays or Saturdays. It is advisable to check prior to making a visit, as these opening hours are subject to change, and to reserve a seat or, where available, a microfilm reader/computer.

## *Bedfordshire*
Bedfordshire and Luton Archives and Record Service, County Hall, Cauldwell Street, Bedford MK42 9AP (tel. 01234 228833/ 228777/363222 ext. 2833; fax 01234 228854)

## *Berkshire*
Berkshire Record Office, Shire Hall, Shinfield Park, Reading RG2 9XD (tel. 0118 901 5132; fax 0118 901 5131)

## *Buckinghamshire*
Buckinghamshire Records and Local Studies Service, County Hall, Aylesbury HP20 1UU (tel. 01296 382587; fax 01296 382274)

## *Cambridgeshire*
Cambridge County Record Office, Shire Hall, Castle Hill, Cambridge CB3 0AP (tel. 01223 717281; fax 01223 717201); also at Grammar School Walk, Huntingdon PE18 6LF (tel. 01480 425842; fax 01480 459563)

## *Cheshire*
Cheshire Record Office, Duke Street, Chester CH1 1RL (tel. 01244 602574; fax 01244 603812)
Chester Archives, Town Hall, Chester CH1 2HJ (tel. 01244 402110; fax 01244 312243)

## *Cornwall*
Cornwall Record Office, County Hall, Truro TR1 3AY (tel. 01872 273698/323127; fax 01872 270340)

Royal Institution of Cornwall, River Street, Truro TR1 2SJ (tel. 01872 272205; fax 01872 240514)

## Cumbria

Cumbria Record Office, The Castle, Carlisle CA3 8UR (tel. 01228 607285; fax 01228 607274); also at County Offices, Kendal LA9 4RQ (tel. 01539 773540; fax 01539 773439); at 140 Duke Street, Barrow-in-Furness LA14 1XW (tel. 01229 894363; fax 01229 894371); and at Scotch Street, Whitehaven CA28 7BJ (tel. 01946 852920; fax 01946 852919)

## Derbyshire

Derbyshire Record Office, New Street, Matlock DE4 3AG (tel. 01629 585347, ext. 35201; searchroom, tel. 01629 585347; fax 01629 57611). Postal address: DRO, County Offices, Matlock DE4 3AG

## Devon

Devon Record Office, Castle Street, Exeter EX4 3PU (tel. 01392 384253; fax 01392 384256)

North Devon Library and Record Office, Tuly Street, Barnstaple EX31 1EL (tel./fax 01271 388608)

Plymouth and West Devon Area Record Office, Unit 3, Clare Place, Coxside, Plymouth PL4 0JW (tel. 01752 305940; fax 01752 223939)

## Dorset

Dorset Record Office, Bridport Road, Dorchester DT1 1RP (tel. 01305 250550; fax 01305 257184)

## Durham

Durham County Record Office, County Hall, Durham DH1 5UL (tel. 0191-383 3253/3474; fax 0191-383 4500)

## Essex

Essex Record Office, County Hall, Chelmsford CM1 1LX (tel. 01245 430067; fax 01245 430085); and Central Library, Victoria Avenue, Southend-on-Sea SS2 6EX (tel. 01702 464278; fax 01702 464253); Colchester and NE Essex Branch, Stanwell House, Stanwell Street, Colchester CO2 7DL (tel. 01206 572099; fax 01206 574541)

## Gloucestershire

Gloucestershire Record Office, Clarence Row, Alvin Street, Gloucester GL1 3DW (tel. 01452 425295; fax 01452 426378)

*Hampshire*
Hampshire Record Office, Sussex Street, Winchester SO23 8TH (tel. 01962 846154; fax 01962 878681)
Portsmouth City Museums and Records Service, Museum Road, Portsmouth PO1 2LJ (tel. 023 9282 7261; fax 023 9287 5276)
Southampton Archives Services, Civic Centre, Southampton SO14 7LY (tel. 023 8083 2251/8022 3855 ext. 2251; fax 023 8033 2156)

*Herefordshire*
Hereford Record Office, The Old Barracks, Harold Street, Hereford HR1 2QX (tel. 01432 265441; fax 01432 370248)

*Hertfordshire*
Hertfordshire Archives and Local Studies, County Hall, Hertford SG13 8EJ (tel. 01992 555105; fax 01992 555113)

*Kent*
Centre for Kentish Studies, County Hall, Maidstone ME14 1XQ (tel. 01622 694363; fax 01622 694379)
East Kent Archive Centre, Enterprise Business Park, Honeywood Road, Whitfield, Dover CT16 3EH (tel./fax 01304 829306). Opening February 2000, two days a week

*Lancashire*
Lancashire Record Office, Bow Lane, Preston PR1 2RE (tel. 01772 263039; fax 01772 263050)

*Leicestershire*
The Record Office for Leicestershire, Leicester and Rutland, Long Street, Wigston Magna, Leicester LE18 2AH (tel. 0116 257 1080; fax 0116 257 1120)

*Lincolnshire*
Lincolnshire Archives Office, St Rumbold Street, Lincoln LN2 5AB (tel. 01522 526204; fax 01522 530047)
North East Lincolnshire Archives, Town Hall, Town Hall Square, Grimsby DN31 1HX (tel. 01472 323585; fax 01472 323582)

*London*
City of Westminster Archives, 10 St Ann's Street, London SW1P 2XR (tel. 020 7641 5180; fax 020 7641 5179)
Corporation of London, London Metropolitan Archives, 40 Northampton Road, London EC1R 0HB (tel. 020 7332 3820; fax 020 7833 9136)

Corporation of London Records Office, PO Box 270, Guildhall, London EC2P 2EJ (tel. 020 7332 1251; fax 020 7332 1119)

## *Manchester*
Greater Manchester Record Office, 56 Marshall Street, New Cross, Manchester M4 5FU (tel. 0161-832 5284; fax 0161-839 3808)

## *Merseyside*
Liverpool Record and Local History Service, Central Library, William Brown Street, Liverpool L3 8EW (tel. 0151-225 5417; fax 0151-207 1342). Now includes records of the Merseyside Record Office

Wirral Archives Service, Birkenhead Reference Library, Borough Road, Birkenhead L41 2XB (tel. 0151-652 6106/7/8; fax 0151-653 7320)

## *Midlands*
Birmingham City Archives, Central Library, Chamberlain Square, Birmingham B3 3HQ (tel. 0121-303 4217; fax 0121-212 9397)

Coventry City Archives, Mandela House, Bayley Lane, Coventry CV1 5RG (tel. 024 7683 2418; fax 024 7683 2421)

Warwick University Modern Records Centre, University Library, Coventry CV4 7AL (tel. 024 7652 4219; fax 024 7657 2988)

## *Norfolk*
Norfolk Record Office, Gildengate House, Anglia Square, Upper Green Lane, Norwich NR3 1AX (tel. 01603 761349; fax 01603 761885)

## *Northamptonshire*
Northamptonshire Record Office, Wootton Hall Park, Northampton NN4 8BQ (tel. 01604 762129; 01604 767562)

## *Northumberland*
Northumberland Record Office, Melton Park, North Gosforth, Newcastle-upon-Tyne NE3 5QX (tel. 0191-236 2680; fax 0191-217 0905)

## *Nottinghamshire*
Nottinghamshire Archives, County House, Castle Meadow Road, Nottingham NG2 1AG (tel. 0115 958 1634/950 4524; fax 0115 941 3997)

## *Oxfordshire*
Oxfordshire Archives, County Hall, New Road, Oxford OX1 1ND (tel. 01865 815203; fax 01865 815429)

*Shropshire*
Shropshire Records and Research Centre, Castle Gate, Shrewsbury
SY1 2AQ (tel. 01743 255350; fax 01743 255355)

*Somerset*
Bath and North East Somerset Record Office, Guildhall, Bath BA1
5AW (tel. 01225 477421; fax 01225 477439)
Bristol Record Office, B Bond Warehouse, Smeaton Road, Bristol
BS1 6XN (tel. 0117 922 5692; fax 0117 922 4236)
Somerset Archive and Record Service, Obridge Road, Taunton TA2
7PU (tel. 01823 278805/337600; fax 01823 325402)

*Staffordshire*
Staffordshire Record Office, County Buildings, Eastgate Street,
Stafford ST16 2LZ (tel. 01785 278379; fax 01785 278384)
Lichfield Record Office, Lichfield Library, The Friary, Lichfield
WS13 6QG (tel. 01543 510720; fax 01543 510715)

*Suffolk*
Suffolk Record Office, Bury St Edmunds Branch, 77 Raingate Street,
Bury St Edmunds IP33 2AR (tel. 01284 352352; fax 01284 352355)
Suffolk Record Office, Ipswich Branch, Gateacre Road, Ipswich IP1
2LQ (tel. 01473 584541; fax 01473 584533)
Suffolk Record Office, Lowestoft Branch, Central Library, Clapham
Road, Lowestoft NR32 1DR (tel. 01502 405357; fax 01502
405350)

*Surrey*
Surrey History Centre (records of Surrey Record Office and Guildford
Muniment Room), 130 Goldsworth Road, Woking GU21 1ND
(tel. 01483 594594; fax 01483 594595)

*East Sussex*
East Sussex Record Office, The Maltings, Castle Precincts, Lewes
BN7 1YT (tel. 01273 482349; fax 01273 482341)

*West Sussex*
West Sussex Record Office, Sherburne House, 3 Orchard Street,
Chichester (tel. 01243 533911; fax 01243 533959). Postal enquiries
to WSRO, County Hall, Chichester, West Sussex PO19 1RN

*Teesside*
Teesside Archives, Exchange House, 6 Marton Road, Middlesbrough
TS1 1DB (tel. 01642 248321; fax 01642 248391)

## Tyne and Wear
Tyne and Wear Archives Services, Blandford House, West Blandford
Square, Newcastle-upon-Tyne NE1 4JA (tel. 0191-232 6789; fax
0191-230 2614); Local Studies Collection, Gateshead Central
Library, Prince Consort Road, Gateshead NE8 4LN (tel. 0191-
477 3478; fax 0191-477 7454)

## Warwickshire
Warwickshire County Record Office, Priory Park, Cape Road,
Warwick CV34 4JS (tel. 01926 412735; fax 01926 412509)

## Isle of Wight
Isle of Wight County Record Office, 26 Hillside, Newport PO30 2EB
(tel. 01983 823820/21; fax 01983 823820)

## Wiltshire
Wiltshire and Swindon Record Office, County Hall, Trowbridge
BA14 8BS (tel. 01225 713136; fax 01225 713993)

## Worcestershire
Worcestershire Record Office, County Hall, Spetchley Road,
Worcester WR5 2NP (tel. 01905 766351; fax 01905 766363);
also St Helen's branch at Fish Street, Worcester WR1 2HN (tel.
01905 765922; fax 01905 765925)

## East Yorkshire
East Riding of Yorkshire Archive Office, County Hall, Beverley
HU17 9BA (tel. 01482 885007; fax 01482 885463)
Hull City Archives, 79 Lowgate, Kingston upon Hull HU1 1HN (tel.
01482 615102/615110; fax 01482 613051)

## North Yorkshire
North Yorkshire County Record Office, Malpas Road, Northallerton
DL7 8TB (tel. 01609 777585; fax 01609 777078). Correspon-
dence address: County Hall, Northallerton DL7 8AF
York City Archives Department, Art Gallery Building, Exhibition
Square, York YO1 7EW (tel. 01904 551878/9; fax 01904
551877)

## South Yorkshire
Barnsley Archive Service, Central Library, Shambles Street, Barnsley
S70 2JF (tel. 01226 773950/773938; fax 01226 773955)
Doncaster Archives Department, King Edward Road, Balby,
Doncaster DN4 0NA (tel. 01302 859811)

Sheffield Archives, 52 Shoreham Street, Sheffield S1 4SP (tel. 0114 273 4756; fax 0114 203 9398)

## West Yorkshire

West Yorkshire Archive Service, Wakefield Headquarters, Registry of Deeds, Newstead Road, Wakefield WF1 2DE (tel. 01924 305980; fax 01924 305983). Branches at Bradford, Halifax, Huddersfield and Leeds

## Scotland

Aberdeen City Archives, The Town House, Broad Street, Aberdeen AB10 1AQ (tel. 01224 522513; fax 01224 522491). Now administers the Grampian Regional Archives

Angus Archives, Montrose Library, 214 High Street, Montrose DD10 8PH (tel. 01674 671415; fax 01674 671810)

Argyll and Bute Council Archives, Manse Brae, Lochgilphead, Argyll PA31 8QU (tel. 01546 604120; fax 01546 606897)

Ayrshire Archives Centre, Craigie Estate, Ayr KA8 0SS (tel. 01292 287584; fax 01292 284918)

Dumfries and Galloway Archives, 33 Burns Street, Dumfries DG1 2PS (tel. 01387 269254; fax 01387 264126)

Dundee City Archives, 1 Shore Terrace, Dundee (tel. 01382 434494; fax 01382 434666). Address for correspondence: Department of Support Services, 21 City Square, Dundee DD1 3BY

Edinburgh City Archives, Department of Corporate Services, City of Edinburgh Council, City Chambers, High Street, Edinburgh EH1 1YJ (tel. 0131-529 4616; fax 0131-529 4957)

Falkirk Council Archives, Falkirk Museum, Callendar House, Callendar Park, Falkirk FK1 1YR (tel. 01324 503770; fax 01324 503711)

Glasgow City Archives, The Mitchell Library, 201 North Street, Glasgow G3 7DN (tel. 0141-287 2910; fax 0141-226 8452)

Highland Council Archive, Inverness Library, Farraline Park, Inverness IV1 1NH (tel. 01463 220330; fax 01463 711128)

Midlothian Council Archives, Library Headquarters, 2 Clerk Street, Loanhead, Midlothian EH20 9DR (tel. 0131-271 3976; fax 0131-440 4635)

North Highland Archive, Wick Library, Sinclair Terrace, Wick KW1 5AB (tel. 01955 606432; fax 01955 603000)

North Lanarkshire Archives, 10 Kelvin Road, Lenziemill, Cumbernauld G67 2BA (tel. 01236 737114; fax 01236 781762)

South Lanarkshire Archives and Information Management Service, 30 Hawbank Road, College Milton, East Kilbride G74 5EX (tel. 01355 239193; fax 01355 242365)

Orkney Archives, Orkney Library, Laing Street, Kirkwall KW15 1NW (tel. 01856 873166/875260; fax 01856 875260)

Perth and Kinross Council Archive, A.K. Bell Library, 2–8 York Place, Perth PH2 8EP (tel. 01738 477012; fax 01738 477010)

Scottish Borders Archive and Local History Centre, Library Headquarters, St Mary's Mill, Selkirk TD7 5EW (tel. 01750 20842; fax 01750 22875)

Shetland Archives, 44 King Harald Street, Lerwick ZE1 0EQ (tel. 01595 696247; fax 01595 696533)

Stirling Council Archives Services, Unit 6, Burghmuir Industrial Estate, Stirling FK7 7PY (tel. 01786 450745)

## Wales

Anglesey County Record Office, Shire Hall, Glanhwfa Road, Llangefni LL77 7TW (tel. 01248 752080)

Carmarthenshire Record Office,County Hall, Carmarthen SA3 1JP (tel. 01267 224184; fax 01267 224104)

Ceredigion Archives, County Office, Marine Terrace, Aberystwyth SY23 2DE (tel. 01970 633697/8; fax 01970 633663)

Denbighshire Record Office, 46 Clwyd Street, Ruthin LL15 1HP (tel. 01824 708250; fax 01824 708258)

Flintshire Record Office, The Old Rectory, Hawarden, Flintshire CH5 3NR (tel. 01244 532364; fax 01244 538344)

Glamorgan Record Office, Glamorgan Building, King Edward VII Avenue, Cathays Park, Cardiff CF1 3NE (tel. 029 2078 0282; fax 029 2078 0284)

West Glamorgan Archive Service, County Hall, Oystermouth Road, Swansea SA1 3SN (tel. 01792 636589; fax 01792 637130)

Gwent County Record Office, County Hall, Cwmbran NP44 2XH (tel. 01633 644886; fax 01633 648382)

Gwynedd Archives Service: Caernarfon Area Record Office, Victoria Dock, Caernarfon (tel. 01286 679095; fax 01286 679637); address for correspondence: County Offices, Shirehall Street, Caernarfon LL55 1SH; Merioneth Archives, Cae Penarlag, Dolgellau LL40 2YB (tel. 01341 424444; fax 01341 424505)

Pembrokeshire Record Office, The Castle, Haverfordwest SA61 2EF (tel. 01437 763707)

Powys County Archives Office, County Hall, Llandrindod Wells LD1 5LG (tel. 01597 826088; fax 01597 827162)

# University Libraries (other than Oxford and Cambridge) with Important Manuscript Collections

Students, undergraduates and graduates of other universities are normally admitted without formality; temporary tickets will be issued to other *bona fide* researchers at the Librarian's discretion. In some cases letters of introduction and/or proof of identity is required. At some libraries there are slightly amended opening hours during vacations. Please note that telepone and fax numbers, as well as opening times, where stated, are for the departments of archives, manuscripts and special collections. In all cases you should write in advance of your visit. The main libraries of the University of Cambridge and the University of Oxford are listed under 'Copyright Libraries' (pages 191–2).

### England

Birmingham University Information Services, Special Collections Department, Main Library, University of Birmingham, Edgbaston, Birmingham B15 2TT (tel. 0121-414 5838; fax 0121-471 4691). Mon–Fri, 9–5. Closed one week in July.

Durham University Library, Archives and Special Collections, Palace Green Section, Palace Green, Durham DH1 3RN (tel. 0191-374 3001; fax 0191-374 7481). Mon–Fri, 9–5, by appointment.

Exeter University Library, Stocker Road, Exeter EX4 4PT (tel. 01392 263870; fax 01392 263871). Mon–Fri, 9–5.

Hull University, Brynmor Jones Library, Cottingham Road, Hull HU6 7RX (tel. 01482 465265; fax 01482 466205). Mon–Fri, 9–1, 2–5.

Keele University Library, Keele ST5 5BG (tel. 01782 583237; fax 01782 711553). Closed for ten days in summer. Mon–Fri, 9–5.

Leeds University, Brotherton Library, Leeds LS2 9JT (tel. 01532 335518; fax 01532 335561). Mon–Fri, 9–7; Sat, 10–1.

Liverpool University, Department of Special Collections and Archives, PO Box 123, Liverpool L69 3DA (tel. 0151-794 2696; fax 0151-794 2681). Mon–Fri, 9.30–4.45.

University of London Library, Palaeography Room, Senate House, Malet Street, London WC1E 7HU (tel. 020 7682 8475; fax 020 7682 8480). Mon, 9.30–8.45; Tue–Fri, 9.30–6; Sat, 9.30–1, 2–5.15.

John Rylands University Library of Manchester, 150 Deansgate, Manchester M3 3EH (tel. 0161-834 5343; fax 0161-834 5574). Mon–Fri, 10–5.30; Sat, 10–1.

Newcastle–upon-Tyne University, Robinson Library, Newcastle-upon-Tyne NE2 4HQ (tel. 0191-222 7671; fax 0191-222 6235). Mon–Fri, 9.15–5.

Nottingham University Library, Hallward Library, University Park, Nottingham NG7 2RD (tel. 0115 951 4565; fax 0115 951 4558). Mon–Fri, 9–5. Closed one week in September.

Reading University Library, Whiteknights, Reading RG6 2AE (tel. 0118 931 8776; fax 0118 931 6636). Mon–Fri, 9–5. Closed in August.

Sheffield University Library, Special Collections and Library Archives Department, Western Bank, Sheffield S10 2TN (tel. 0114 222 7230; fax 0114 222 7290). Mon–Fri, 9.30–1, 2–4.30.

Southampton University Library, Highfield, Southampton SO17 1BJ (tel. 023 8059 3724/8059 2721; fax 023 8059 3007). Mon, Tue, Thu, Fri, 9–5; Wed, 10–5.

Sussex University Library Manuscripts Collections, Falmer, Brighton BN1 9QL (tel. 01273 606755; fax 01273 678441). Mon–Fri, 9.15–5.

Warwick University Modern Records Centre, University Library, University of Warwick, Coventry CV4 7AL (tel. 024 7652 4219; fax 024 7657 2988). Mon–Thu, 9–1, 1.30–5; Fri, 9–1, 1.30 4. Closed one week at Easter.

York University, Borthwick Institute of Historical Research, St Anthony's Hall, Peasholme Green, York YO1 2PW (tel. 01904 642315; fax 01904 633284). Mon–Fri, 9.30–12.50, 2–4.50. Closed one week at Easter.

## *Scotland*

Aberdeen University Library, Department of Special Collections and Archives, King's College, Aberdeen AB24 3SW (tel. 01224 272598; fax 01224 273891). Mon–Fri, 9.30–4.30.

Dundee University Library, Archives and Manuscripts Department, Tower Building, Dundee DD1 4HN (tel. 01382 344095; fax 01382 345523). Mon–Wed, 9–5; Thu, 9–1.30, 5–8; Sat 10–1. Vacation Mon–Wed, Fri, 9.30–12.30; Thu, 9.30–1.30.

Edinburgh University Library, Special Collections Department, George Square, Edinburgh EH8 9LJ (tel. 0131-650 3412; fax 0131-650 6863). Mon–Fri, 9–5. Closed second week in August.

Glasgow University Library, Department of Special Collections, Hillhead Street, Glasgow G12 8QE (tel. 0141-330 6767; fax 0141-330 3793). Mon–Thu, 9–8.30; Fri, 10–5; Sat, 9–12.30 (term); Mon–Fri, 9–5; Sat, 9–12.30 (vacation).

St Andrews University Library, North Street, St Andrews KY16 9TR (tel. 01334 462324; fax 01334 462282). Mon–Wed, Fri, 9–5; Thu, 9–9; Sat, 9–12.15 (term only). Vacation, 9–5.

*Wales*
University of Wales, Bangor, Department of Manuscripts, Bangor LL57 2DG (tel. 01248 351151 ext. 2966; fax 01248 382979). Mon–Fri, 9–1, 2–5; Wed to 9 (term only).

# Cathedral Archives and Libraries

Canterbury Cathedral Archives, The Precincts, Canterbury, Kent CT1 2EH (tel. 01227 463510; fax 01227 865222). Mon–Thu, 9–5; 1st and 3rd Sat of each month, 9–1. Reader's ticket required (take 2 passport-size photographs and means of identification).
Durham Dean and Chapter Library, The College, Durham DH1 3EH (tel. 0191-386 2489). Mon–Fri, 9–1, 2.15–5. Closed in August.
Exeter Cathedral Library, Old Bishop's Palace, Diocesan House, Palace Gate, Exeter EX1 1HX (tel. 01392 272894). Mon–Fri, 2–5. Archives, tel. 01392 495594 (administered by Devon Record Office, see page 195).
Salisbury Cathedral Chapter Archives, 6 The Close, Salisbury SP1 2EF (tel. 01722 555100), by appointment (written application required).
York Minster Library, Dean's Park, York YO1 2JD (tel. 01904 611118; fax 01904 611119), by appointment.
Westminster Abbey Muniment Room and Library, Westminster Abbey, London SW1P 3PA (tel. 020 7222 5152 ext. 228; fax 020 7233 2072). Written application to Librarian or Keeper of the Muniments required.
Westminster Diocesan Archives (Roman Catholic), 16a Abingdon Road, London W8 6AF (tel. 020 7938 3580), by appointment.
Winchester Cathedral Library, 5 The Close, Winchester SO23 9LS (tel. switchboard, for general enquiries, 01962 857200). Written application required, opening times vary.

# Other Major Reference Libraries

Belfast: Irish and Local Studies Department, Central Library, Royal Avenue, Belfast BT1 1EA (tel. 028 9024 3233; fax 028 9033 2819)
Birmingham and Midland Institute, 9 Margaret Street, Birmingham B3 3BS (tel. 0121-236 3591)
Birmingham Reference Library, Central Library, Chamberlain Square, Birmingham B3 3HQ (tel. 0121-303 4511; fax 0121-303 4458)

Cardiff Arts and Social Studies Resource Centre, University of Wales, PO Box 430, Colum Drive, Cardiff CF10 3XT (tel. 024 7687 4818; fax 024 7637 1921)

Edinburgh City Libraries, Central Library, George IV Bridge, Edinburgh EH1 1EG (tel. 0131-225 5584; fax 0131-225 8783)

Glasgow City Libraries and Archives: Mitchell Library, North Street, Glasgow G3 7DN (tel. 0141-287 2999; fax 0141-287 2815)

Liverpool City Libraries, Central Library, William Brown Street, Liverpool L3 8EW (tel. 0151-225 5429/5435/5436; fax 0151-207 1342)

London: Westminster Reference Library, 35 St Martin's Street, London WC2H 7HP (tel. 020 7641 4636; fax 020 7641 4606)

Manchester: Central Library, St Peter's Square, Manchester M2 5PD (tel. 0161-234 1900; fax 0161-234 1963)

## Private Subscription Libraries

Highgate Literary and Scientific Institution Library, 11 South Grove, Highgate Village, London N6 6BS (tel. 020 8340 3343). Tue–Fri, 10–5; Sat, 10–4. £40.00 per year (£63.00 family subscription).

London Library, 14 St James's Square, London SW1Y 4LG (tel. 020 7930 7705; fax 020 7766 4766; email inquiries@londonlibrary. co.uk; Website webpac.londonlibrary.co.uk). Mon–Sat, 9.30–5.30; Thu to 7.30. £130.00 per year.

Space does not permit a complete listing of the nineteen other surviving private subscription libraries in the provinces, but these will be well known to readers living locally; or consult the yellow pages of the local telephone directories. A descriptive leaflet is available from the Association of Independent Libraries, c/o The Leeds Library, 18 Commercial Street, Leeds LS1 6AL (tel. 0113 245 3071).

## Short List of Subjects and Sources

*Advertising*

Advertising Association Library, Abford House, 15 Wilton Road, London SW1V 1NJ (tel. 020 7828 2771; fax 020 7931 0376). Closed for refurbishment, due to reopen January 2000 (telephone for details of opening hours).

History of Advertising Trust, Unit 12, The Raveningham Centre, Raveningham, Norwich NR14 6NU (tel. 01508 548623; fax 01508 548478). Mon–Fri, 9–5.

## Agriculture

Rural History Centre, Reading University, PO Box 229, Whiteknights, Reading RG6 2AG (tel. 0118 931 8666; fax 0118 975 1264). Mon–Thu, 9.30–1, 2–5; Fri, 9.30–1, 2–4.30, by appointment.

## Air Force

Royal Air Force Museum, Department of Aviation Records, Grahame Park Way, Hendon, London NW9 5LL (tel. 020 8205 2266; fax 020 8200 1751). Written enquiries only.
See also Ministry of Defence Whitehall Library under '*Military*', and under '*World Wars I and II*'.

## Architecture

British Architectural Library, Royal Institute of British Architects, 66 Portland Place, London W1N 4AD (tel. 020 7580 5533; fax 020 7631 1802; public information line 0891 234 400). Mon, 1.30–5; Tue, 10–8; Wed, Thu, Fri, 10–5; Sat, 10–1.30. Closed in August. Free to RIBA members; non-members may purchase day tickets. Priced research service.

## Art

Art and Design Library, Westminster Reference Library, 2nd floor, 35 St Martin's Street, London WC2H 7HP (tel. 020 7641 4638; fax 020 7641 4604). Mon–Fri, 10–8; Sat, 10–5.
British Museum, Department of Prints and Drawings, Great Russell Street, London WC1B 3DG (tel. 020 7636 1555). Proof of identity required. Mon–Fri, 10–1, 2.15–4; Sat, 10–1.
Courtauld Institute of Art Library, Somerset House, London WC2R 0RN (tel. 020 7873 2707; fax 020 7873 2887). Mon–Fri, 10–7 (term); 10–6 (vacation). Closed in August.
National Art Library, Victoria & Albert Museum Library, Cromwell Road, London SW7 2RL (tel. 020 7938 8315; fax 020 7938 8275; email enquiries@nal.vam.ac.uk). Tue–Sat, 10–5. N.B. A specially endorsed reader's ticket is required for access to certain MSS and reserved material in the National Art Library.
National Portrait Gallery Heinz Archive and Library, 2 St Martin's Place, London WC2H 0HE (tel. 020 7306 0055 ext 257; fax 020 7306 0056). Tue–Sat, 10–5, by appointment only.

**Recommended title:**
*Dictionary of Art*, ed. Jane Turner, Macmillan, London, 34 vols, 1996

## Banking and Commerce

Bank of England Library and Information Services, Threadneedle

Street, London EC2R 8AH (tel. 020 7601 4715; fax 020 7601 4356). Telephone or written enquiries only. The Bank of England and other major banks will grant access to historical records only when applications are supported by a university or other centre of research.

Westminster Reference Library, 35 St Martin's Street, London WC2H 7HP (tel. 020 7641 4634; fax 020 7641 4606). Mon–Fri, 10–8; Sat, l0–5. Computer search and information for business services available.

### Births, Marriages and Deaths
Family Records Centre, 1 Myddleton Street, London EC1R 1UW (tel. general enquiries, 020 8392 5300; certificates, 0151-471 4800). See under 'General Register Offices' (page 193) and '*Genealogy*'.

### Broadcasting and Television
BBC Written Archives Centre, Peppard Road, Caversham Park, Reading RG4 8TZ (tel. 0118 946 9280/1/2; fax 0118 946 1145). Open to *bona fide* researchers for reference only, Wed–Fri, 9.30–5.30, by appointment. Some services are charged.

British Library National Sound Archive (NSA), 96 Euston Road, London NW1 2DB (tel. 020 7412 7440; fax 020 7412 7441; email nsa@bl.uk). Mon–Fri, 10–5. The Recorded Sound Information Service is based in the Humanities 2 Reading Room; users require a valid British Library pass. There is free public access to the Listening & Viewing Service, by appointment (tel. 020 7412 7418), in the Rare Books and Music Reading Room. Northern Listening Service at the British Library's Document Supply Centre, Boston Spa, Wetherby, West Yorkshire LS23 7BQ (tel. 01937 546070).

British Universities Film and Video Council (BUFVC), 77 Wells Street, London W1P 3RE (tel. 020 7393 1500; fax 020 7393 1555). *Bona fide* researchers may use the library for reference purposes.

### Business
British Library Business Collections, Science 3 Reading Room, British Library, 96 Euston Road, London NW1 2DB. Mon, 10-8; Tue, Wed, Thu; 9.30–8; Fri, Sat, 9.30–5. For quick information telephone British Library-Lloyds TSB Business Line (020 7412 7454/020 7412 7977; email business-information@bl.uk), Mon–Fri, 9–5. The British Library Business Information Research Service (tel. 020 7412 7457; fax 020 7412 7453) will undertake in-depth research at commercial rates.

Business Archives Council, 3rd/4th Floors, 101 Whitechapel High Street, London E1 7RE (tel. 020 7247 0024; fax 020 7422 0026). Will assist in tracing business histories and business archives. By appointment.

Business Archives Council of Scotland, c/o Glasgow University Archives and Business Record Centre, 77–81 Dumbarton Road, Glasgow G11 6PW (tel. 0141-330 4543; fax 0141-330 4158). Written and telephone enquiries only.

City Business Library, 1 Brewers' Hall Garden, London EC2V 5BX (tel. 020 7638 8215; fax 020 7332 1847). Mon–Fri, 9.30–5.30.

Companies Registration Office, Companies House, Crown Way, Maindy Pool, Cardiff CF14 3UZ; London search room at Companies House, 21 Bloomsbury Street, London WC1B 3XD. (For general enquiries, tel. 029 2038 0801). Personal enquiries only at London office, Mon–Fri, 9–5 (last search 3 p.m.). N.B. There is a search fee of £3.50 per company. Microfiche copies of company records in London, files in Cardiff. In Scotland, 37 Castle Terrace, Edinburgh EH1 2EB (tel. 0131-535 5800).

Westminster Reference Library, Business & Official Publications section, 35 St Martin's Street, London WC2H 7HP (tel. 020 7641 4634; fax 020 7641 4606). Mon–Fri, 10–8; Sat, 10–5.

**Recommended titles:**

*Business: A Guide to Searching in Published Sources*, by Nigel Spencer, *How to Find* series, British Library, London, 1995

*Instant Guide to Company Information Online – Europe*, ed. Nigel Spencer, *Key Resource* series, British Library, London, 3rd edn, 1998

### Cartoons and Caricature

Cartoon Art Trust, 7 Brunswick Centre, Bernard Street, London WC1A 1AF (tel. 020 7278 7172; fax 020 7278 4234). Mon–Fri, 12–6.

The Centre for the Study of Cartoons and Caricature, The Templeman Library, University of Kent at Canterbury, Canterbury, Kent CT2 7NU (tel./fax 01227 823127). Mon–Fri, 9–5.

*Punch* Library, Trevor House, 100 Brompton Road, London SW3 1ER (tel. 020 7225 6710; fax 020 7225 6712). Mon–Fri, 10–1, 2.30–5.30, by appointment only.

**Recommended title:**

*The Dictionary of British Cartoonists and Caricatures 1730–1980*, compiled by Mark Bryant and Simon Heneage, Scolar Press, London, 1994

**Census Returns**
Family Records Centre, 1 Myddelton Street, London EC1R 1UW
(tel. 020 8392 5300; fax 020 8392 5307). Mon, Wed, Fri 9–5;
Tue, 10–7; Thu, 9–7; Sat, 9.30–5. Open to the public without
ticket. Census returns for England and Wales 1841–1891.

**Children's Books**
Bethnal Green Museum of Childhood, Cambridge Heath Road,
London E2 9PA (tel. 020 8983 5200; fax 020 8983 5225). Renier
Collection of Historic and Contemporary Children's Books; also
Young Book Trust Collection (after two years) and some smaller
collections. Computerised catalogue in preparation; access by
appointment (contact Curator of Children's Books, tel. 020 8983
5217). N.B. The Museum is closed on Fridays, but open
Mon–Thu and Sat, 10–5.50 and Sun 2.30–5.50.
National Art Library, Victoria & Albert Museum, Cromwell Road,
London SW7 2RL (tel. 020 7938 8315; fax 020 7938 8275).
Tue–Sat, 10–5. Reader's ticket required (letter of introduction in
first instance). Closed for three weeks after August bank holiday.
Young Book Trust Children's Reference Library, Book House, 45
East Hill, London SW18 2QZ (tel. 020 8516 2977; fax 020 8516
2978). Access for reference only, by appointment, Mon–Fri, 9–5.
Information service and membership by subscription.

**Costume**
Fashion Research Centre, 4 Circus, Bath, Somerset BA1 2EW (tel.
01225 477752; fax 01225 444793). By appointment: reference
library Thu, Fri, 10–12.30, 2–4.30; study collection Mon, Tue,
Wed, 10.30 and 2.30.
London College of Fashion Library, 20 John Prince's Street, Oxford
Circus, London W1M 0BJ (tel. 020 7514 7400). Open to the
public for reference only, Mon–Thu, 9–7; Fri, 9.30–4.45.
Museum of Costume, The Assembly Rooms, Bennett Street, Bath
BA1 2QH (tel. 01225 477789; fax 01225 444793). Daily 10–5.

**European Commission**
Commission of the European Communities, Press and Information
Office, Jean Monnet House, 8 Storey's Gate, London SW1P 3AT
(tel. 020 7973 1992). Mon–Fri, 10–1. Not open to students.
Enquiries should be referred through a local public library.

**Films and Cinema History**
British Film Institute National Library, 21 Stephen Street, London
W1P 1PL (tel. 020 7255 1444; fax 020 7436 2338). Mon, Fri,

10.30–5.30; Tue, Thu, 10.30–8; Wed, 1–8. *Note.* The telephone enquiry service is in operation only from 10–5. Open to non-members for reference only, limited day membership available.

British Universities Film and Video Council (BUFVC), 77 Wells Street, London W1P 3RE (tel. 020 7393 1500; fax 020 7393 1555). Houses the British Universities Newsreel Project (database of records of British cinema newsreels 1910–1979). By appointment to *bona fide* researchers.

### Folklore

The Folklore Society, c/o University College, Gower Street, London WC1E 6BT (tel. 020 7387 5894). Written and telephone enquiries only.

Vaughan Williams Memorial Library, English Folk Dance and Song Society, Cecil Sharp House, 2 Regent's Park Road, London NW1 7AY (tel./fax 020 7284 0523). Mon–Fri, 9.30–5.30. Non-members pay daily fee for access, reference only.

### Recommended title:

*Larousse Dictionary of World Folklore*, Larousse, London, 1995

### Genealogy and Heraldry

College of Arms, Queen Victoria Street, London EC4 4BT (tel. 020 7248 2762; fax 020 7248 6448). Mon–Fri, 10–4; Sat by appointment. N.B. There are no public search rooms. Research is undertaken only by the Heralds and their staff, on a fee-paying basis (brief preliminary search is free).

Family Records Centre, 1 Myddleton Street, London EC1R 1UW (Census and general enquiries, tel. 020 8392 5300; fax 020 8392 5307; births, marriages, deaths enquiries, tel. 0151-471 4800). Mon, Wed, Fri, 9–5; Tue, 10–7; Thu, 9–7; Sat, 9.30–5.

French Protestant Church of London, 8 & 9 Soho Square, London W1V 5DD (tel. 020 7437 5311). Library open Tue, Thu only, 10.30–1 and 2.15–4.45, by appointment with archivist.

Hyde Park Family History Center of the Church of Jesus Christ of Latter-Day Saints (of Salt Lake City, Utah, USA), 64–68 Exhibition Road, London SW7 2PA (tel. 020 7589 8561). Tue–Fri, 10–7; Sat, 10–3. Closed on Mondays. Appointment advisable to reserve a computer.

Institute of Heraldic and Genealogical Studies Library, 79–82 Northgate, Canterbury, Kent CT1 1BA (tel. 01227 768664; fax 01227 765617). Mon, Wed, Fri, 10–5, by appointment.

Religious Society of Friends, Friends House, Euston Road, London NW1 2BJ (tel. 020 7663 1135; fax 020 7663 1001). Tue–Fri, 10–5;

closed for one week before Spring Bank Holiday and one week at end of November. *Bona fide* researchers providing suitable introductions/letters of recommendation may use the Library on payment of a search fee, or searches will be carried out by staff at a fee.

Society of Genealogists' Library, 14 Charterhouse Buildings, Goswell Road, London EC1M 7BA (tel. 020 7251 8799; fax 020 7250 1800; email info@sog.org.uk; Website http://www.sog.org.uk/). Tue, Fri, Sat, 10–6; Wed, Thu, 10–8; closed on Mondays. Non-members pay search fees (currently £3.00 for one hour; £8.00 for half day (4 hours); £12.00 for a day or a day and an evening). Closed for one week in February and on Friday afternoons and Saturdays prior to bank holidays.

## Geography and Maps

British Library Maps Reading Room, British Library, 96 Euston Road, London NW1 2DB (tel. 020 7412 7702; fax 020 7412 7780). British Library reader's pass required. Mon from 10; Tue–Sat from 9.30 (tel. for details of closing times).

Royal Geographical Society/Institute of British Geographers Library, Kensington Gore, London SW7 2AR (tel. 020 7591 3040; fax 020 7591 3001). Mon–Fri, 11–5. Access restricted to Fellows and members; Map Room open to general public (closed 1–2).

## Government and Official Information

British Library Social Policy Information Service, Science 2 North Reading Room, British Library, 96 Euston Road, London NW1 2DB (tel. 020 7412 7536; fax 020 7412 7761). British Library reader's pass required. Mon from 10; Tue–Sat from 9.30 (tel. for details of closing times).

Central Office of Information, Hercules Road, Westminster Bridge Road, London SE1 7DU (tel. 020 7928 2345). Telephone or written enquiries only.

Foreign & Commonwealth Office Library, King Charles Street, London SW1A 2AH (tel. (enquiries) 020 7270 3050). Open to *bona fide* researchers only, by appointment.

Office for National Statistics Information & Library Service, 1 Drummond Gate, London SW1V 2QQ (tel. 020 7533 6262; fax 020 7533 6261). Mon–Fri, 9.30–4.30.

Oriental and India Office Collections Reading Room, British Library, 96 Euston Road, London NW1 2DB (tel. 020 7412 7873; fax 020 7412 7641; email oioc-enquiries@bl.uk). The former India Office Library. Mon from 10; Tue–Sat from 9.30 (tel. for closing times).

Public Record Office, Ruskin Avenue, Kew, Richmond, Surrey TW9 4DU (tel. 020 8876 3444; fax 020 8878 8905; email

enquiry@pro.gov.uk; Website http://www.pro.gov.uk/). Admission by reader's ticket. Mon, Wed, Fri, Sat, 9.30–5; Tue, 10–7; Thu, 9.30–7. (Last document orders on Saturdays, 2.30 p.m.). Closed for stocktaking two weeks usually early December. *Note.* The Public Record Office in Chancery Lane is now closed.
See also under '*Parliament*'.

### International Affairs
Royal Institute of International Affairs Library, Chatham House, 10 St James's Square, London SW1Y 4LE (tel. (enquiries) 020 7957 5723 or 020 7314 2783). Open to non-members by arrangement with the librarian. *Note:* The press cuttings collection for the period 1940–71 has been transferred to the British Newspaper Library, Colindale (indexes at Chatham House).

### Recommended title:
'*Never Complain, Never Explain*': *Records of the Foreign Office and State Paper Office 1500–c. 1960*, by Louise Atherton, PRO Publications, London, 1994

### Law
Use of the law libraries in London is limited to members of the legal profession, but *bona fide* researchers may be able to obtain information by telephone or written enquiry. There are law libraries at a number of universities in the UK. (For these and other law libraries, see the *Aslib Directory of Information Sources in the UK*.)

Gray's Inn Library, 5 South Square, Gray's Inn, London WC1R 5EU (tel. 020 7242 8592; fax 020 7831 8381)
Holborn Library (London Borough of Camden public library), 32–38 Theobalds Road, London WC1X 8PA (tel. 020 7413 6345/6; fax 020 7413 6356). Mon, Thu, 10–7; Tue, Fri, 10–6; Sat, 10–5. Closed on Wednesdays.
Inner Temple Library, Inner Temple, London EC4Y 7DA (tel. 020 7797 8218/19/20)
Institute of Advanced Legal Studies Library, University of London, 17 Russell Square, London WC1B 5DR (tel. 020 7637 1731)
The Law Society Library, 113 Chancery Lane, London WC2A 1NB (tel. 020 7320 5946). (Holds records of solicitors from 1907; also LEXIS index to newspaper law reports.) Members only.
Lincoln's Inn Library, Lincoln's Inn, London WC2A 3TN (tel. 020 7242 4371; fax 020 7404 1864)
Middle Temple Library, Middle Temple Lane, London EC4Y 9BT (tel. 020 7427 4830; fax 020 7427 4831)

Royal Courts of Justice Library, Strand, London WC2A 2LL (tel. 020 7936 6000)

**Recommended title:**
*Legal Information – What it is and where to find it*, by Peter Clinch, Aslib, London, 1995

*London*
Corporation of London Records Office, PO Box 270, Guildhall, London EC2P 2EJ (tel. 020 7332 1251; fax 020 7332 1119). Mon–Fri, 9.30–4.45. Proof of identity required.
Guildhall Library, Aldermanbury, London EC2P 2EJ (tel. 020 7332 1868/1870; fax 020 7600 3384). Mon–Sat, 9.30–4.45.
London Metropolitan Archives Library, 40 Northampton Road, London EC1R 0HB (tel. 020 7332 3822; fax 020 7833 9136; email LMA@ms.corpoflondon.gov.uk). Mon, Wed, Fri, 9.30–4.45; Tue, Thu, 9.30–7.30.
Westminster City Archives, 10 St Ann's Street, London SW1P 2XR (tel. 020 7641 5180; fax 020 7641 5179). Mon, Tue, Thu, Fri, 9.30–7; Wed, 9.30–9; Sat, 9.30–5.

*N.B.* A number of London borough public libraries hold sizeable local history collections. Consult the current edition of *Record Repositories in Great Britain*, PRO Publications, London, and *Greater London History and Heritage Handbook*, Peter Marcan, London, 1999. A recent title from the British Records Association is *Sources for the History of London, 1939–45: A Guide and Bibliography*, by Heather Creaton, London, 1998, an invaluable reference work for the writer setting a story in wartime London.

*Medicine*
Marylebone Public Library Health Information Library, 109–117 Marylebone Road, London NW1 5PS (tel. 020 7798 1039; fax 020 7641 1044). Mon, Tue, Thu, Fri, 9.30–8; Wed, 10–8; Sat, 9.30–5, Sun, 1.30–5. Reference and lending facilities (tickets from other public libraries are accepted).
Royal College of Physicians of London Library, 11 St Andrew's Place, London NW1 4LE (tel. 020 7935 1174; fax 020 7487 5218). Mon–Fri, 9.30–5.30. *Bona fide* researchers not members of the profession may use the reference facilities (proof of identity required). Holds *Munk's Roll* (lives of Fellows of the Royal College of Physicians from the 16th century to the present day).
Royal College of Surgeons of England Library, 35–43 Lincoln's Inn Fields, London WC2A 3PN (tel. 020 7973 2138; fax 020 7405

4438). Letter of introduction required. Mon–Fri, 9–6. Closed in August.

Royal Society of Medicine Library, 1 Wimpole Street, London W1M 8AE (tel. 020 7290 2940; fax 020 7290 2939). Mon–Fri, 9–8.30; Sat, 10–5. Access for reference only, by introduction.

Wellcome Institute for the History of Medicine Library, 183 Euston Road, London NW1 2BE (tel. 020 7611 8582; fax 020 7611 8703). Mon, Wed, Fri, 9.45–5.15; Tue, Thu, 9.45–7.30; Sat, 9.45–1. By appointment. Reader's ticket required.

For further information see the *Directory of Medical and Health Care Libraries in the British Isles*, Library Association, London (latest edition, 10th, 1997).

## Military

Liddell Hart Centre for Military Archives, King's College, Strand, London WC2R 2LS (tel. 020 7873 2187/2015; fax 020 7873 2760). Access by written application (letter of introduction required). N.B. 20th-century records only.

Ministry of Defence Whitehall Library, 3–5 Great Scotland Yard, London SW1A 2HW (tel. (general enquiries) 020 7218 4445; fax 020 7218 5413). Telephone or written enquiries only.

National Army Museum, Royal Hospital Road, London SW3 4HT. Library and Department of Archives, Photographs, Film and Sound (tel. 020 7730 0717 ext. 2222; fax 020 7823 6573). Admission by reader's ticket. Tue–Sat, 10–4.30. Handles research enquiries for Society for Army Historical Research.

Public Record Office, Ruskin Avenue, Kew, Richmond, Surrey TW9 4DU (tel. 020 8876 3444; fax 020 8878 8905; email enquiry@pro.gov.uk; Website http://www.pro.gov.uk/). Admission by reader's ticket. Mon, Wed, Fri, Sat, 9.30–5; Tue, 10–7; Thu, 9.30–7. (Last document orders on Saturdays, 2.30 p.m.) Closed for stocktaking two weeks usually early December. *Note*. The Public Record Office in Chancery Lane is now closed.

**Recommended title:**

*Records of the War Office and Related Departments, 1660–1964*, by Michael Roper, PRO Publications, London, 1998

See also under '*World Wars I and II*'.

## Music

British Library Rare Books and Music Reading Room, British Library, 96 Euston Road, London NW1 2DB (tel. 020 7412 7673; fax 020 7412 7577; email rare-books@bl.uk). British Library reader's pass required. Mon, 10-8; Tue, Wed, Thu, 9.30–8; Fri, Sat, 9.30–5. Access to printed and manuscript material and to the Listening and Viewing Service of the National Sound Archive (see page 207).

Royal College of Music Reference Library, Prince Consort Road, London SW7 2BS (tel. 020 591 4325; fax 020 7589 7740). Admission by reader's ticket. Mon–Thu, 9.30–6.15; Fri, 9.30–5.30 (term); Tue–Fri, 10–1, 2–4.30 (vacation); closed for two weeks at Christmas and at Easter.

Royal Opera House Archives, Royal Opera House, Covent Garden, London WC2E 9DD (tel. 020 7240 1200; fax 020 7212 9489). Currently closed during rebuilding of Royal Opera House, but due to re-open early 2000.

Vaughan Williams Memorial Library, English Folk Dance and Song Society, Cecil Sharp House, 2 Regent's Park Road, London NW1 7AY (tel./fax 020 7284 0523). Mon–Fri, 9.30–5.30. Non-members pay daily fee for access, reference only.

Westminster Music Library, Victoria Library, 10 Buckingham Palace Road, London SW1W 9UD (tel. 020 7641 4292; fax 020 7641 4281). Mon–Fri, 11–7; Sat, 10–5.

**Recommended title:**
*The New Grove Dictionary of Music and Musicians*, ed. Stanley Sadie, 20 vols, Macmillan, London, 1980; paperback edn, 1995

### Natural History

Natural History Museum Library, Cromwell Road, London SW7 5BD (tel. 020 7938 9191; fax 020 7938 9290). Mon–Fri, 10–4.30. Proof of identity required for reader's ticket (telephone for appointment).

Royal Botanic Garden Library, 20a Inverleith Row, Edinburgh EH3 5LR (tel. 0131-552 7171; fax 0131-552 0382). By appointment, letter of introduction required.

Royal Botanic Gardens Library and Archives, Kew, Richmond, Surrey TW9 3AE (tel. 020 8332 5414; fax 020 8332 5278). Tue–Thu, 10–5. By appointment, reader's ticket required.

See also under 'Zoology'.

### Naval

Caird Library, National Maritime Museum, Greenwich, London SE10 9NF (tel. 020 8312 6528/6673; fax 020 8312 6632; email library@nmm.ac.uk; Website http://www.nmm.ac.uk). Mon–Fri, 10–4.45; Sat, by appointment. Reader's ticket required. For those unable to visit the Library an independent professional researcher can be provided on a fee-paying basis. Computerised catalogue (Tin lib system) also on Website.

Royal Naval Historical Library, at Ministry of Defence Whitehall Library, see under '*Military*' on page 214.

## Newspapers and Periodicals

British Library Newspaper Library, Colindale Avenue, London NW9 5HE (tel. 020 7412 7353; fax 020 7412 7379; email newspaper@ bl.uk; Website http://www.bl.uk/collections/newspaper/). Admission by British Library reader's pass or Newspaper Library pass. Mon–Sat, 10–4.45; closed for the week following the last complete week in October.

British Library Humanities Reading Rooms, British Library, 96 Euston Road, London NW1 2DB (tel. 020 7412 7676; fax 020 7412 7609). Mon, 10-8; Tue, Wed, Thu, 9.30–8; Fri, Sat, 9.30–5. Reader's ticket required. Some reference material relating to periodicals is on open access. Journals held at the British Library Document Supply Centre, Boston Spa, Wetherby, West Yorkshire LS23 7BQ may be borrowed on request (through British Library or local public library).

## Parliament

House of Lords Record Office, House of Lords, Palace of Westminster, London SW1A 0PW (tel. 020 7219 3074; for appointments 020 7219 5316; fax 020 7219 2570). Mon–Fri, 9.30–5, when House is sitting. Intending searchers should write to the Clerk of the Records in advance, giving at least one week's notice and details of the nature of their research and/or specific documents they wish to consult. Confirmation of appointment and proof of identity will be checked at Pass Office prior to admission.

*Note:* The libraries of the House of Commons and House of Lords are for the use of Members only. Outside enquiries may be addressed to the House of Commons Information Office, Department of the Library, House of Commons, London SW1A 0AA (tel. 020 7219 4272).
See also under '*Government and Official Information*'.

## Politics (20th-century)

British Library of Political and Economic Science,London School of Economics, 10 Portugal Street, London WC2A 2HD (tel. 020 7955 7229; fax 020 7955 7454), by appointment.

Churchill Archives Centre, Churchill College, Cambridge CB3 0DS (tel. 01223 336087; fax 01223 336135). Mon–Fri, 9–5, by appointment with the Archivist (proof of identity required). N.B. Certain collections are subject to special conditions of access.

## Printing and Publishing

St Bride Printing Library, Bride Lane, London EC4Y 8EQ (tel. 020 7353 4660; fax 020 7583 7073). Mon–Fri, 9.30–5.30.

## Recorded Sound

British Library National Sound Archive, British Library, 96 Euston Road, London NW1 2DB (tel. 020 7412 7440; fax 020 7412 7441; email nsa@bl.uk). British Library reader's pass required. The Recorded Sound Information Service (tel. Mon–Fri 10–5, 020 7412 7440; fax 020 7412 7441) is based in the Humanities 2 Reading Room; the Listening & Viewing Service is in the Rare Books and Music Reading Room (appointments through the Recorded Sound Information Service, as above). Northern listening service at British Library Document Supply Centre, Boston Spa, Wetherby, West Yorkshire LS23 7BQ (tel. 01937 546070)

## Religion

Catholic Central Library, Lancing Street, London NW1 1ND (tel. 020 7383 4333; fax 020 7388 6675). Non-members for reference and research only. Mon, Tue, Thu, Fri, 10.30–5; Wed, 10.30–8.

Church of England Record Centre, 15 Galleywall Road, South Bermondsey, London SE16 3PB (tel. 020 7231 1251; fax 020 7231 5243). Mon–Fri, 10–5, by appointment.

Dr Williams's Library, 14 Gordon Square, London WC1H 0AG (tel. 020 7387 3727; fax 020 7388 1142). Mon, Wed, Fri, 10–5; Tue, Thu, 10–6.30; closed first two weeks in August. Admission by subscription for borrowers; non-members for reference only.

Lambeth Palace Library, London SE1 7JU (tel. 020 7928 6222; fax 020 7928 7932). Mon–Fri, 10–5; closed for ten days at Easter. Letter of introduction required.

Methodist Archives and Research Centre, John Rylands University Library, University of Manchester, 150 Deansgate, Manchester M3 3EH (tel. 0161-834 5343; fax 0161-834 5574). Mon–Fri, 10–5.30; Sat, 10–1.

Parkes Library (Jewish studies), University of Southampton Library, Highfield, Southampton SO17 1BJ (tel. 023 8059 3335). Mon–Thu, 9–5; Wed, 10–5.

Religious Society of Friends (Quakers) Library, Friends House, 173–177 Euston Road, London NW1 2BJ (tel. 020 7663 1135; fax 020 7663 1001). Mon, Tue, Thu, Fri, 1–5; Wed, 10–5. Letter of introduction required for non-members.

Sion College Library, Victoria Embankment, London EC4Y 0DN (tel. 020 7353 7983). Mon–Fri, 10–5. Annual subscription rates and temporary membership available.

See also under '*Cathedral Archives and Libraries*'.

**Recommended title:**
*Keyguide to Information Sources on World Religions*, compiled by Jean Holm, Mansell, London, 1991

*Royal Archives*
By special permission of the Keeper of the Queen's Archives, Windsor Castle, Berks SL4 1NJ. Apply in writing.

*Science and Technology*
British Library Science, Technology and Business Service (formerly the Science Reference and Information Service), British Library, 96 Euston Road, London NW1 2DB. Five reading rooms: Science 1 South (British and European patents and trademarks), tel. 020 7412 7919/fax 020 7412 7495; Science 1 North (foreign patents), tel. 020 7412 7901/fax 020 7412 7912); Science 2 South (Life sciences and technologies, medicine and chemistry, *classmarks A–J*), tel. 020 7412 7288/fax 020 7412 7217); Science 2 North (Official publications and social sciences, engineering, *classmarks R–W*), tel. 020 7412 7536/fax 020 7412 7761; Science 3 (Business information, physical and earth sciences), *classmarks K–Q*), for business information telephone/fax lines, see under '*Business*', pages 207–8; other enquiries tel. 020 7412 7288/fax 020 7412 7217.
Imperial College of Science, Technology and Medicine, South Kensington, London SW7 2AZ. Central Library (tel. 020 7594 8820; fax 020 7584 3763) and various departmental libraries. Mon–Fri, 9.30–9; Sat, 9.30–5.30 (term); Mon–Sat, 9.30–5.30 (vacation).
Royal Society of London Library, 6 Carlton House Terrace, London SW1Y 5AG (tel. 020 7451 2606; fax 020 7930 2170). Mon–Fri, 10–5. Admission on introduction by a Fellow: *bona fide* researchers by application (proof of identity required).
Science Museum Library, Imperial College Road, off Exhibition Road, London SW7 5NH (tel. 020 7938 8234; fax 020 7938 9714). Mon–Fri, 9.30–9 (closes at 5.30 during vacations); Sat, 9.30–5.30. Access for reference only. Operates jointly with Imperial College Central Library (see above).
See also the Highgate Literary and Scientific Institution Library, listed under '*Private Subscription Libraries*'.

**Recommended titles:**
*ISIS Cumulative Bibliography* and the *History of Technology* series, both published by Mansell, London

**Science Fiction**
Science Fiction Foundation Research Library, Liverpool University Library, PO Box 123, Liverpool L69 3DA (tel. 0151-794 2733/ 2696; fax 0151-794 2681). By appointment.

Recommended title:
*Encyclopedia of Science Fiction*, compiled by John Clute and Peter Nicholls, Orbit, London, rev. edn, 1993

**Theatre**
Raymond Mander and Joe Mitchenson Theatre Collection, The Mansion, Beckenham Place Park, Beckenham BR3 2BP (tel. 020 8658 7725; fax 020 8663 0313). Open to *bona fide* researchers by appointment.
Society for Theatre Research, c/o Theatre Museum, 1e Tavistock Street, Covent Garden, London WC2E 7PA. Written enquiries only.
Theatre Museum Library and Archive, 1e Tavistock Street, London WC2E 7PA (tel. 020 7836 7891; fax 020 7836 5148). Study Room open Tue–Fri, 10.30–4.30, strictly by appointment, preferably ten days in advance. Entrance to the Study Room is not the Museum entrance, but round the corner in Tavistock Street at basement level, approached by a ramp. The collection includes that of the Enthoven Collection, previously at the Victoria & Albert Museum, and the library of the former British Theatre Association.

Recommended titles:
*Biographical Dictionary of Actors, Actresses, Musicians, Dancers, Managers and Other Stage Personnel in London 1660–1800*, by P.H. Highhill, K.A. Burnim and E.A. Langhans, Southern Illinois University Press, USA, 16 vols, 1973–93
*A Directory of Theatre Research*, ed. Francesca Franchi, Society for Theatre Research/Library Association, London, 3rd edn, 1998
*International Dictionary of Theatre*, St James Press, Detroit, 3 vols, 1992–4
*The London Stage* (day-by-day calendar of plays produced at the major London theatres 1890–1959), Scarecrow Press, Lanham, Maryland (formerly Metuchen, N.J.), 1976–93

**Transport**
Civil Aviation Authority Library and Information Centre, Aviation House, Gatwick Airport South, West Sussex RH6 0YR (tel. 01293 573725; fax 01293 573181). Mon–Fri, 9.30–4.30.
Department of the Environment, Transport and the Regions, Library and Information Service, Ashdown House, 123 Victoria Street,

London SW1E 6DE (tel. 020 7890 3039; fax 020 7890 6098). Written and telephone enquiries in first instance.

Leicester University Library, Transport History Collection, University Road, Leicester LE1 9QD (tel. 0116 252 2042; fax 0116 252 2066). Mon–Fri, 9–5.

London Transport Museum Library, 39 Wellington Street, Covent Garden, London WC2E 7BB (tel. 020 7379 6344; fax 020 7565 7252). Mon–Fri, 10–5.

National Railway Museum Library and Archive, National Railway Museum, Leeman Road, York YO26 4XJ. By appointment (tel. 01904 686235; fax 01904 611112).

Royal Aeronautical Society Library, 4 Hamilton Place, London W1V 0BQ (tel. 020 7499 3515; fax 020 7499 6230). Mon–Fri, 10–5.

### United Nations

United Nations Library and Information Centre, Millbank Tower (21st floor), 21/24 Millbank, London SW1P 4QH (tel. 020 7630 1981; fax 020 7976 6478). Reference library, 9–1, 2–5, by appointment. Information Centre, Mon–Fri, 9.30–1, 2–5.30.

### Weather

National Meteorological Library and Archive. The Library is at London Road, Bracknell, Berks RG12 2SZ (tel. (information officer) 01344 854841; fax 01344 854840; email metlib@meto.gov.uk). The Archive is nearby, at The Scott Building, Sterling Centre, Eastern Road, Bracknell, Berks RG12 2PW (tel. 01344 855960; fax 01344 855961). Mon–Fri, 8.30–4.30, advance notice of visit required.

### Wills

Borthwick Institute of Historical Research (York University), St Anthony's Hall, Peaseholme Green, York YO1 2PW (tel. 01904 642315; fax 01904 633284). Mon–Fri, 9.30–12.50, 2–4.50, by appointment; closed for one week at Easter. (PCY wills).

Family Records Centre, 1 Myddleton Street, London EC1R 1UW (tel. 020 8392 5300; fax 020 8392 5307). Mon, Wed, Fri, 9–5; Tue, 10–7; Thu, 9–7; Sat, 9.30–5. (PCC wills 1383–1858)

Principal Registry of the Family Division, First Avenue House, 42–49 High Holborn, London WC1V 6NP (tel. 020 7936 7000/6948). Mon–Fri, 10–4.30 (wills and administrations since 1858).

### Women's Studies

Fawcett Library, London Guildhall University, Calcutta House, Old Castle Street, London E1 7NT (tel. 020 7320 1189; fax 020 7320 1188). Term-time, Mon, 10.15–8.30; Wed, 9–8.30; Thu–Fri, 9–5;

vacation, Mon, Wed, Thu, Fri, 9–5. Annual subscription or one-day pass for non-members. The library will move to new premises in Aldgate, East London, in autumn 2000.

Feminist Library Resource and Information Centre, 5 Westminster Bridge Road, London SE1 7XW (tel. 020 7928 7789). Tue, 11–8; Wed, 3–8; Sat, 2–5. Free access for reference; books may be borrowed on payment of fee.

**Recommended titles:**

*The She Women's Directory*, by Loulou Brown, *She* Magazine and Cassell, London, 1998

*Women's Studies: A Guide to Information Sources*, by Sarah Carter and Maureen Ritchie, Mansell, London, 1990

### World Wars I and II

Churchill Archives Centre, Churchill College, Cambridge CB3 0DS (tel. 01223 336087; fax 01223 336135; email archives@chu.cam.ac.uk; Website http://www.chu.cam.ac.uk/archives/home.htm). Mon–Fri, 9–5, by appointment with the Archivist. Proof of identity required. (Papers of military and naval commanders, politicians and scientists; certain collections subject to special conditions of access.)

Imperial War Museum Library, Lambeth Road, London SE1 6HZ (tel. 020 7416 5000; fax 020 7416 5374). Mon–Sat, 10–5, by appointment. Closed last two full weeks in November.

Wiener Library, Institute of Contemporary History, 4 Devonshire Street, London W1N 2BH (tel. 020 7636 7247/8; fax 020 7436 6428). Letter of introduction required. Subscription payable for extensive research, but short-term use of reference facilities free. Mon–Fri, 10–5.30. N.B. The collection of books was mostly transferred to Tel Aviv University in 1980, but the bulk of the material has been retained on microfilm in London.

**Recommended titles:**

*The First World War*, by John Keegan, Hutchinson, London, 1998; paperback edn, 1999

*The Oxford Companion to the Second World War*, ed. I.C.B. Dear, Oxford University Press, Oxford, 1995

*The Second World War: A Guide to Sources*, by J.D. Cantwell, PRO Publications, London, 1998

### Zoology

Zoological Society of London Library, Regent's Park, London NW1 4RY (tel. 020 7449 6293; fax 020 7586 5743). Mon–Fri, 9.30–5.30. Access for non-members on payment of fee.

# Appendix II

## Reference Books for the Writer

Good reference books, microfiches and CD-ROMs are expensive, and the average writer cannot afford to compete with a library in keeping his personal collection fully up to date. He would be foolish even to try. What he buys, therefore, must be related to his own pocket, mobility and access to a well-stocked reference library, as well as to the special nature of his work.

Some basic suggestions for a writer's bookshelf are listed below. It is recommended that a plan for systematic renewal should be worked out, whereby you replace the essential yearbooks annually and other books in rotation. Sell those which you discard to a secondhand book-dealer and put the proceeds towards the purchase of new editions. Excellent reference works may often be picked up in secondhand bookshops for a fraction of their original cost and are a good buy for those not engaged on highly topical work; the information they contain can be supplemented or updated by the occasional visit to the library or, in case of urgent need, by a telephone call to the reference librarian. Now that the Net Book Agreement has gone, discount bookshops are springing up all over the country, and you will find real bargains there. You should keep an eye open for special offers advertised by book clubs. Look out also for publishers' 'reference shelf' or similar offers: these are good value for the writer beginning to build up a library and usually include a dictionary, a thesaurus, a dictionary of quotations and possibly a single-volume encyclopedia or one or two other titles, at a very competitive price. If you have a CD-ROM drive you may like to consider the *Penguin Hutchinson Reference Library*; or Oxford University Press's *Writers' Shelf*, marketed both on CD-ROM and on floppy disks (Windows and Macintosh), and consisting of sixteen titles on the one disk, including the *Pocket Oxford Dictionary*, the *Oxford Dictionary for Writers and Editors*, the *Oxford Guide to English Usage*, the *Oxford Minidictionary of Quotations*, *A Compact Encyclopedia*, the *Dictionary of Computing*, the *Oxford Dictionary for Scientific Writers and Editors*, a *World Gazetteer*, mini-dictionaries in French, German, Italian and Spanish, and several other useful texts.

Paperback reference titles are by no means to be scorned. Naturally they will not stand up to as much handling as hard-covers, but you will be less reluctant to offload them when revised editions become available – and less guilty about giving them the full 'working tool' treatment, annotating and marking them as your research proceeds.

At the end of a major project you may decide to dispose of a number of books in order to create shelf space for a new set related to your next work, and here again the secondhand bookseller with whom you are in the habit of dealing should give you a fair price. Do not however be too ruthless! (How to locate specialist booksellers will be found on page 43 and details of bookfinding services on page 52.)

# Suggested Basic Reference Library for the Writer

The essential items are:

1   A good English dictionary.
    *The Oxford English Dictionary* (OED), 2nd edition, 20 volumes, 1989, is obviously ideal, but probably beyond the pocket (and shelf-space) of the average writer for home use. There is a second edition of the *Compact OED*, in slipcase with magnifying glass (1991). The *OED* (2nd edn), the *New Shorter OED* (2 vols, 1993) and the *Concise OED* (9th edn, 1995) are also marketed in electronic form (CD-ROM and magnetic tape). New as this book goes to press is the 10th edn of the *Concise OED* (1999; CD-ROM forthcoming). A three-volume set, *The Oxford English Dictionary Additions Series*, the first major update of the OED for ten years, was published in 1997. (*Note:* a third edition of the full *OED* is in preparation and scheduled for publication in 2005.) Among single-volume dictionaries recommended are the *Oxford Paperback Dictionary and Thesaurus* (1997), *Collins English Dictionary* (millennium edn, 1998) and the *Chambers Dictionary* (7th edn, 1997; now also on CD-ROM). For American meanings and spellings you should consider acquiring one of the *Webster* dictionaries available in the UK, such as *Webster's New World Dictionary* (4th edn, 1994)\* or the

---

\*Rights have been aquired by Penguin Books, but at the time of writing no date has been set for a new edition. Less comprehensive, but highly recommended (and inexpensive) alternatives are *Webster's II New College Dictionary*, Houghton Mifflin International, Boston, Mass., 1995; updated paperback edn 1999, or the paperback *Webster's New World Basic Dictionary American English*, published by Macmillan Publishing USA, Indianapolis, 1998.

*American Heritage College Dictionary* (with CD-ROM), published by Houghton Mifflin International (3rd edn, 1997). It is a good idea to keep a smaller dictionary handy for quick reference, even if your word processor has a spell-checker, and there are many to choose from. Remember that language is forever changing: ideally you should update your main dictionary every ten years or so, or at least supplement it with a dictionary of current use, such as *The Oxford Dictionary of New Words* (1997). Especially valuable to writers is the *Oxford Writers' Dictionary* (1990), mentioned in chapter 10.

2    An encyclopedic dictionary.
     Again, there are many to choose from. The *Chambers Encyclopedic English Dictionary* (1995) is wide-ranging and reliable.

3    One or two biographical dictionaries.
     An up-to-date *Who's Who*, if you can afford it. *Who Was Who*, if you do historical writing. The 3-volume *Concise Dictionary of National Biography* is not cheap, but invaluable. The best relatively inexpensive buy is *Chambers Biographical Dictionary*, centenary edn, 1997 (available in hardback and paperback). Other compilations include the *Cambridge Biographical Encyclopedia* (1994) and *The Pocket Oxford Dictionary of Biography* (1997).

4    A good atlas, plus, if possible, a world gazetteer.
     *The Times Comprehensive Atlas of the World* is unrivalled; currently in its 9th edition (last revised 1997), a millennium edition is due at the end of 1999. The smaller *Times Concise Atlas of the World* is good value, as are any of the atlases from Collins or Philip's, or from the two big American publishers, Rand MacNally and National Geographic. The compact edition of *The Times Atlas of the World* (1997, reprinted with revisions 1998) is useful for quick reference. *Webster's New Geographical Dictionary* (revised edition 1997) is an excellent cross between an atlas and a gazetteer. It is unlikely that individual readers will wish to acquire for home use the three-volume *Columbia Gazetteer of the World*, published in 1998 and retailing at a mere £500.00, but this *is* the definitive book in the field; you will of course find it in a good map library. Among the many atlases on CD-ROM the *Microsoft Encarta World Atlas* is highly recommended. *N.B.* Atlases are brought up to date every few years, and it is wise to buy the latest edition and the best you can afford. Take the advice of a firm

like Stanford's, 12–14 Long Acre, London WC2E 9LP (tel. 020 7836 1321; fax 020 7836 0189).

5   A road atlas/gazeteer of the British Isles.
These also go out of date very quickly, and you should replace them regularly. The *AA Big Road Atlas Britain* (scale 3 miles to 1 inch) (latest edn 1999) is currently excellent value. An up-to-date copy of *London AZ* is also a good investment.

6   An encyclopedia (or two).
Here the choice depends very much on your needs and your budget. The newest state-of-the-art encyclopedias are 'multimedia', presenting information not only in print but with the accompaniment of sound and video. Supreme among the traditional compilations, *The New Encyclopedia Britannica* runs into thirty-two volumes in printed form but is now available at a reasonable cost in two different CD-ROM editions and a DVD edition. You can choose between a single-disk non-multimedia CD version or a 2-disk multimedia version. Alternatively, for not much more money, provided you possess a suitable PC, you might go for the fully interactive single-disk multimedia *Britannica DVD99*, whose features include sophisticated filters through which you can refine your research, a search engine that will answer with a list of relevant articles any question you care to type in, and the ability to connect to some 33,000 Internet links. The world English edition of the US *Microsoft Encarta* comes in three CD-ROM formats, all multimedia: standard, de luxe (with additional articles) and 'reference suite' which includes not only additional material and curriculum guides, but an atlas and a yearbook (updated online every month). Outstanding among the single volume encyclopedias are *The Macmillan Encyclopedia*, *The Hutchinson Encyclopedia* and *The Cambridge Encyclopedia*. Unless you live a long way from a good reference library, where you can consult the multi-volume encyclopedias, it makes sense to buy one of these concise editions and renew them frequently; most are now updated annually. However, if you have the chance to acquire a secondhand set of the 9th (the so-called 'scholars' edition) or the 11th *Britannica* (with supplements, the most extensive), do not pass it by; these contain much information not included in modern editions. That said, one word of warning: do not be tempted to acquire too many different encyclopedias, or when you come to look things up, you will be driven crazy by conflicting facts!

7   A dictionary of quotations (preferably more than one).
    Standard works are *The Oxford Dictionary of Quotations* (4th
    edn, revised, 1996) and *Bartlett's Familiar Quotations* (latest
    edn, 1992). Paperback editions for quick reference include *The
    Bloomsbury Dictionary of Quotations* (1997), *The Concise
    Oxford Dictionary of Quotations* (rev. 3rd edn, 1997), *The
    Little Oxford Dictionary of Quotations* (1994), the *New
    Penguin Dictionary of Quotations* (6th edn, 1998) and the *New
    Penguin Dictionary of Twentieth Century Quotations* (3rd edn,
    1997). Also recommended are *The Oxford Dictionary of Phrase,
    Saying and Quotation* (1997) and the *Cassell Dictionary of
    Proverbs* (1997). The *Penguin Thesaurus of Quotations* (1998;
    paperback edn due spring 2000) is especially useful in that the
    quotations are grouped under 800 different themes. The *Cassell
    Companion to Quotations*, compiled by Nigel Rees (1997)
    contains explanatory footnotes on the provenance of the
    quotations included. In recent years there have been many
    specialist compilations ranging from biographical to war
    quotations, even the erotic, the humorous and the insulting – too
    numerous to list here. Buy a standard work and one or two
    others that best reflect your writing interests.

8   A dictionary of dates and/or chronology of historical events.
    Highly recommended and fully up to date, but expensive, is the
    expanded version of *The Hutchinson Chronology of World
    History* (4 vols, Helicon, Oxford, 1999; also on CD-ROM).
    There is a compact edition of the *Chronology* (2nd edn, 1998).
    The Oxford University Press paperback, *A Dictionary of Dates*
    (2nd edn, 1997) is a good buy, and so is the classic S.H.
    Steinberg's *Historical Tables 58 BC–AD 1990* (Macmillan, 12th
    edn, 1991). Sadly, *Everyman's Dictionary of Dates* has gone out
    of print and is unlikely to be reprinted; but it is worthwhile
    searching for secondhand.

9   A concise world history.
    *Chambers Dictionary of World History* (Larousse, 1993,
    reprinted 1994; new edn scheduled for autumn 2000) is an
    excellent reference tool. See also *The Hutchinson Chronology of
    World History*, mentioned above.

10  A thesaurus.
    *Roget's Thesaurus of English Words and Phrases* is the standard
    work; revised and brought up to date by E.M. Kirkpatrick,
    Longman, 1996, it is currently out of print in hardback but

available as a Penguin paperback (1998). A different style of compilation is *The Oxford Thesaurus*, compiled by Laurence Urdang (Oxford University Press, 2nd edn, 1997). Other editions include the *Concise Oxford Thesaurus*, compiled by Betty Kirkpatrick (1995, reprinted 1997), *The Little Oxford Thesaurus* (rev. edn, 1998) and *The Oxford Minireference Thesaurus* (1992, reprinted 1997), both compiled by Alan Spooner. There is also the *Chambers Combined Dictionary Thesaurus* (Larousse, 1995).

11  A guide to English usage.
Fowler's *A Dictionary of Modern English Usage* has long been the standard. There is a revised edition by Sir Ernest Gowers (Oxford University Press, 2nd edn, 1965; paperback edn, 1983); also *The New Fowler's Modern English Usage*, revised by R.W. Burchfield (Oxford University Press, 3rd edn, 1996). A highly recommended modern work is Godfrey Howard's *The Good English Guide: English Usage in the 1990s* (Pan Macmillan, 1993; paperback edn, 1997). By the same author is a handy reference title, *The Macmillan Good English Handbook*, 1998, available in both hardback and paperback.

12  *Brewer's Dictionary of Phrase and Fable*, originally published in 1870 and now in its 15th edition (Cassell, 1995) is available in a concise edition, revised by Betty Kirkpatrick (Helicon, 1992, reprinted 1999; paperback, 1996, reprinted 1997). There is also Adrian Room's *Brewer's Dictionary of Names: People & Places & Things* (Helicon, 1995).

13  A current yearbook.
*Whitaker's Almanack* is a classic. You should however be careful before opting for the concise edition, as some sections are omitted altogether (these are listed). A newcomer to this field is *The Hutchinson Almanac 1999*, highly recommended.

14  *Writers' & Artists' Yearbook*, published annually by A & C Black. Every writer should possess a current edition. This is one reference book that should be renewed each year.

15  One or more other directories reflecting the writer's chief interests. For example, the *Cassell Directory of Publishing*; *Benn's Media*; *Willing's Press Guide*; *The Media Guide* – all listed in the bibliography at the end of chapter 3. The radio and television writer will want Barrie Macdonald's *Broadcasting in*

*the United Kingdom* (Mansell, rev. 2nd edn, 1994; new edn in preparation) and *Contacts*, an annual publication from Spotlight (7 Leicester Place, London WC2H 7BP; tel. 020 7437 7631) which lists all the main addresses of the radio and television companies, names of heads of department, agents, etc.

The above titles form a first-class nucleus reference library, which can be built up over the years according to the dictates and fluctuations of the bank balance and work requirements. Some further suggestions (many of which have been mentioned in various chapters of this book) are:

*Britain: An Official Handbook*, published annually by The Stationery Office (formerly HMSO), London

*The Companion to British History*, by Charles Arnold-Baker, Longcross Press, Tunbridge Wells, 1996

*Debrett's Correct Form*, Headline, London, 1992; new edn, 1999

*Europa World Year Book*, published annually by Europa Publications, London

*Hollis Press & Public Relations Annual*, published annually by Hollis Directories, Teddington, Middx

*International Authors' & Writers' Who's Who*, Melrose Press, Cambridge; updated every few years (16th edn, 1999)

*International Who's Who*, published annually by Europa Publications, London

*Oxford Companion to English Literature*, Oxford University Press (5th edn, edited by Margaret Drabble, 1985); concise edition (paperback), edited by Margaret Drabble and Jenny Stringer, 1987; reissued 1992

*Pears Cyclopaedia*, published annually, now by Penguin Books, London, 107th edn, 1998

*Record Repositories in Great Britain*, Royal Commission on Historical Manuscripts, PRO Publications, London, updated every few years; 11th edn, ed. Ian Mortimer, 1999

*The Statesman's Year-Book*, published annually by Macmillan, London

*Walford's Concise Guide to Reference Material*, compiled by A. Chalcroft *et al.*, Library Association, London, 2nd edn, 1992

*Who Was Who*, published by A & C Black, London, 9 vols to date, covering the period 1897–1995; also *Cumulated Index 1897–1990*. Available on CD-ROM as *Who's Who 1897–1996*, published jointly by A & C Black and Oxford University Press

*The Writer's Handbook*, ed. Barry Turner, published annually by Macmillan, London

*Note*. Many reference books are now produced in electronic form. In order to access some of this (mostly academic) data you (or your library) must be a subscriber. But more and more standard general titles, such as books of quotations, are becoming freely available. *Roget's Thesaurus*, for example, can be searched at http://www.thesaurus.com. (Personally, I find it easier to flip through the pages of the printed book. On which note, with heartfelt thanks to Dr Roget and to all other compilers of our great reference tools, I end this sixth edition.)

# Index

*Note:* It would be impossible to include in this index every library, institution and book or newspaper title referred to in the text. Entries are therefore confined to those of major importance and those with special mention in the book. Users will quickly locate other material by looking up the relevant subject entry and by consulting the bibliographies at the end of the various chapters.

accuracy, importance of, 2–3, 31–2, 150
acknowledgments, 38, 118, 181
address, forms of, 96
administrations, *see* wills and administrations
Adopted Children's Register, 141
advertisements, 87
advertising
    as means of seeking information, 119–20
    sources, 205
Africa, 165, 166
agriculture, 206
Air Force records, 124, 125, 206
*All England Law Reports*, 129
America, *see* Latin America; United States of America
anachronisms, 96
Ancestral File, 143
ancestry research services, 159
Arab States, 167
archaeological societies, 139, 140
    publications, 57–8, 149
architecture, 206
archive centres, regional (UK), 194–201
archives, British
    guides to, 62, 119
arms, coats of, 150

Army records, 124–5, 214
art, 206
Asia, 167
Association for Information Management (Aslib)
    *Directory of Information Sources in the UK*, 47, 164, 191, 212
    other publications, 47, 64
associations, professional and trade, 83, 94
atlases, 61, 224–5
    historical, 99
Australasia, 168, 169
Australia, 170
    Sir Robert Menzies Centre for Australian Studies (London), 166
Austria, 172
Authors, Society of, 11, 35, 46, 185
    *The Author*, 10, 27, 130, 157
    *Information Sheets*, 16, 26, 41
    *Quick Guides*, 35, 41, 105
    Translators Association, 160
Authors' Licensing and Collecting Society, 34
autobiographical research, 116–31
autobiographies, 97–8
    *see also* memoirs

background research, 6, 92–3, 94
banking, 206–7
baptismal records, 139, 144, 145
Baptist records, 149
baronetages, 149
BBC Sound Archives, 65
BBC Written Archives Centre, 65,
    127, 207
behavioural studies, 94
Belgium, 172–3
*Benn's Media*, 54, 227
bibliographies, xviii, 48, 49, 85, 96,
    122–3, 162, 163
    preparation of, 32, 128, 180, 182
    *see also British National
        Bibliography*
*Bio-Bibliographicus Notorum
    Hominum, Index*, 122
*Biographical Archives*, 120–1
biographical dictionaries and
    indexes, 96, 120–2, 163, 224
biographical research, 6, 20, 60–1,
    116–31, 158
biography, unauthorised, 118
*Biography and Genealogy Master
    Index*, 121
Birmingham Central [Reference]
    Library, 61, 204
birth certificates, 11, 141–2
birth records, 128, 140, 141–4,
    145, 207
Bishop's Transcripts, 145
BLAISE (British Library Automated
    Information Service), 50, 51, 60,
    179
Bodleian Library (Oxford), 44, 46,
    192
book information services, 49–50
Book Trust, 50
    *see also* Young Book Trust
*BookBank*, 43
bookfinding services, 52
books
    as reference tools, xix, 42
    borrowing from libraries, 43–4
    buying, 43, 222–3
    care of, 22
    obtaining foreign language
        titles, 163

out-of-print titles, xviii, 51–3
    tracing, 43–4, 51
*Books on Demand*, 52–3
*Bookseller, The*, 43, 51
booksellers
    antiquarian, secondhand and
        specialist, 43, 51–2
    London, 43, 52
*Boyd's Marriage Index*, 145–6
British Broadcasting Corporation
    (BBC), 65
    *see also* BBC Sound Archives;
        BBC Written Archives Centre
British Copyright Council, 33, 35
British Film Institute, 66, 209–10
British history sources, 62, 72, 85,
    96–7
British Library, 29, 44, 45–6, 157,
    191–2
    automated book request
        system, 48–9
    Automated Information Service
        (BLAISE), 50, 51, 60, 179
    Business Information Research
        Service, 82, 126, 207
    Department of Manuscripts/
        Manuscripts reading room,
        45, 61, 119, 193
    Document Supply Centre,
        43–4, 45, 55, 207, 216, 217
    *General Catalogue of Printed
        Books*, 48, 54, 55, 69
    Humanities reading rooms, 45,
        216
    *Keyword Index to Serial Titles*,
        55
    King's Library, 45
    Maps reading room, 45, 61, 211
    move to St Pancras, 45
    National Bibliographic Service,
        50
    National Sound Archive, 45,
        65–6, 95, 126–7, 207, 217
    newspaper and periodicals
        collections, 53, 55
    Newspaper Library, 45, 53–4,
        56, 58, 128, 163, 216
    Open Access Catalogue, 44, 48,
        51, 55

Oriental and India Office
   Collections, 45, 64, 165, 168,
   193, 211
Rare Books and Music reading
   room, 45, 66, 214–15
reader's tickets, 29, 53, 61, 82
Science reading rooms, 45, 218
Science, Technology and
   Business Service, 58, 82, 218
*Serials in the British Library*, 55
Social Policy Information
   Service, 58–9, 81, 211
British Library-Lloyds Bank
   Business Line, 82, 207
*British National Bibliography*, 24,
   39, 58, 107, 118
*British Newspaper Index*, 56, 81
British Records Association, 63
*British Standards*, 181, 182, 185,
   187, 188–9
British Universities Film and Video
   Council, 66, 207, 210
British Universities Newsreel
   Project, 66
broadcast material, 65–6, 126–7,
   207
Broadcasting Act 1990, 65, 66
buildings, 93, 99
   *see also* architecture
burial records, 139, 144, 145
Burke's Ancestry Research, 159
*Burke's Peerage* publications, 140,
   149
Business Archives Council, 125, 208
Business Archives Council of
   Scotland, 125, 208
business records, 125–6, 207–8

Caird Library (National Maritime
   Museum Library), 29, 44, 61,
   63, 119, 127, 215
calendar, Old Style and New Style,
   86
Cambridge University Library, 44,
   46, 55, 192
camera-ready copy, 181, 183
cameras, 12
Canada, 170–1

card indexes
   personal, 19, 20, 21, 128, 140
   *see also* catalogues, library
      and archive centre
Caribbean sources, 177–8
cartoons and caricature, 87, 208
cassette recorders, 12, 37, 38
catalogues, library and archive
   centre, 28–30, 48, 55
cathedral archives and libraries,
   204
CD-ROM, xv, xviii, 162
census returns, 63, 142, 147–8, 209
Childhood, Bethnal Green Museum
   of, book collections, 104, 209
children's books, 104–5, 209
China, 169
chronologies
   published, 98, 226
   working, 20
Church of Jesus Christ of Latter-Day
   Saints (Mormon Church), 42–3,
   210
Church records, 204, 210, 217–18
Churchill Archives Centre, 64, 119,
   216, 221
cinema, *see* films and cinema
clothes, *see* costume
College of Arms, 140, 158–9, 210
commerce, *see* banking; business
   records; company histories
Commonwealth, British
   libraries and study centres (UK),
      165, 166
   sources, 58, 169–70
Commonwealth of Independent
   States, *see* Russian Federation
Companies House/Companies
   Registration Office, 125, 208
company histories, 125
computer pens, 17
computer search services, xvi,
   49–50, 80
computer terminals, ordering books
   and documents on, 48–9, 63
computers
   personal (PCs), 12, 13, 14–17
   portable (laptops, PDAs), 16

concordances, 60
conflicting authorities, 86
contracts, publishers', 11, 117, 159, 185
copy editing, 181, 184, 185
copy editors, 184
copy shops, 33
copyright
    British, 33–6
    Crown, 36
    EC Directive on, 34
    'fair dealing', 35
    international, 34
    quotation of material in, 11, 35–6
    reprography and, 32–3
    United States, 34
Copyright, Designs and Patents Act 1988, 34
copyright libraries (UK), 28, 29, 44, 46, 163, 191–2
    reader's tickets, 29, 46
Copyright Licensing Agency, 33
cost of living (historical), 101–2
costs, *see* research costs
costume, 6, 102–3, 209
Costume Society, The, 102
county histories, 150, 151
county record offices, 58, 61, 149, 157, 158, 194–201
    depositing papers at, 152
    parish registers at, 144
    using, 139–40, 150
crime writing, 94, 105
curiosity, the researcher's, 3–4
currencies, world (historical), 102
current affairs, 81
cybercafés, xvi, 27

*Daily Telegraph*, 123, 129
databases
    access to, xv, 49–50
    personal, 18, 39
    *see also* computer search services
dates
    copying, 31
    dictionaries of, 98, 226
    in correspondence, 129–30
    in historical research, 86–7, 99, 151

death certificates, 11, 141–2
death duty registers, 142
death records, 128, 140, 141–4, 145, 207
Debrett Ancestry Research, 159
Debrett's publications, 96, 121, 149
Denmark, 176
Dewey Decimal Classification, 30
dialects, 6, 95
diaries, 94, 97, 98, 123
dictionaries
    encylopedic, 96, 224
    English language, 223
    *see also* biographical dictionaries; dates, dictionaries of; quotations, dictionaries of
*Dictionary of National Biography*, 120, 224
Digitisation Licensing Scheme, 33
diplomatic representation, 164
directories, 60, 80, 83
discussion groups, 25
dissertations, *see* theses
divorce records, 128, 146
documents, care of, 21, 22, 62–3

eating habits and diet, 6, 103
electronic note-takers, *see* cassette recorders
electronic storage of material, 18–19, 39
electronic typescripts (disks), 181
email, xv, 23, 24, 25, 26, 162
email addresses, xviii–xix, 26
embassies, foreign (in UK), 54, 158, 164
*Encarta*, 225
*Encyclopedia Britannica*, 225
encyclopedias, 80, 85, 122, 225
    foreign language, 162, 163
*English Short Title Catalogue*, 50, 59–60
English usage, 227
entertainments (historical), 87
    *see also* films and cinema; theatre

equipment, 12–17
  use of, in libraries and record
    offices, 36–7, 63
*Essay and General Literature
  Index*, 59
etiquette 103
  *see also* address, forms of
European Commission, 59, 209
  Directive on copyright, 34
  publications, 59
European sources, 171–7, 178
  social histories, 85, 96–7
  statistics, 81, 85
  *see also under individual
    countries*
expenses, *see* research costs
experts, how to contact, 61, 83–4

factual research, 5, 6, 79–84
  *see also* statistics
fairy tales, 104
Family History Library Catalog, 143
family history publishers, 138–9
family history research, 61, 137–50,
  158
family history societies, 138, 149
Family History Societies, Federation
  of, 138
  publications, 139, 146, 149, 156
Family Records Centre, 63, 128,
  141, 142, 143, 147, 193, 207,
  209, 210, 220
*Family Search* database, 142, 143
*Family Tree Magazine*, 139, 156
family trees, 141, 159
  *see also* Ancestral File
Far East, 168–9
fashion, 87, 102–3
  *see also* costume
Fashion Research Centre, 102, 209
fax machines, 17
fiction
  children's, 104–5
  crime, 105
  finding out about published,
    105–6
  research for, 6, 92–106
  science, 105

*Fiction Index*, 105, 106
fictional characters, 104, 106
figures, copying, 31
filing systems, 19, 20, 21–3
films and cinema, 66–7, 209–10
First Avenue House, 119, 128, 142,
  146–7, 193, 220
Fleming, Peter, 7
folklore, 99, 210
food, *see* eating habits and diet
foreign countries, sources of
  information on, 58, 162–79
foreign libraries (in UK), 164,
  165–6
foreign publications, how to obtain,
  163
Forsyth, Frederick, 5
France, 173–4
  embassy (London), 174
  French Institute library
    (London), 165
Freelance Editors and Proofreaders,
  Society of, 184
French Protestant Church of
  London, 144, 210
Friends, Religious Society of, 143,
  210–11, 217

gazetteers, 9, 224–5
genealogical research, 137–50,
  158–9, 210
genealogical research services, 159
genealogists, professional, 128, 137,
  158, 161
Genealogists, Society of, 116,
  137–8, 142, 145, 149, 152, 159
  *Computers in Genealogy*, 138
  *Genealogists' Magazine*, 138, 159
  Library, 138, 140, 143, 211
  publications, 60, 87, 138, 139,
    145
  research service, 138, 159
Genealogists and Record Agents,
  Association of, 158
Genealogists and Record Agents,
  Association of Scottish, 158
Genealogists in Ireland, Association
  of Professional, 158

General Register Offices, 141, 142, 193
*Gentleman's Magazine*, 57, 100, 123
Geographers, Institute of, Library, *see* Royal Geographical Society/ Institute of Geographers Library
geographical sources, 211
Germany, 174
 libraries and information services (UK), 165
gestures, 94
government publications, 58–9, 211–12
government records, *see* official records; Parliamentary records
graphology, 130
Graphology Bureau Ltd, The, 130
Greece, 174–5
*Grey Literature in Europe*, 50
*Guardian, The*, 123
Guild of One-Name Studies, 138
Guildhall Library, 60, 64, 213

hairstyles (historical), 103
handwriting
 analysis of, 130
 in research notes, 31
 old, study of, *see* palaeography
*Hansard*, 59, 126
Hemingway, Ernest, *quoted*, 1
Her Majesty's Stationery Office (HMSO), *now* The Stationery Office Ltd, *q.v.*, xii, 36
 former publications, 59
Heraldic and Genealogical Studies, Institute of, 137, 146, 210
heraldry, 149–50, 158–9, 210
Herrick, Robert, *quoted*, 8
high commissions (in UK), 54, 158, 164
Highgate Literary and Scientific Institution Library, 47, 205, 218
Historical Association, 84
 publications, 84, 87, 151
Historical Manuscripts Commission, *see* Royal Commission on Historical Manuscripts

historical novels
 published, 106
 research for, 6, 96–103
historical research, 5, 6, 84–7
Historical Research, Institute of, 85
 database, 85
 publications, 48, 65, 91, 126
hotel registers, 127
House of Lords Record Office, 64, 126, 146, 216
Huguenot records, 143–4, 149
Hyde Park Family History Center, 143, 210
hymns, 60

idiom, *see* language
illustrations, 11, 159–60
Imperial War Museum Library, 29, 44, 64, 221
incumbents' search fees, 144
indexers
 authors as, 186
 professional, 186, 188
Indexers, Society of, 186, 187
 *Indexers Available*, 186, 188
 Training course, 187
indexes
 cost of, 185–6
 preparation of, 185–8
 subject indexes, *see* catalogues, library and archive centre
 *see also* newspapers, indexes to; periodicals, indexes to
indexing tutorials, 187
India, 64, 168, 171
India Office Library, former, *see under* British Library: Oriental and India Office Collections
Information Bureau, The, 81–2
information technology, xv, xvii, 6, 39
international affairs, 58, 164, 212
International Genealogical Index, 142–3
Internet, the, xv, xvi, 9, 14, 79
Internet bookshop, 43
Internet research, 23–8, 39
Internet service providers, 10, 25

Internet training, 26–7
interviewing, 37–8
Ireland, Northern
    General Register Office, 141, 193
    Public Record Office, 64, 192
Ireland, Republic of (Eire)
    General Register Office, 141, 193
    National Archives, 175
    National Library of Ireland, 64,
      175
    Trinity College Library (Dublin),
      44, 64, 192
Italy, 175
    Italian Institute library
      (London), 165

Japan, 168–9
Jewish records, 121, 144, 217
John Rylands University Library of
    Manchester, 44, 202
Johnson, Dr Samuel, *quoted*, 3
journalists, freelance, 83

*Keesings' Record of World Events*,
    81
*Keyword Index to Serial Titles*, 55
Korea, 169

language, 6, 95–6, 101, 105
Latin, use of (in genealogical and
    local history research), 149, 151,
    158
Latin America, 177–8
law libraries, 212–13
law reports, 129
letters, 123
    copyright in, 35, 118
    problems of dating, 87, 129–30
libraries (abroad)
    guides to, 47, 164
    *see also under relevant country*
libraries (UK)
    catalogues and guides, 28–30,
      47, 48, 82
    computer search services, xvi,
      49–50, 80
    copyright libraries, 29, 44, 46,
      163, 191–2

foreign libraries, 164–6
    opening hours, 46
    ordering procedures, 28–9
    private subscription libraries, 28,
      43, 47, 205
    public libraries, 28, 43, 57, 98,
      139, 140
    reader's tickets, 29, 53
    reference libraries, 44–7, 204–5
    special libraries, 28, 47–8
    university libraries, 29, 163,
      202–4
    *see also* British Library
Library Association, 47, 49
Listening and Viewing Service, *see*
    *under* National Sound Archive
literary manuscripts (English), 62
*Literature Online*, 106
local history publishers, 138–9
local history research, 137–40,
    150–2, 158
local history societies, 84, 128, 138
    publications, 57–8
*Local Newspapers in Peril*, 56
London
    buildings, 99
    City records, 64, 213
    Corporation of London Record
      Office, 197, 213
    historical sources, 150, 213
    public libraries, 46, 129, 213
    street directories, 60
    Westminster City Archives
      Centre, 196, 213
    Westminster Reference Library,
      45, 46, 59, 205
*London Gazette*, 59
London Library, 46–7, 205
London Metropolitan Archives,
    142, 196, 213
London University Library, 44,
    202

magazines, *see* periodicals
manners, 6
    *see also* behavioural studies;
      etiquette; gestures
manorial records, 150–1

manuscripts, 180–1
  sources, 61–3, 193–4, 202–4
maps, 9, 61, 63, 150, 211
marriage certificates, 11, 141–2,
  145
marriage indexes, 145–6
marriage records, 128, 139, 140,
  141–3, 144, 146, 207
Maugham, W. Somerset, *quoted*, 5
media, guides to the, 54, 65, 227–8
medicine, 58, 213
  *Index Medicus*, 58
Members of Parliament, 126
memoirs, 94, 116, 123
Meteorological Library and
  Archive, National, 100–1, 220
Methodist records, 149, 217
microfiche, catalogues and source
  material on, xviii, 30, 37
microfilm
  catalogues and source-material
    on, xvi, xviii, 32
  newspapers on, 53, 55, 56
  public records on, 63
microform readers (for microfiche
  and microfilm), 37
Middle East, 167
military records, 124–5, 214
misprints, 2, 32
Mizner, Wilson, *quoted*, 188
money, 102
moral rights, 33–4, 35
Mormon Church (London
  Mission), *see* Hyde Park Family
  History Center
multimedia, 16
music, 60, 66, 214–15

names, 95, 129, 140
  copying, 31
  *see also* nicknames; place-names;
    pseudonyms
National Art Library, 104, 209
National Film and Television
  Archive, 66
*National Index of Parish Registers*,
  144, 145, 154–5
*National Life Story Collection*, 67

National Maritime Museum
  Library, *see* Caird Library
National Meteorological Library
  and Archive, 100–1, 220
National Register of Archives, 62,
  118–19, 123, 193
National Sound Archive, British
  Library, 65–6, 95, 126–7, 207,
  217
  catalogue (CADENSA), 66
  Listening and Viewing Service,
    66, 207, 215, 217
  Northern Listening Service, 45,
    66, 207, 217
  Recorded Sound Information
    Service, 45, 207, 217
*National Union Catalog*, 51
Natural History Museum Library,
  45, 215
natural history sources, 215
naval records, 124, 125, 215–16
Netherlands, The, 175
New Zealand, 171
newsgroups, 25
Newspaper Library, British Library
  (Colindale), 45, 53–4, 56, 58,
  128, 163, 216
newspapers, 53–7, 101, 123, 216
  bibliographies, 54
  catalogues and guides to, 53,
    54
  Early English, 54, 56
  foreign, 53, 54, 163
  indexes to, 56–7
  local, 56, 93, 123, 128, 129
newsreels, 66
nicknames, 94, 129
Nonconformist records, 142,
  143–4
Norway, 176
notes and references, 31–2, 180,
  182
note-taking, 4–5, 18, 19–20, 31–2
novels, research for
  historical, 96–103
  modern, 92–6
*NUJ Freelance Directory*, 83–4
nursery rhymes, 60, 104

obituaries, 123
Office for National Statistics, 81, 142, 193, 211
official publications, 58–9, 211
official records, 63–4, 84, 211–12
online, going, xvi, 16, 24–7
Online Public Access Catalogue (OPAC), 44, 48, 51, 55
online research methods, 23–8
'open access' material, 28, 45
oral history collections, 67
Ordnance Survey maps, 61, 99
organisation of material, 4–5, 9, 18–23
original material, care of, 22
out-of-print titles, xviii, 51–2

page references, 31
palaeography, 137, 151, 158
*Pallot's Marriage Index*, 146
parish histories, 99
parish registers, 139, 144–5
Parliamentary records, 59, 64, 126
patents, 58, 82, 218
PCs, *see* computers, personal
peerages, 149
people
  fallibility of memories of, 131
  finding out about, 93–5
periodicals, 53–6, 57–8, 216
  catalogues and guides to, 54–55
  foreign, 53, 55, 163
  indexes to, 57–8
  local, 57–8, 93
  recommended, for historical research, 87
  scientific and technical, 58
permissions clearance, 35–6
personal digital assistants, *see* computers, portable
photocopiers, 14, 17
photocopying, xvi, 32–3, 46
  costs, 11, 53–4, 183–4
photographs, care and storage of, 21, 22
picture research, 158, 159–60
Picture Research Association, 159

picture researchers, freelance, 159
place-names, 93
  copying, 31
places, research into, 92–3, 99
plagiarism, 36, 188
*Play Index*, 105
pocket memos, *see* cassette recorders
*Poetry, Granger's Index to*, 60
police procedures, 94, 105
Polish Library (London), 165
politics (20th century), 64, 84, 216
prelims, 180, 181
Prerogative Court of Canterbury (PCC) wills, 63, 142, 147, 220
Prerogative Court of York (PCY) wills, 147, 220
press and public relations officers, making use of, 83, 94, 164
Press Association News Library, 58
press cuttings, 22, 32, 58, 212
prices (historical), 87, 101–2
Principal Registry of the Family Division 128, 146, 193, 220
printed sources, 42–61
printers, 13, 14
printing and publishing, 217
private individuals, information from, 37–8, 131
private papers, 61–3, 118–20, 162
  dating problems in, 87
  depositing, 116, 152
probate records, 146–7, 220
proof-correction, 2, 8, 80, 185
pseudonyms, 94
  literary, 106
public libraries, 28, 43, 46, 56, 98, 129, 140, 149, 213
public library lending service, xviii, 43
Public Record Office (Kew), 61, 63–4, 84, 119, 127, 142, 157, 192, 211–12, 214
  document ordering procedures, 63–4
  *Guide to the Public Record Office*, 64
  other guides to records, 63, 124

reader's tickets, 63
*Record Repositories in Great
    Britain*, 64, 139, 191, 213
staff research library, 64
Public Record Office of Northern
    Ireland, 64, 192
Publishers Association, 35
punctuation, 181, 184

Quaker records, 143, 149, 217
quotations
    checking, 60
    dictionaries of, 226
    from material in copyright, 11,
        35

'Recent Acquisitions' (library), 30
record agents, 10, 137, 140, 157,
    161
record offices, *see* county record
    offices; Public Record Office
*Record Repositories in Great
    Britain*, 64, 139, 191, 213
recorded material, 66–7, 126–7, 217
Rees-Mogg, Lord, *quoted*, xvii
reference books, suggested nucleus
    library of, 222–9
reference libraries, major (UK),
    44–7, 204–5
reference material, guides to, 48, 62
religious records, 204, 217–18
Religious Society of Friends, 143,
    210–11, 217
reproduction fees (illustrations), 11
research costs, 9–11, 117
    for genealogical research, 138,
        141, 142, 144, 146, 147, 159,
        211
    professional research assistance,
        82, 161
research methods, xvii, 6–7, 9,
    23–39, 127–9
researcher, the writer as, xiv–xv,
    1–8
researchers, freelance, 10, 128,
    157–8, 161
    *see also* genealogists; picture
        researchers; record agents

*Roget's Thesaurus*, 226, 229
Roman Catholic records, 144, 217
Rowse, Dr A.L., *quoted*, 7
Royal Archives, 218
Royal Botanic Gardens Library and
    Archives, 29, 45, 215
Royal Commission on Historical
    Manuscripts, 62, 118–19,
    150–1, 193
    *Guide to Sources for British
        History*, 62, 72, 126
    *Record Repositories in Great
        Britain*, 64, 139, 191, 213
    other publications, 62, 126, 149,
        151
Royal Geographical Society/
    Institute of Geographers Library,
    61, 211
Royal Historical Society
    publications, 84–5, 91, 126
Royal Institute of International
    Affairs Library, 58, 212
Russian Federation, 178

St George Saunders, Joan, *quoted*, 7
Scandinavian sources, 176
School of Oriental and African
    Studies Library, 165, 166, 169
school records, 124
school stories, 104
science and technology, 58, 82–3,
    218
science fiction, 105, 219
Science Museum Library, 45, 55,
    218
Science, Technology and Business
    Service, British Library, 58, 82,
    218
    SCICAT catalogue, 82, 91
Scotland
    General Register Office, 141, 193
    National Library of Scotland,
        44, 64, 192
    National Register of Archives,
        64, 193
    record offices, 200–1
    reference libraries, 205
    university libraries, 203

Scottish Record Office, 64, 192
search engines, 25
Service records, 124–5, 206, 214, 215–16
shipping records, 127
shopping, 101–2
*Short Story Index*, 105
shredders, 13, 17
slang, 6, 95–6, 101
social histories, 96, 97
societies and institutions, transactions and proceedings of, 55, 126
software, computer
    genealogical, 140
    indexing, 186–7, 190
    optical character, 17
    word-processing, 15–16
song indexes, 60
source notes, importance of keeping, 4–5, 23, 31–2, 188
sources, basic, 42–78
Spain, 176–7
    Cervantes Institute library (London), 165
special libraries, 28, 47–8
specialist research, 157–61
speeches, public and broadcast, 126–7
Stationery Office Ltd, The, xii
statistics, 59, 80, 81, 85
Stevenson, Robert Louis, *quoted*, 4
storage of material, 4–5, 9, 18–23
street directories, 60
subject indexes, *see* catalogues, library and archive centre; newspapers, indexes to; periodicals, indexes to
subscription libraries, 28, 43, 47, 205
subscriptions to foreign newspapers and periodicals, 163
Sweden, 176
Switzerland, 177
Sydney Jones Library (Liverpool University), 44

tape recorders, 12, 13, 37
tax, expenses to set against, 10
technology, new, *see* information technology
technology sources, 83
telephone directories, 60–1
    *see also* yellow pages
televised material, 65–6, 207
theatre, 219
thesauruses, 226–7, 229
theses, 64–5
*Times, The*, xvii, 55, 56, 81, 129, 157
    *Index*, 56, 81, 123, 126, 129
    law reports, 129
    obituaries, 123
    weather reports, 100
*Times Literary Supplement*, 56, 157
titles (rank), 129
    *see also* baronetages; peerages
titles, protection of, 33, 35, 105
topographical research, 92–3, 99
tourist information offices, 92, 164
trade journals, 94, 123
translation, 60, 158, 160
    *Index Translationum*, 60
Translation and Interpreting, Institute of, 160
translators, professional, 160
transport and travel, 93, 103, 127, 219–20
travel guides, 93, 164
travelling (for research), 9, 128
Trinity College Library (Dublin), 44, 64, 192
Twain, Mark, xvii
typescripts, preparation of, 180–4

unauthorised biographies, 118
United Nations Library and Information Centre (London), 59, 220
    publications, 59
United States of America, 178–9
    *Books in Print*, 51, 179
    indexes to newspapers and periodicals, 56–7

Information Service Reference
Center (London), 166
Library of Congress, 50, 178–9
National Archives and Records
Administration, 179
*National Union Catalog*, 51,
178–9
Public Affairs Information
Service Index (PAIS), 164
statistics, 81
theses, 65
university libraries (UK), 29, 163,
202–4
University of London Library, 44,
202
university registers, 124
unpublished material, finding aids
to, 48, 61–3

verbal information, 31, 131

wages (historical), 101
Wales
National Library of Wales, 44,
192
record offices, 201
University of Wales libraries,
204, 205
weather records, 100–1, 220
Web browser programs, 25
Websites, xviii, 23, 24, 26
Westminster Reference Library, 45,
46, 59, 205, 208
*Whitaker's Almanack*, 80, 83, 87,
94, 99, 100, 130, 140, 227

Whitaker's bibliographic
publications, 43, 51
*Who's Who* volumes, 121, 122,
124, 163, 228
*Willing's Press Guide*, 54, 227
wills and administrations, 63, 128,
142, 146–7, 220
women's magazines, 55, 101
women's studies, 220–1
word processing, 10, 27, 182–3
*World Bibliographical* series, 49,
162
*World Biographical Index*, 120–1,
163
world history sources, 85–6, 98
World Wars I and II, 64, 101, 221
World Wide Web, xv, xvi, 14, 24
*Writers' & Artists' Yearbook*, 27,
34, 157, 160, 181, 185, 227
*Writers and their Copyright
Holders*, 36
Writers' Guild of Great Britain, 36,
166
*Writer's Handbook, The*, 27, 157,
160, 185, 228

Xerox, *see* photocopying

yearbooks, 59, 80, 227
yellow pages, 60, 83, 160
Young Book Trust, 104, 209

zoology, 221

*Personal Notes*

*Personal Notes*

*Personal Notes*

*Personal Notes*

*Personal Notes*